Resources for Reform

Resources for Reform

Oil and Neoliberalism in Argentina

Elana Shever

Stanford University Press
Stanford, California

Stanford University Press
Stanford, California

Printed in the United States of America on acid-free, archival-quality paper

Library of Congress Cataloging-in-Publication Data

Shever, Elana, author.
  Resources for reform : oil and neoliberalism in Argentina / Elana Shever.
    pages cm
  Includes bibliographical references and index.
    ISBN 978-0-8047-7839-8 (cloth : alk. paper) — ISBN 978-0-8047-7840-4 (pbk. : alk. paper)
    1. Petroleum industry and trade—Political aspects—Argentina. 2. Petroleum industry and trade—Social aspects—Argentina. 3. Neoliberalism—Argentina. 4. Protest movements—Argentina. 5. Kinship—Political aspects—Argentina. 6. Citizenship—Argentina. I. Title.
    HD9574.A72S47 2012
    338.2'72820982—dc23
                                        2012004363

Typeset by Bruce Lundquist in 10/14 Minion

For Jonathan

Contents

List of Illustrations

Acknowledgments

I HAVE ACCRUED MANY DEBTS in the course of researching and writing this book. I thank the National Science Foundation, the Fulbright Commission, and, at UC Berkeley, the Office of Graduate Fellowships, the Center for Latin American Studies, and the Human Rights Center for supporting my fieldwork. The Regents of the University of California, the UC Berkeley Department of Anthropology, and Phi Beta Kappa of Northern California supported my writing. I am especially indebted to the Watson Institute for International Studies at Brown University, where I was a postdoctoral research fellow in 2008–2009, for providing a year of writing in an atmosphere that was highly conducive to the task. Keith Brown, Cathy Lutz, Jessaca Leinaweaver, and Dan Smith were instrumental in making my time there both productive and enjoyable. I thank Karen Brison and Linda Cool at Union College for helping me carve out time for this project amid teaching. I am grateful to Carolyn Hsu, Mary Moran, and Nancy Ries at Colgate University for helping me get over the final hurdles of publishing this book. I am also thankful for small grants from the Colgate University Research Council and the Division of Social Sciences.

I began this project while in the Department of Anthropology at UC Berkeley, and I benefited greatly from the theoretical rigor, analytical acumen, and incisive critiques of Lawrence Cohen, Cori Hayden, Donald Moore, Alexei Yurchak, and Michael Watts. I am deeply grateful for all the support I have received from Donald, who has so generously shared his invaluable criticism, his talent for making connections among both people and ideas, his tactical advice, and his caring friendship over the long haul from jumbled ideas to finished book. I also very much appreciate the comments I received on early drafts from Laura Bear, Monica DeHart, Jessica Greenberg, Jane Guyer, John Kelly, Tim Mitchell, Hiro Miyazaki, Andrea Muehlebach, Marina Welker, Noa Vaisman, and Sylvia Yanagisako. I want to thank the participants in the School of Advanced Research Seminar, "The Difference That Kinship Makes," for their dynamic discussion of my work, and I especially appreciate co-organizers Susie McKinnon and Fenella Cannell for including me in this remarkable group of scholars. I am also thankful for the feedback I received from participants in the University of Chicago Workshop on the Anthropology of Latin America and my writing group. This project has been further enriched by conversations with Robert Johnston, Jake Kosek, Nancy Postero, Dinah Rajak, and Annelise Riles.

I had the good fortune of having two outstanding reviewers of my book in Susie McKinnon and Steve Striffler. They not only gave me insightful comments on the entire manuscript, but went above and beyond their role in making themselves available to me as I revised. Joa Suorez, my editor at Stanford University Press, has been an enthusiastic champion of this project and a helpful sounding board for ideas. I thank Karen DeVivo and Jessie Dolch for helping me polish the final manuscript, Lara Scott for expertly crafting a map for it, Scott Smiley for making the index, and the Special Collections Department at the University of Washington Library for locating and reproducing the poster included in Chapter 1. I also greatly appreciate the hard work of Kate Wahl, Carolyn Brown, and the whole production team at Stanford University Press for shepherding this book to publication.

I owe my biggest debt to people in Cutral Có, Plaza Huincul, Dock Sud, and Buenos Aires, as this book emerged out of my encounters with them. I could not have carried out this research without the hospitality of Inés Ditines and the extended Velasquez family. I thank them for their generosity in repeatedly opening their homes and lives to me. Carlos, Carlos, Gustavo, Marcelo, Monica, Norma, Nelly, Nelida, Raúl, Ricardo, Silvia, Silvia, Silvina, and Suni each have shared their knowledge, experience, losses, hopes, dreams, and hard-earned provisions with me. I feel enormously privileged to have known and learned from numerous others in Argentina as well. I have benefited from the extensive knowledge of Argentine scholars Javier Auyero, Claudia Briones, Gastón Gordillo, Mark Healey, Mariana Llanos, and Natalia Milanesio. In addition, I have been assisted time and again by the nuanced knowledge of *castellano argentino* of Inés Ditines, Sachi Feris, and Pedro Sancholuz Ruda.

Finally, I am very grateful to my friends and family who have supported me over the course of this project. I especially thank Julia Schaffer, who also has provided invaluable counsel on the arts of writing, listening, and holding on to dreams. My parents always have encouraged my independence, critical thinking, and continuing education. My sister Samara supplied words of support and pleasurable breaks when I badly needed them. Above all else, I owe more than can be expressed to Jonathan Levine, who lovingly accompanied me back and forth between the United States and Argentina several times, and read this manuscript even more times. I deeply appreciate all his questions and suggestions, even the ones I did not take. Let it not be said that his title for this book, *Oil, Soil, Toil, and Trouble*, did not make it into print. He kept the fire burning beneath this project even when I was ready to abandon it. Ariella Shever, who came into the world between drafts of this book, added joy and levity in the perfect moments and is a constant reminder that my research and writing are motivated by the dream of a more just world for her.

Resources for Reform

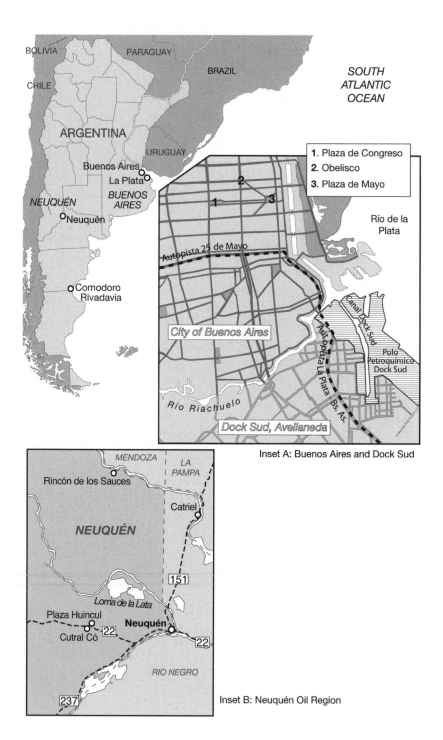

Map of Argentina with field sites enlarged. Illustration by Lara Scott.

Introduction

Oil and Neoliberalism in Argentina

THE FALL AFTERNOON was unseasonably warm as I stood on the grassy median of the wide Avenida 9 de Julio in downtown Buenos Aires. Groups of poor Argentines filled the sidewalks and plaza surrounding the Obelisco, the modernist monument commemorating the 1536 founding of the city. They were gathering for a protest march and rally in support of the national boycott of two of the world's largest oil companies. The swelling crowd was composed of people of all ages. They wore nylon vests in the celestial blue and white of the national flag that were painted with big black letters indicating the social movements they represented. These people, with their bright vests but threadbare shirts, flimsy cloth shoes, and missing teeth, did not usually frequent the downtown where professionals and tourists move among government buildings, corporate offices, posh stores, and restaurants. They were clearly too poor to own cars, yet they gathered to protest recent gasoline price hikes. I was intrigued.

Although they looked out of place to many who passed by them, the people around me did not seem uncomfortable as they stood or sat in small groups, chatting and sharing soda or the traditional tealike drink *mate*. Children squealed as they ran amid the adults, playing games. As I leaned against a railing along the median, five people sat down in the grass at my feet and began to pass around a plastic bottle of cola. They included a heavy-set man with curly brown hair and three teenage girls I took to be his daughters. I asked them to tell me about what was going on. With the accent of someone from the north of Argentina with little formal education, the man told me why he joined the march using words I would hear many times in the coming months: they were protesting against the oil companies because if the people did not do something about the rise in fuel prices, the price of everything else would go up too. He was unemployed and relied on a welfare check of 150 pesos (approximately $50) a month to provide for his family. Gesturing to his daughters squabbling over the one bottle of soda, he said that even a small rise in fuel costs would raise the price of beef and other staples to beyond what he could afford. The situation, the man asserted in a gruff but not angry tone, was dire. This did not stop him from offering me a sip from the bottle of warm brown soda.

At the appointed time, a group of young men and women filed into the street, lined up side by side in the crosswalks, and stopped traffic. Other youths distributed small paper flyers to bystanders and drivers, who looked annoyed but not surprised at the imminent delay in their activities. As the traffic lanes cleared, the protesters took their places behind large banners that flapped with the brisk wind in the deserted street. Drummers beat a steady rhythm as approximately seven thousand people began to walk slowly down the broad avenue toward the once elegant Congressional Palace (see Figure 1 and Map, Inset A). The group grew denser as it arrived in the Plaza del Congreso, where a stage was set up for a rally beside the congressional building. The slightly bit-

Figure 1. Protesters begin marching down the wide Avenida 9 de Julio toward the Plaza de Congreso, as a tourist takes a photo. The banner reads "No to Shell and Exxon's Increase."

ter smell of mate mixed with the smoky smell of chorizo, cigarettes, and sweat. Young children who had been running around in excited circles a few hours earlier now fell asleep in their parents' arms as the adults stood listening to the speeches by politicians and union and social movement leaders who spoke passionately about national energy independence and restoring the dignity of the working class.

The speakers asserted that the recent price increases at Shell and Exxon gas stations were signs that foreign dictators still ruled the national economy. For this reason, the event seemed a return to the famous "petroleum nationalism" (Solberg 1979) of twentieth-century Argentina. Yet it undoubtedly also represented the popular politics of the twenty-first-century. This protest march followed a form that had become common in Buenos Aires since 2001, when a major uprising ousted the elected president in a remarkable popular impeachment. The march and rally demonstrated the contemporary networks of "personalized political mediation" (Auyero 2000) in which poor people publicly showed their political support for the Peronist Party (Partido Justicialista) in exchange for material support for their daily survival from party brokers. The event, however, represented more than the merging of old and new politics. The Shell and Exxon boycott was framed as a protest against *neoliberalismo*, a shorthand for the state and economic "reforms" that have reconfigured Argentine society and everyday lives over the past two decades. Yet, despite the boycott's explicit rejection of neoliberalism, I argue that the boycott is better understood as a reconfiguration of key features of Argentine neoliberalismo, particularly because it framed the purchase of certain brands of gasoline as a political action that could effect social change. The boycott shows that neoliberalismo has continued to be a crucial force shaping Argentina.

The protest against the oil companies in 2005 hints at how much oil matters to millions of people, even to those without the financial resources to use many hydrocarbon-based products. Oil is at the center of many of the most crucial economic, political, and social processes defining the contemporary world. Although a small rise in the price of gasoline at Shell and Exxon stations seems inconsequential in light of the march participants' struggles for daily provisioning, the protesters reminded me that oil and its politics affect everyone's lives. Oil is the motor of global capitalism, a driving force undergirding transnational alliances and international conflicts, and a powerful symbol of social achievement the world over. I first became interested in the oil industry because of the juxtaposition of its importance in underwriting contemporary capitalism and its invisibility as a productive force in everyday life. Since

I began investigating these issues in the late 1990s, some of that invisibility has disappeared. The importance of oil is now far more widely recognized but still not well understood.

Debates over oil politics now have spread far beyond boardrooms and courtrooms to public plazas, residential neighborhoods, and even shanty settlements. Yet much of the commentary on the oil industry is quite simplistic, frequently falling back on "big man" theories of power. *Resources for Reform* closely examines how oil intersects with the lives of people who are both near to and far from the inner workings of the petroleum industry by exploring the lives of oil producers and oil consumers in Argentina. Argentina is a fascinating case not because it is a major producer of petroleum, for it is not, but because it has a long history of struggling with questions about the roles of state, citizenry and business in the development of the economy and the nation, and about the place of oil in society. These questions came to a head during the recent state and economic restructuring—carried out in the name of neoliberalism—which placed great emphasis on reorganizing the oil industry as a means of fixing myriad social, economic, and political problems.

Argentina is a particularly intriguing place to look at oil production and consumption because of its remarkable history. It was among the first countries in the world to, first, establish a state-owned oil company when the petroleum industry arose around the world at the beginning of the twentieth century, and then to fully privatize it as a wave of neoliberal "state reforms" and "structural adjustments" swept across the globe at the end of the century. Throughout these changes, the role of oil in society has remained a critical matter of debate. In "oil nations" such as Venezuela, it goes without saying that oil is central to the government, the economy, and the popular imagination of the nation (Coronil 1997). In Argentina, however, this is not a settled case but a series of hotly debated questions. Who should control the petroleum reserves buried beneath the national territory? Who owns the oil extracted from them? What should it be used for? How should the material and financial resources generated by oil extraction be distributed? Who should benefit? Is oil consumption a right that is necessary for full participation in contemporary society, or a privilege that must be restricted? Argentina offers insights into the significance of oil not only for nationalism, but also for globalization, and even more broadly, for state governing, social life, and the subjectivity of ordinary people.

Resources for Reform is the result of the research I conducted in Argentina between 2002 and 2006 on the conversion of Argentina's venerable state oil company, called YPF (Yacimientos Petrolíferos Fiscales, pronounced *ee-pe-efe*), into a transnational corporation, now named YPF-Repsol, and on the emergence of private corporations as major actors in the national oil market.[1] The book analyzes how the reorganization of the oil industry fits into both large-scale transformation of Argentine society and its global engagements, and the microscale transformation of people's relationships and subjectivities. In particular, the privatization of the Argentine oil industry provides a window into the translocal process known as neoliberalism, which has been of great consequence in recent decades and will continue to reverberate for a long time to come. The twists and turns in the story of oil in Argentina that this book recounts confound any linear or unidirectional understanding of this social transformation.

Most broadly, *Resources for Reform* examines the intersection of oil and neoliberalism. How do these two seemingly incommensurable things mix? Oil is a natural resource, a physical substance created by geological processes we cannot control but upon which we depend. It is hidden beneath the surface of the earth in the crevices of porous rocks until it is pumped out by rigs in far-off places; transported in pipes, barrels, and tanks; and then transformed in our workplaces, in our homes, and even in our bodies. How many of us who use oil almost every minute of the day are aware of all that is involved in bringing it into these spaces? The vast majority of consumers only experience oil once this natural resource has been altered into thousands of derivatives. Although we do not see oil as we go about our daily lives, we know it to be a powerful substance, capable of creating both unprecedented luxury and unfathomable destruction.

Oil is powerful because it is "a perfect specimen" of the commodity form (Retort 2005: 38) and a basic building block of modern capitalism. In classical Marxist terms, we can say that oil has both exceptionally high use-value and exchange-value. First, it is valuable because it packs a huge amount of energy into a small mass and burns quickly, making it especially convenient as a power source. Oil's high energy density also facilitates its transportation in large quantities, enabling its consumption geographically far from where it is extracted. Oil is thus an extraordinarily useful substance in our fast-paced world. In fact, one could argue that it makes this pace possible. Oil is valuable, second, because it can function like money, as a (nearly) universal medium of exchange.[2] In the capitalist exchange of oil for other things, the circumstances under which oil is produced become hidden from its consumers, most of whom do not even realize they are consuming petroleum at all while they, say, eat their dinner and then brush their teeth. Oil's exchange-value thus enables the current global capitalist arrangement, with all its inequities among regions and peoples. Yet all this goes unnoticed when people use hydrocarbon-powered machines and petroleum-based goods to undertake the tasks and pleasures that are seen as the stuff of modern life.

If oil is a largely invisible substance, neoliberalism is an elusive concept. It has been variously defined as a set of specific policies, a hegemonic ideology, a new form of government, and a series of specific political-economic projects. Neoliberalism is widely seen as having spread globally with remarkable speed and penetrated new sites with apparent ease. But what precisely is it that is traveling the world over? For many, neoliberalism is the newest form of capitalist globalization. Bauman (1998) wryly criticized the use of the term globalization as "a shibboleth, a magic incantation, a passkey meant to unlock the gates of all present and future mysteries" (1). The same may now be said of neoliberalism. As other scholars who surveyed the field have noted, there is so much "overreach and underspecification" in the use of the term neoliberalism that it has become "something of a *rascal concept*—promiscuously pervasive, yet inconsistently defined, empirically imprecise, and frequently contested" (Brenner, Peck, and Theodore 2010b: 184). For too long anthropologists took neoliberalism as the ground undergirding the problems they were analyzing but not as an object of analysis itself. Although this has begun to change, the term is still in need of greater analytical precision.

I discuss later in this introduction how I understand neoliberalism and respond to the warranted criticism of its imprecise use in scholarship. But here, I take a second look at both oil and neoliberalism to point out that these objects of analysis are more alike than they first appear to be. Oil is not only a powerful substance, but also a powerful idea. A necessary amendment to the classical Marxist understanding of value is the recognition that oil also derives its value from its role as a depository of meaning. In Argentina, as elsewhere, oil can stand for movement, innovation, modernity, development, improvement, and progress. It can also stand for greed, corruption, violence, and environmental catastrophe. Neoliberalism, likewise, is not only a set of ideas, it is also a cluster of concrete events and their material effects. These include the privatization of the state oil company, the increase in foreign investment, and the informalization of labor in Argentina. *Resources for Reform* thus presents oil and neoliberalism as inseparably semiotic *and* material forces, that is, as symbols *and* substances, and as representations *and* entities.

The chapters that follow scrutinize the conversion of Argentina's state-owned and state-managed oil industry into a privately owned and privately managed one as a way to grasp a mutually political, economic, and social process that is transforming things, spaces, people, meanings, and values. How have oil production and consumption been reconfigured by the process of neoliberal structural adjustment undertaken in Argentina? And how did the deeply sedimented structures of the Argentine oil industry lay the path taken by neoliberal "reform"? Examination of this dual process reveals that oil and neoliberalism are not quite what they seem. But before we return to these questions, it is important to place recent events in their historical context.

A Brief History of Oil in Argentina

Argentina is a fascinating place to examine oil and neoliberalism because the reconfiguration of the ownership and management of the oil industry has been a central part of the larger experiment in remaking the state, the economy, and society. Argentines have debated questions such as: What is the role of oil in pursuing national security, progress, and sovereignty? Do foreign, private national, or state-owned oil companies offer the surest path to economic development for the country and its citizens? Who owns the oil and how should its rewards be distributed? Through policy shifts from encouraging foreign companies to exploit the Argentine subsurface, to restricting their roles to contractors for the state entity, to welcoming them as key players once again, oil has been understood as an inalienable national treasure *and* as a natural resource in short supply. In the course of developing a national oil industry, state agents have promoted oil both as an important resource *for* social and economic development and as the reward *of* it.

Argentina is unique in the prominent role that the national government has played in the oil industry since its initiation. State institutions were largely responsible for exploration and extraction beginning with the discovery of deposits in Patagonia in 1907.[3] The state oil company, YPF Estatal, was founded in 1922, long before similar companies were established elsewhere in the world.[4] YPF quickly became involved in refining and commercializing oil as well as locating and extracting it. In fact, the company was the first vertically integrated state oil company in the world outside of the Soviet Union (Solberg 1979: vii). It managed the national oil industry, from exploration to consumer sales, for seven decades. Other state institutions also have had major effects on oil consumption. Policies such as price controls, taxes, and subsidies and programs like advertising campaigns, consumer education, and boycotts have encouraged citizens of all classes to use petroleum in their daily lives.

The early creation of a national company prevented foreign corporations from dominating the development of the oil industry in Argentina as they did in most other countries in the Global South. This is not to say that private oil companies have not been active in Argentina. Standard Oil (including its heirs and subsidiaries) was one of the most important corporations in Argentina for a long time. While foreign and national private companies were central to the development of the Argentine industry, their roles were defined and managed by state institutions for most of the twentieth century. Yet the power dynamic and the distribution of responsibilities among YPF Estatal, foreign oil corporations, and national companies changed multiple times. At some points, drilling and refining by foreign companies was seen as the surest way to provide for Argentina's development. At others, YPF was envisioned as the only company that could ensure the security, progress, and sovereignty of the country. Throughout these changes, petroleum was both the input necessary for economic activity and the prized end product of economic development. Moreover, oil paradoxically represented both an inalienable treasure belonging to the nation and a scarce resource whose use by citizens needed to be rationed. It was the national state that both produced this treasure and restricted access to it.

One cannot understand events in Argentina since the 1940s without understanding Peronism, and this is true of oil politics as much as anything else. Peronism is a social movement, a political party, a cultural force, and a popular social identity that is organized around the figure of Juan Domingo Perón but far transcends him. Perón, the man, rose from within the military to become president from 1946 to 1955 and again from 1973 until he died in 1974. He emerged as a national figure in the context of Argentina's rapid industrialization during the period between the global recession of the 1930s and World War II. By the end of the war, Argentina's industrial production had more than doubled and national wealth had significantly increased, yet the masses of industrial workers had seen their economic standing decline (James 1988: 8). When Perón served as secretary of labor under the military government in the early 1940s, he began to put in place policies that assisted these disenfranchised workers in gaining economic benefits and political power. He built an effective labor movement around him, while undermining communist and other groups that were organizing workers through other channels. By 1948, Perón had established a highly centralized union structure through which employers were legally bound to negotiate with their workers. Perón asserted that workers, as the citizens creating Argentina's economic growth, not only had a right to "labor with dignity," but also had a right to shape the development of the country (James 1988). Yet, at the same time that workers acquired substantive representation within the state through their unions, they became dependent on welfare from paternal state institutions. The Peronist state's commitment to ensuring workers' representation, rights, and welfare frequently conflicted with its aim to increase industrial production and domestic consumption.

The conflicts within Peronism among the goals of increasing workers' political power, citizens' welfare, and national economic growth played out particularly dramatically in the oil industry. Under the military government, Perón encouraged unionization in the oilfields for the first time. The state oil workers' union, the Sindicato Unidos Petroleros del Estado (Syndicated Unions of State Oilmen, hereafter SUPE), incorporated recent immigrants and longtime residents into a highly centralized governing structure and national movement. Oil workers gained wage increases, improved labor and living conditions, and an extensive array of social benefits, such as medical services, retirement payments, and vacation leave. Yet they did so in exchange for ending their adversarial stance against YPF and becoming state agents. Once president, Perón supported greater nationalization of strategic industries and utilities, including oil. He gave the national government jurisdiction over oil concessions but stopped short of expropriating foreign oil companies' operations. Despite the intense pressure on the state to take over foreign oil companies, as it did the French-owned railroads and the U.S.-owned telephone company, the Perón administration instead encouraged YPF to increase its production. It was not possible for YPF alone to keep up with the demand for oil created by the continued industrialization of the country and the increased disposable income of its citizens. The country thus became dependent on foreign imports of both the equipment needed to increase fuel production and fuel itself. In the face of severe shortages, Perón changed course and, in 1955, made a deal with a subsidiary of Standard Oil of California (SOCAL) to extract petroleum in Patagonia. However, a military coup overthrew Perón before his contract with SOCAL could be implemented. General Eduardo Lonardi, the first provisional military president, cited Perón's agreement with the despised North American oil company as a justification for the military coup (Solberg 1979: 163–66). This ended Perón's nine years of formal rule but not his influence on Argentina.

Perón quickly became a powerful symbol that has been used to mobilize and justify a wide range of political-economic projects from Import Substitution Industrialization to neoliberal reform. Peronism does not represent a consistent set of policies regarding the oil industry but a broad commitment to petroleum nationalism that has taken several different forms. Perón's early

support of a state oil monopoly and his subsequent turn toward foreign investment in the oil industry were both made in the name of strengthening the nation. As historian Carl Solberg (1979) carefully showed, petroleum nationalism
denotes the conviction that state control of oil is essential for the well-being of
the country and its citizenry. The strong support for petroleum nationalism in
Argentina, however, has sat uneasily with the continual importance of foreign
capital, equipment, and oil to meet the demand for fuel in the country.

In the years following Perón's death in 1974, Argentines lived through a
series of brutal military dictatorships that encouraged foreign investment in
the oil industry, once again in the name of national independence and self-
sufficiency. In order to finance the arms purchases that supported their reign of
terror, the military rulers started the process of converting YPF from an autonomous state enterprise into a joint-stock corporation. Beginning in the 1970s,
the dictatorship introduced the first steps in what became signature neoliberal
policies—including privatization, deregulation, and deunionization—while
still maintaining tight government control over the company (Solberg 1979:
174). These moves only fueled the inflation, unemployment, and misery that
contributed to the military's downfall in 1983.

Economic collapse both helped to end the dictatorship and continued to
plague Argentina in the post-dictatorship period. As Chapter 2 discusses in
greater depth, the increasingly dire economic situation following the end of
military rule enabled the Peronist Carlos Menem to carry out one of the most
exhaustive state and economic restructuring programs in the world. The fact
that Menem was a long-time Peronist leader further indicates that the relationship between the state and the oil industry has continued to be as complex in
recent years as it had been in the past. The story of the privatization of the petroleum industry told in the chapters that follow shows how the neoliberal restructuring represented a departure from much of the history outlined here but
could not erase the legacies of petroleum nationalism, company paternalism,
Peronism, or state involvement in the oil industry. The privatization reworked
different parts of this history in surprising ways.

Argentine Neoliberalismo

Neither oil nor neoliberalism is a simple object of analysis, and defining neoliberalism is particularly difficult. The term has been used so widely that it has
lost precise meaning. While some scholars have advocated abandoning the
word because of this, I retain it with some hesitation and several caveats. I do
so, first, because I believe that the popularity of the term within and beyond

academic circles indicates that its meaning matters. I do not want to see anthropologists shy away from engaging in debates that extend beyond our discipline; instead, we should aspire to play a role in shaping the terms of debate on the most important issues of our time. Oil and neoliberalism are certainly among them. Moreover, avoiding the word *neoliberalism* has not, in my opinion, eliminated the need to name a crucial phenomenon that exists in the world, even if that phenomenon is not internally consistent but instead is complex, contingent, and dependent upon its context. Replacing a commonly used word with jargon-filled phrases is no solution to the problem that neoliberalism never has, or ever will, exist in a single ideal form.

The second and more important reason I use the word is because it is an emic term in my research. When living in Argentina, I heard the word *neoliberalismo* said in businesses, community centers, and homes, on the television and on the street. I heard it said with a spit of anger, a sigh of regret, or sometimes with a self-deprecating laugh. Whereas in the United States neoliberalism has become a catchall for myriad phenomena in the contemporary moment, in Argentina it has a more precise meaning. I use the Spanish form of the word, *neoliberalismo*, as an unobtrusive way to remind the reader of this precision of meaning.

The privatization of state entities and services, the opening of national markets to transnational corporations, and the weakening of organized labor are three crucial aspects of a profound state and economic restructuring Argentines know as neoliberalismo. Though it is important to recognize the roots of neoliberalismo in earlier administrations, it was during Menem's presidency from 1989 to 1999 that the Argentine government, economy, and society were most profoundly transformed along neoliberal lines. In fact, many Argentines use the term *menemismo* interchangeably with neoliberalismo to refer to the policies, programs, and discourse about "reform" that were rapidly implemented during these years. These changes were enacted under the premise that the state should no longer regulate the national economy directly by running companies, providing services, or regulating markets but indirectly by enabling corporations to govern the economy with little to no restraint. For instance, although General Jorge Rafael Videla, the de facto president under the military dictatorship from 1976 to 1980, changed YPF's legal status from an autonomous state enterprise into a joint-stock corporation, he did so in order to increase government control over the company (Solberg 1979: 174). The Menem administration, in contrast, was the one that transferred management of the company to private hands. The state remained YPF's only shareholder until 1993, when officials began selling YPF shares on stock markets around the world. In 1999, the Menem administration definitively relinquished state control over the company when it sold its remaining stake to the Spanish firm Repsol. As Chapter 1 discusses, these changes came as great shocks to state oil workers and their families and led to profound transformations of their lives.

Repsol was hardly the only private oil company to benefit from the privatization movement. During the same period, private companies, both domestic and transnational, acquired unprecedented access to markets, natural resources, and consumers in Argentina. Moreover, the restructuring of the oil industry was not unique; privatization was the centerpiece of Menem's program. During his decade-long presidency, the state transferred ownership and control of 90 percent of the national companies and public services to conglomerates of business firms and banks (IMF 1998: 5). These privatizations embraced a wide range of public enterprises in addition to oil and gas—from domestic utilities (for example, telecommunications, water supply, and electric power plants) to transportation (airlines, railways, and urban subways) to industries (steel manufacturing and defense equipment) (Alexander, Corti, and World Bank 1993). YPF's privatization shows that the process of neoliberal restructuring did not eliminate market regulation, as some have suggested, but rather replaced state management with corporate management.

Although neoliberalismo is closely identified with Menem, the former has outlived the reign of the latter. The Menem era formally came to a close with Fernando de la Rúa's narrow defeat of the president's chosen successor, Eduardo Duhalde, in the 1999 presidential election, when the aftershocks of Menem's rule were being felt strongly across the country. Since then, neoliberalismo has been identified with the ongoing consequences of this intense period of change. For millions of Argentines, neoliberalismo represents the polarized inequalities that have translated into poverty, hunger, and disease in a country that once prided itself on having the largest middle class in Latin America. De la Rúa did not break with Menem's economic policies, yet he promised to address their social costs. However, he became president in the midst of a prolonged recession and could not even begin to fulfill his pledge to relieve the growing levels of destitution. When it became clear that the state was insolvent, the national economy fell apart as foreign investors fled and the International Monetary Fund (IMF) suspended assistance. De la Rúa's economic team froze bank accounts in a desperate attempt to halt the run on the banks. In this moment, middle-class Argentines joined their working-class compatriots in banging pots and pans outside banks, rallying at supermarkets, and setting up emergency soup kitchens in the streets. In December 2001, millions of people gathered outside the presidential palace in the Plaza de Mayo and in other plazas across the country, chanting, "*Que se vayan todos!*" ("All of them [the politicians] must go!"). The crowd included many of the impoverished people living on the outskirts of the city who would return four years later for the smaller march and rally in support of the Shell and Exxon boycott.

President de la Rúa resigned, but, unlike in the past, a military government did not take over. Instead, after a succession of five nominal civilian heads of state in ten days, Congress appointed Duhalde to finish out the last two years of the term of his 1999 rival, de la Rúa. While this was happening, the state defaulted on more than $130 billion in debt, the largest sovereign default to that point in history. More than half the population had fallen below the official poverty line by that time, and at least 20 percent of Argentines could not afford daily food (INDEC 2001; Rock 2002: 2).

In the next presidential election, a little-known governor from Patagonia named Néstor Kirchner defeated Menem, who sought to recapture the presidency for a third term, in an election that turned into an internal struggle within the Peronist Party.[5] While Menem stood for neoliberalismo, Kirchner stood for its antithesis. He campaigned on a platform of ridding the country of the vestiges of his rival's earlier "reforms." He censured foreign corporations for monopolizing national markets and criticized foreign companies for making enormous profits by extracting resources from the national territory and labor from the people. After winning the presidency, Kirchner again asserted his anti-neoliberalism when he refused to accept the foreign bankers' terms for loan repayment and renegotiated the country's defaulted debt. Bolstered by the popular support this gained him, Kirchner announced an anti-inflation campaign that aimed to ensure that the prices of staple commodities would not rise further. This campaign, he claimed, would restore the "purchasing power" that Argentine citizens had lost during the Menem years.

This brings us back to the protest scene that opens this book. The march I describe was part of a boycott of Shell and Exxon, undertaken across Argentina in 2005, that began after the two companies raised the price of fuel at their gas stations. The price increase seemed at first an unremarkable occurrence, quite common with the creeping inflation in Argentina and the upward trend in oil prices on global markets. As Chapter 3 explains more fully, car-owning Argentines did not appear to see the price hike as a major event until Kirchner called for a national boycott from the presidential palace. Shell, and then also Exxon, had defied the ongoing negotiations between his administration and the oil industry that were aimed at curbing inflation, and Kirchner decided to make a point of it. The president's action was not out of character, given his anti-neoliberal rhetoric, nor was he exceptional within the region. Kirchner joined Luiz Ignacio da Silva (Lula) in Brazil and Hugo Chávez in Venezuela in proclaiming the end to neoliberalismo across South America. Two years into his presidency, the boycott of two foreign oil giants captured the widespread anti-neoliberal sentiment of the moment. The incident seemed the perfect example of Argentines' response to the intersection of neoliberalismo and the oil industry, so I stopped the series of interviews with petroleum industry professionals I was doing at the time and threw myself into learning about the boycott firsthand. Whereas I had been focusing my attention on people working in the oil industry, I now saw those formally outside of it as equally crucial to understanding its transformation. This is how I found myself in the midst of the crowd of boycott supporters on Avenida 9 de Julio and in conversation with people I did not expect to be part of my study of the oil industry.

Argentines who owned cars participated in the boycott by "voting" with their gasoline purchases, while their impoverished compatriots took part by occupying gas stations and joining protests like the march and rally I attended in downtown Buenos Aires. As I listened to the speeches at the rally that day, I was struck by the incongruity of the political rhetoric celebrating the value of the working class being delivered to a crowd composed of people who did not fit the image of the Peronist worker being hailed from the stage. The people who participated in this demonstration were mostly unemployed or worked in informal and odd jobs without stable wages or benefits, not to mention union representation or the ability to afford a car. The majority of the protesters identified as *piqueteros*, members of popular social movements that organized the unemployed, underemployed, and marginally employed through informal networks in poor neighborhoods and shanty settlements across Argentina. Their vests and banners identified the neighborhood subgroups of the national associations to which they belonged. As they walked toward the Plaza del Congreso, they shouted chants that included both ones popular at protest marches of this sort and ones that specifically addressed the boycott, connecting Shell and Exxon with greed, illegitimate power, and even treason. Despite the angry words, the mood was not hostile and the crowd not violent. Yet apprehension was evident all around me. Like their wealthier counterparts, the piqueteros saw the boycott as a way to support President Kirchner's anti-neoliberal position and to express opposition to neoliberalismo. They also endorsed the president's message that participation in the boycott demonstrated their belonging to the nation. Impoverished Argentines in particular envisioned the boycott as defending petroleum consumption as part of their economic right to support themselves and their families. What had brought them into alliance with middle-class gasoline consumers, oil workers' unions, and the president was not only their concern with oil prices, but also with neoliberalism and how it was reconfiguring daily life. By linking people's everyday activities to global political-economic processes, the boycott demonstrated the continued importance of oil and neoliberalismo in shaping Argentina.

How should we understand the anti-neoliberal stance of the boycott in light of Argentina's history? The boycott was both a resurgence of the petroleum nationalism that characterized twentieth-century Argentina and an expression of the contemporary configuration of society, with its polarization of wealth and privilege. It was not, however, a popular expression of resistance to neoliberalismo and the growth of corporate power in Argentina. Why? The boycott was not a "grassroots" action because it did not begin when consumers saw new prices at their local gas stations or markets, but only after the president urged them to stop buying Shell gasoline. As I describe later in the book, the boycott was carefully staged and orchestrated by the Kirchner administration and allied organizations. State representatives deployed affective ties of kinship to discourage certain purchases, and promote others. In doing so, they invoked a sense of filial obligation to domestic economy, in the double sense of the national market and household finance.

It is important to recognize that, although the boycott pushed Argentines to collectively use their "purchasing power" to shape the oil market, it was not a *gasoline* boycott, but a *brand* boycott. It did not urge Argentines to abstain from using oil or even to find less-hydrocarbon-intensive forms of transport but directed their consumption *toward* products that were presented as good for the family and nation. For middle-class citizens, these "goods" were certain brands of gasoline, ironically including the privatized state company. Buying YPF-Repsol fuel became an expression of national belonging, even though it moved through the same transnational networks as other brands. This incongruity leads me to argue that the boycott was not a protest *against* neoliberalismo but *a continuation of it*, albeit in a novel form. Despite the anti-neoliberal rhetoric, I assert that the boycott represents crucial features that have characterized Argentine neoliberalismo from its emergence in the late 1970s through its development in the mid-2000s. I want to highlight here two ways in which it reworked crucial features that have characterized Argentine neoliberalismo and the global family of phenomena to which it belongs.

First, the boycott strengthened neoliberalismo by increasing the ability of transnational corporations to export resources and profits. This takes a bit of explanation: At the beginning of the privatization process, corporate executives took the place of state regulators in setting policies for everything from extraction and refining rates to distribution patterns, pricing, and environmental standards. As a senior official in the Energy Department stated: "the lawyers of the involved oil companies actively participated in the drafting of the decrees that established the oil sector deregulation. In fact, it could be said that the [private companies'] lawyers . . . wrote those decrees" (Etchemendy 2005: 67 fn 3). Corporate control over oil became more complicated after the 2001 political-economic collapse. Price ceilings were reintroduced, and oil companies were legally required to satisfy the domestic market before they could export fuel. This latter provision was added because price ceilings made it more lucrative for oil companies to sell their products outside of Argentina than within the country. Yet the law stated that once a company sold as much fuel as Argentines wanted to buy, they could export the rest. This is exactly what Shell and Exxon did during the month-long boycott.

The Kirchner administration did not move to lower the price ceiling or otherwise change the law regulating the oil market. Instead, the president and his supporters used affective techniques to encourage Argentines to choose certain brands of gasoline over others. Therefore, even though the boycott led to lower consumer fuel prices, the decrease in Shell's and Exxon's domestic market shares that occurred as a result of the protest was actually financially advantageous for the two transnational oil giants because it enabled them to export more fuel. This meant, paradoxically, that the boycott actually *increased* both corporate profits and the integration of Argentina into the regional and global oil markets.

Second, the national boycott of Shell and Exxon extended neoliberalismo by promoting commodity consumption as an act of democratic citizenship and an expression of national belonging. The boycott reinforced the neoliberal idea that today people are, and should be, bound together through market relationships. To borrow Néstor García Canclini's reworking of Benedict Anderson, neoliberalismo implies that what makes a country an "imagined community" in the contemporary moment is the collective sum of citizens' individual purchases. In his words, people today are "brought together as consumers even when we are being addressed as citizens" (García Canclini [1995] 2001: 15–16). Although his statement applies to the boycott, this event illustrates that commodity purchases are not necessarily the autonomizing acts that García Canclini sees but can be unifying ones that merge calculation and affect.

The boycott supporters used petroleum's powerful symbolism to unite Argentines as a community of consumers who are dedicated to their nation, yet it did so in class-specific ways. While the boycott urged car-owning Argentines to assert their political opinion by choosing among differently branded (but identical) products, it encouraged impoverished Argentines to reassert their place in the nation by demanding that oil consumption be extended to the very citizens who had been driven farther from such citizenship by the earlier process of neoliberal structural adjustment. As Chapter 3 documents, the piqueteros took this claim a step further and contended that universal suffrage required universal commodity consumption. The boycott strengthened the idea that Argentines are connected to each other as a network of consumers by demanding the extension of consumer citizenship across class divides. The boycott thereby embodied a neoliberal notion that the market is the preeminent site for democracy and community by asserting that all Argentines should be able to purchase petroleum products.

My claim that the boycott was profoundly neoliberal, despite its anti-neoliberal frame, obviously rests on a particular understanding of Argentine neoliberalismo and its relationship to neoliberal projects elsewhere in the world.[6] In order to rigorously analyze Argentina's configuration of neoliberalism, I now situate it within a transnational network of neoliberalisms and connect it to the intellectual debates surrounding the concept and its uses.

Analyzing Neoliberal Projects

Much of the pioneering anthropological scholarship on neoliberalism portrays it as an ideology and set of policies that created a dramatic shift from an era of state-led social welfare and national economic development to an era of intensified globalization. While other scholars have concentrated on policy changes, anthropologists have largely followed Jean and John Comaroff's assertion that neoliberalism needs to be understood as changing "the phenomenology of being in the world" (2000: 305). Anthropological scholarship has emphasized how the penetration of market relations into new sites and the privatization of state resources are driving forces for changes in subjectivities and social relations. It has drawn attention to the spectacular failures of privatization schemes to live up to their promises, their dramatic escalation of poverty and inequality, and their fragmentation of communal belonging.[7] Recent ethnographic investigations of "actually existing neoliberalism" (Brenner and Theodore 2002) have provided nuance to the earlier broad-brushed portraits of neoliberalism as the newest capitalist logic or ideology. They also have identified telling cracks in what was once taken as a hegemonic order. Yet the existing scholarship still tends to neglect the lines of continuity between neo-liberal and previous regimes of rule. In analyzing current problems, scholars have inadvertently romanticized the developmentalist and welfare states of the past, overlooking their repeated failures to provide what they legally guaranteed. In this book, I aim to heed E. P. Thompson's warning that "too often in our histories we foreshorten the great transitions" and mistake assertions of a new economic rationality by a small group of privileged actors for its acceptance by a stratified population ([1971] 1991: 253). One way that this book does this is by exploring how the privatization of YPF Estatal and the ascendance of transnational giants like Shell reasserted some aspects of state and company paternalism within the privatized oil industry, at times with a feminine veneer.

Many of the anthropologists who have critiqued the characterization of neo-liberalism as a hegemonic project driven by the internal gears of capitalism do so using an approach inspired by Michel Foucault's discourse analysis. They have engaged scholars in other disciplines who have scrutinized the development of neoliberal rationality or "style of thinking" and the norms of human behavior it suggests.[8] Because this literature has emphasized discursive over labor practices, it has identified a greater homogeneity among neoliberal phenomena than I believe really exists. A careful comparison of neoliberalisms suggests that what these scholars have identified as akin processes are frequently only similar vocabularies. A discourse about the free market, competition, economic efficiency, consumer choice, entrepreneurship, self-responsibility, and the like has traveled around the world through the educational programs, publications, conferences, and marketing campaigns of multilateral financial institutions, research centers, policy think tanks, and universities (Garth and Dezalay 2002; Babb 2004; Harvey 2005). Yet this does not mean that the practices these words describe are as similar as they seem. Despite transnational talk of how competition among private firms increases the efficiency of utility markets and consumers' ability to choose among commodities, for instance, Argentine neoliberalismo did not introduce competition into most of the industries, markets, and services that were privatized. Consequently, the privatization of state-owned industries means significantly different things in Poland (Dunn 2004), China (Rofel 2007), andArgentina. My argument does not imply that neoliberal discourse has no material effects but instead that this discourse masks crucial differences among sites and processes, thereby suggesting their homogeneity. The transnational discourse of neoliberalism thus insinuates that the same changes will inevitably spread to every corner of the world. The study of peoples' everyday lives, however, tells another story, one full of the contingency of events shaped by multiple forces.

Anthropologists have more productively employed the Foucauldian concept of governmentality to conceptualize neoliberalism as a set of techniques that are used by a wide range of actors, both within and outside of official state institutions, in order to govern themselves and other people. Studies in this tradition persuasively show that the shift from state-led to market-based government has involved far more than removing state and social controls over economic relations. Neoliberal forms of governing are carried out by nonstate actors representing political parties, civic organizations, social movements, corporations, and multilateral financial institutions, among others.[9] Julia Paley (2001), for instance, documented how nongovernmental organizations (NGOs) and neighborhood groups took over the provisioning of health care from state agents as part of the shift from dictatorship to democracy in Chile. She charted how shantytown residents responded to this change by both adopting and resisting the new way of understanding the responsibility for health. While anthropologists' tendency to focus on people's resistance to neoliberalism has led to questioning its hegemony, it also has led to overlooking the ways in which a wide range of people actively participate in *advancing* neoliberal projects. In particular, scant ethnographic attention has been paid to the corporate actors who frequently lead neoliberal projects such as privatizations.[10] Part I of this book highlights the crucial role played by corporate managers who negotiated the new relationship between the privatized YPF SA and its subcontractors, while Part II emphasizes the importance of Shell's public relations staff.

My approach may be closest to that of Lisa Rofel, who has examined the creation of neoliberal subjectivity in China. She rightly has criticized analyses of neoliberalism as the newest form of governmentality for asserting an erroneous consistency among changes in economic policy, discourse, ideas, and personhood. Like Rofel (2007), I aim "to forestall a sense that neoliberalism is a universal set of principles from which derives, in a deterministic fashion, a singular type of neoliberal subject" (2). This book builds on her work by highlighting several crucial aspects of Argentine neoliberalismo that would be overlooked without close attention to affect, familial sentiments, and kinship practices. I follow Sylvia Yanagisako's use of the term "sentiment" (2002: 10–12) to blur assumed divides between emotion and thought and between affective desires and economic goals. Yet I draw greater attention to the political-economic and statal processes that strongly shape both discursive practice and subject formation than previous scholars have done.

Resources for Reform examines a range of actors differently related to neoliberalismo in Argentina and explores how they have been involved in shaping it.

These include former state oil workers, their wives who raised children in company towns, and their children who are trying to find a place for themselves in the privatized oil industry; men and women who currently work on oil rigs and in refineries as employees, contractors, or day laborers as well as those who have sought but been denied these jobs; oil executives, public relations managers, and business consultants who whiz through shanty settlements in armored cars on their way to work; and the recipients of oil companies' philanthropy who live in these precarious settlements that exist in the shadow of the refineries. Together, these people who are living in the oil towns of Northwest Patagonia, the shantytowns of metropolitan Buenos Aires, and the national capital itself provide compelling evidence that Argentines of all sorts participated in the creation and development of neoliberalismo, whether intentionally or unintentionally. They were neither helpless victims trapped by forces beyond their control, nor were they Davids who valiantly fought a giant Goliath, although they have been portrayed as both in numerous popular and scholarly accounts, and they sometimes even described themselves in these terms. They were not suffering from "false consciousness," persuaded by state and corporate representatives to believe that policies that were hurting them—such as those that encouraged the poor people living amid the pollution from the Dock Sud refineries to take personal responsibility for their own poor health—were really in their best interests. Nor were they exemplars of *Homo economicus*, self-interested individuals who calculate the value of things and relationships, weighing each decision on a scale of benefits and costs and then choosing those that maximize their individual gain. Instead, this book portrays Argentines enmeshed in neoliberal processes as people working collectively to carve out a livable space for themselves between not one, but many, rocks and hard places.

I have noted that the bourgeoning interest in neoliberalism in anthropology and allied fields has, unfortunately, led to overextension and underspecification of the meaning of the term. When nearly everything in the contemporary world is portrayed as neoliberal, labeling it so accomplishes little. Yet to narrow neoliberalism to an explicit ideology or a predetermined list of policies is to miss much of what neoliberalism is about. A recent survey of the field contends that "*all* prevalent uses of the notion of neoliberalism involve references to the tendential extension of market-based competition and commodification processes into previously insulated realms of political-economic life" (Brenner 2010a: 329, emphasis in original). This does not, however, accurately describe Argentine neoliberalismo. For instance, although the privatization of the oil industry illustrates the increased commodification of natural resources, it also exhibits a *decrease* in "market-based competition." More generally, there are fewer oil companies in the world today than only a few decades ago (mostly because of mergers). As Tara Schwegler's study of changes in Mexican social security shows, policies that seem "the epitome of neoliberal logic," such as privatization, do not necessarily represent a consistent ideology but instead can embody the competing ideas of a diverse set of policymakers (2008: 683). Although the concept of neoliberalism is in need of greater precision, it is too complex to define in terms of essential tenets.

My response to the need to sharpen the analytic of neoliberalism, while not reducing its complexity, takes inspiration from Ludwig Wittgenstein's concept of "family resemblance." Wittgenstein observed a "tendency to look for something in common to all the entities that we commonly subsume under a general term." He wrote: "We are inclined to think that there must be something in common to all games, say, and that this common property is the justification for applying the general term 'game' to the various games; whereas games form a *family*, the members of which have family likenesses. Some of them have the same nose, others the same eyebrows, and others again the same way of walking; and these likenesses overlap" (1958: 17, emphasis in original). Wittgenstein's crucial insight is explaining how phenomena can be grouped together in a way that does not rely on an essence or ideal type. He used the notion of family resemblance to show that we can understand the commonalities among phenomena that are grouped together under a term like neoliberalism as overlapping in multiple respects without suggesting that they all share one or more characteristics or all derive from an abstract model of the ideal member of the group. In his words, "I am saying that these phenomena have no one thing in common which makes us use the same word for all, but that they are related to one another in many different ways" (27). Instead of imagining neoliberalism's family as a tree with a single trunk and distinct branches, one might imagine a creeping vine with multiple roots and tangled shoots whose web is denser in some spots than in others.

Understanding neoliberalism as a family resemblance avoids several of the aforementioned pitfalls of the existing scholarship, particularly the tendency to overstate the newness and uniqueness of neoliberal phenomena. The neoliberal "family" includes novel and previously existing concepts, techniques, and discourses that became powerfully "married" in the late twentieth century. This neoliberal family is as differentiated and internally inconsistent as any human family I know; yet its members are infused with a sense of belonging, and they resemble each other in multiple complex ways. Many of them share a tendency toward quantification, commoditization, and evaluation through market principles. Another resemblance, one that is usually overlooked, is the way neoliberal projects can generate, and work through, affective attachments, a theme I return to in Chapter 1. An analytic based on family resemblance allows acknowledgment that some likenesses are more prominent than others—but only in particular sites and moments, not absolutely. A fine-grained understanding of the relationships among a sometimes unified, sometimes scattered group of people, institutions, events, discourses, and practices allows for analysis of how neoliberalism works as a powerful productive force in the world but does not constitute The Force.

An analytic of family resemblance also highlights that the bonds among the phenomena we call neoliberal are not innate yet they are not fleeting or easily dissolved either. While several anthropologists have turned to Gilles Deleuze and Félix Guattari's notion of assemblage to emphasize the emergent and shifting character of neoliberal forms, my use of Wittgenstein's concept of family resemblance reminds us that some formations are particularly enduring and hard to break. To continue his metaphor, a family is not simply an idea or a feeling but a sometimes pleasurable, sometimes hurtful reality that cannot be easily remade or disregarded. The obstinacy of familial bonds helps explain the difficulties that those in Argentina and elsewhere who oppose neoliberalism face when attempting to break out of its framework. This is manifest, for instance, in the boycott leaders' advocacy of commodity consumption as oppositional politics. It also helps explain continuities between neoliberal and previous regimes of rule such as the reliance on paternal authority.

One potential danger of the analytic for neoliberalism I am proposing is that it could naturalize an understanding of family resemblance based on genetic commonality, physiological likeness, or innate affinity. How should we interpret Wittgenstein's suggestion that some groups have "the same nose, others the same eyebrows, and others again the same way of walking"? I intend the notion of family resemblance to capture the overlapping likenesses among a large group of policies, programs, ideas, and people that have cohabited for a significant period of time, not that share some genetic, ideological, or other essence. The members of the neoliberal family have learned from each other, have come to speak with similar words and syntax, and are expected to have deep ties to one another. They have supported one another, both financially and symbolically, as together they rose from relative obscurity to worldwide celebrity and as they faced criticism and sometimes violent opposition. But like all families, their members also clash at other times. Emphasizing this unromantic conception of the family resemblance among neoliberalisms is especially important given my concern with kinship and sentiments in this book.

I call attention above to the affinities among neoliberalisms that are created when some resemblances are highlighted and others are discounted. Scrutinizing these processes of inclusion and exclusion is as important when examining different regions of Argentina as it is when comparing neoliberal projects in disparate parts of the world. To conclude, I describe the two principal sites of my fieldwork in Argentina and examine their interconnections. I ground this book in some of the spatial particularities and pressing concerns of two regions of the country and their people.

Attending to Argentina

The Argentine aphorism *Dios está en todas partes pero atiende en Buenos Aires* (God is everywhere, but attends [that is, to supplicants, patients, or customers] in Buenos Aires) was said repeatedly to me over the course of my fieldwork. Much scholarly work reflects this maxim and allows Argentina's cosmopolitan capital to stand in for the whole country. Though I open with a scene from the ostensible epicenter of Argentine politics in downtown Buenos Aires, *Resources for Reform* works against the centripetal trend in Argentine scholarship by paying equal attention to Patagonia. Rather than formulate questions in the presumed national core and follow them out to the southern periphery, this research grounds its questions and much of its ethnographic and historiographic investigation in the often neglected southern part of the country. It was, in fact, a suggestion from a man in Patagonia that led me to conduct part of my investigation in Buenos Aires and thus to be there during the national boycott of Shell and Exxon.

This research began in the twin oil towns of Plaza Huincul and Cutral Có, which together form an isolated settlement in Neuquén Province on the desert plateau of northern Patagonia near the Chilean frontier (see Map, Inset B). The region long has been considered peripheral to the nation, except in its role as a supplier of energy. It is best known as one of the three principal oil regions in the country.[11] Neuquén was not converted from a national territory into a province until 1958, and it remains among the most sparsely populated provinces in the country. Yet, the history of state involvement in the oil industry has meant that Plaza Huincul, long an official YPF company town, and neighboring Cutral Có never formed an oil enclave comprising a gated community of expatriates, like company towns in other parts of the world (see, for example, Ferguson 2005: 378; Vitalis 2007). Instead, these towns have long been thoroughly Argentine places that have celebrated the accomplishments of the nation.

Plaza Huincul began as a post on the trade route across the Andes and was transformed when it became an oil exploration camp in 1915. Chapter 1 describes how Cutral Có grew up beside it as an informal worker settlement when petroleum production began. As more people arrived to work in the oilfields and towns and the industry expanded, the two towns grew together. Today, a dry canal bed filled with garbage is the only thing that marks the administrative border between them. In contrast, the cities' outer edge is clearly defined by the line where paved streets abruptly end and the reddish sandy soil of the Patagonian desert begins. The houses are mostly single-story ranches of sturdy construction, built with small windows to prevent breakage during sandstorms (see Figure 2). Still, when these strong winds sweep across the plateau in winter, they often knock out the electricity. This happened when I was interviewing a retired YPF couple at their home in Cutral Có (see Chapter 1). Whenever this occurred, the residents of the oil towns would sigh in resignation that a region so rich in natural resources suffered frequent power outages, and then would stalwartly go on with their activities.

Observers began calling Cutral Có and Plaza Huincul a "ghost town" in the 1990s because the population declined precipitously when YPF Estatal was dismantled and then YPF-Repsol moved its regional headquarters to Neuquén

Figure 2. An example of the uniform housing blocks built for YPF worker families, with small, set-back, shuttered windows to prevent damage during sandstorms.

City, the provincial capital that sits on the border with Río Negro Province (see Map, Inset B). Today, the eighty thousand people who live in Plaza Huincul and Cutral Có are on average older than the national population, with a large percentage now in their sixties and older (INDEC 2001). Walking around town, I frequently passed empty playgrounds. On the other hand, over the years that I returned to northern Patagonia, I witnessed several casinos open and thrive, and I saw the renovation and expansion of the local museum. Cutral Có and Plaza Huincul are relatively young towns compared with those in the pampas and north of the country that date to the colonial period, and the ink of their history is still wet. As I visited the museum with two friends who served as my informal guides, they marveled that people and places they knew from their childhood had become History.

The Buenos Aires metropolitan area provides another window for discerning how the privatization of the oil industry has remade people's everyday lives, relationships, and subjectivities. My research here was focused in Dock Sud, a neighborhood of interspersed industrial sites, residential blocks, and shanty settlements named after the port on its eastern edge. Dock Sud is a swampy zone sitting just south of the city of Buenos Aires in the municipality of Avellaneda (see Map, Inset A). Avellaneda was a major center for Argentina's extensive rail system until its privatization and dismantling in the early 1990s. It continues to be a hub for the remains of the country's light industry. Dock Sud contains the most extensive industrial installations within the municipality, including port facilities, metallurgical works, an electricity plant, and the Polo Petroquímico Dock Sud (Dock Sud Petrochemical Complex) where Shell houses its only South American refineries. This campus of refineries and petrochemical plants forms a peninsula that juts into the Río de la Plata, receiving much of its crude oil from Patagonia by ship. The various businesses there turn this crude into a range of hydrocarbon fuels, asphalt, and solvents such as turpentine.

Many small shanty neighborhoods fill the pockets between the officially recognized residential blocks, the industrial plants, and the port facilities in Dock Sud. Goldendas, the shanty settlement in which I conducted my most extensive fieldwork, was once a swamp.[12] Its few blocks of extralegal settlement were constructed on successive layers of landfill, some of which contain toxic waste from the petrochemical complex. The houses are made out of a collage of cement blocks, scrap wood, corrugated metal, cardboard, and plastic sheeting and are densely packed together and connected by a maze of narrow, unpaved alleys. The residents are mostly migrants from the north of Argentina who came to the capital in search of work during Menem's presidency or who lost houses in other parts of metropolitan Buenos Aires more recently. My survey in 2006 revealed that Goldendas contained 113 households, almost exclusively composed of women and men in their thirties or younger and their children. Because there are no state-sponsored utilities in Goldendas, residents have snaked black plastic tubing along the ground to carry water from house to house, have dug canals alongside the alleys to drain wash water, and have built privies (which a municipality truck does empty on an irregular basis). Electricity enters the shanty residences through a tangle of extralegal lines that connect to power cables on the official side of Dock Sud, but they do not carry enough power in the evenings to run the nebulizers the children need to calm their chronic asthma. As Chapter 3 explains, residents carry in small canisters of propane for cooking, if they use gas fuel at all.

Despite the myriad difficulties of life in Goldendas, it is considered among the most desirable shanty neighborhoods in metropolitan Buenos Aires because it is relatively free of crime and drugs. Several residents hold legal employment, and a few even consider themselves almost middle class. People who live there are proud of their settlement. Their pride was evident, for example, when my husband and I attended the neighborhood Children's Day celebration. As we watched shoes being handed out to the most destitute children, a man pulled my husband aside and explained to him that only *some* poor people lived there. Several of my friends in Goldendas had asked me to bring my husband that day, I believe, to show him what they wanted an outsider to know about this shanty settlement—how they put together a celebration for all the children in the neighborhood, rather than how many of them eat in a communal soup kitchen or cannot afford to buy shoes. The Children's Day celebration highlighted the contagious optimism alive in Goldendas (see Figure 3).

I did not select the Neuquén oil towns and the Dock Sud neighborhood as field sites out of some misguided notion that they would represent the breadth of Argentina but because they represent sites in which petroleum and its politics often have sparked significant conflicts. Petroleum is not the only thing that links Plaza Huincul and Dock Sud, but oil's political and material volatility makes the interconnections most tangible. Although it is often helpful to "follow the thing" (Marcus 1998), my investigation of oil and neoliberalism in Argentina moves beyond exposing links between sites. While George Marcus and others have pointed to the endemic problems with territorialized anthropological investigations, much multisited ethnography still presents fieldwork sites as ahistorical, distinct, and fixed locations that capital, materials, and anthropologists connect. Instead, I follow Donald S. Moore (2005) in showing that particular

Figure 3. Two men dressed up in homemade clown costumes lead children in games during the Children's Day celebration in Goldendas.

histories of struggle produce "an *entangled landscape* in which multiple spatialities, temporalities, and power relations combine" (4, emphasis in original). In the present case, they form intertwined spaces of oil and habitation. Northwest Patagonia and metropolitan Buenos Aires are not separate locations that petroleum production has united, but sites that have been carved out, and isolated as much as connected, through the development of the petroleum industry. Furthermore, each one itself entails vertically and horizontally overlapping spaces. For instance, Plaza Huincul has been variously demarcated as a petroleum reserve, a company camp, a state administrative district, and more recently, a zone of piquetero protest. Likewise, Dock Sud has been defined both as a space for "the community," where Shell supported—and shaped—some community programs, and as a space of "insecurity," where the company established private security escorts for professional employees and visitors. These corporately defined spaces intersect with residents' spatial configurations of politics, danger, security, and protest. Dock Sud was also created by the conflicts among the overlapping jurisdictions of the state, the provincial police, and the national coast guard (*prefectura*). This often meant that only residents responded to problems like robberies in Goldendas because the police claimed that the shanty neighborhood was under the authority of the coast guard, while the coast guard claimed that the police were responsible for responding to calls there.

Plaza Huincul exemplifies how the reorganization of petroleum production intersects with the reconfiguration of nation, community, family, and self. Dock Sud, in comparison, more explicitly illustrates how changes in patterns of oil consumption intertwine with changes in the relationships among state entities, corporations, and citizens. Neuquén and Buenos Aires together show how diverse actors in different locations with distinct relationships to the oil industry have shaped neoliberalismo, not merely reacted to it. The inhabitants of both places are, sometimes contrary to their aims, crucial for the success of the private companies that now control the oil industry.

While this introduction has briefly discussed some of the themes that carry through this book, it does not lay out a complete argument to be elaborated and demonstrated in the succeeding chapters. Part I of *Resources for Reform* examines the intersection of neoliberalismo and oil production with the generative power of kinship; Part II connects neoliberalismo, oil consumption, and transformations in citizenship.

Part I takes a close look at the privatization of YPF from the vantage point of the state oil workers and their families living in the oil towns of Northwest Patagonia. These workers have long called themselves YPFianos, and many continued to use this term even after YPF Estatal was dissolved. Their naming practice indicates how central YPF has been to their work and home lives, and their sense of self. Chapter 1 traces the intertwined history of the Argentine state in Patagonia, YPF Estatal, and the twin oil towns of Plaza Huincul and Cutral Có in order to see how YPF kinship was constructed and then redeployed as YPFianos transformed their work units into independent subcontracting businesses during the privatization process. Chapter 2 examines how oil became private property, how the state-owned oil industry was converted into one that was privately owned and managed, and how state workers' subjectivities were remade through changes in legal, financial, and labor practices.

Part II scrutinizes the rise in importance of transnational corporations such as Shell from the perspective of oil consumers, especially the impoverished ones living in the capital region. Chapter 3 takes a closer look at the national boycott of Shell and Exxon within the context of other projects to make buying and using hydrocarbon fuels into political acts. Chapter 4 analyzes Shell's move from corporate philanthropy to corporate social responsibility and the concomitant regendering of the public face of the company to show

how changes in the company's public relations strategy shifted responsibility for problems of ill health and poverty in Dock Sud from the company to newly "empowered" individuals and community groups. Each of the chapters in *Resources for Reform* thus engages problems that cut across the Argentine oilfields and the anthropological theoretical fields and compels them to speak to each other: neoliberalismo, YPF kinship, and worker subjectivity; private property, the public domain, and social exclusion; citizenship and commodity consumption; corporate personhood, health care, and environmental justice. Chapter 1 begins the ethnographic exploration of these themes by turning back to the history of the national oil industry in the early twentieth century and examining the linked development of the national state, the oil towns of Northwest Patagonia, and the YPF families.

Neoliberal Kinship

1 Affective Reform

DIEGO PARMADO WAS DEVASTATED.[1] He had been born and raised in a Patagonian oil town and followed his father and uncles into YPF Estatal at the age of fourteen, expecting to retire from the company as they had. He had worked in the Neuquén oilfields for almost thirty years when he was dismissed during the privatization of YPF Estatal. He was thus younger than fifty years old at the time he left the company and, like most state oil workers, was too young to receive a retirement pension but too old to be hired by another oil company or to retrain for another career. He was overwhelmed because leaving YPF represented more than the loss of a job. In the early 1990s when the company was being restructured, Diego was one of fifty-one thousand workers who called themselves YPFianos after the state entity for which they labored. This self-designation begins to illustrate how attached the workers were to the state oil company. Not only Diego's work life, but also his sense of himself and his family life revolved around YPF.

As the state oil company was converted into a privately owned corporation, Diego and the workers in his division were dismissed from their jobs. They were not, however, entirely pushed out of the oil industry. They were told to re-form their production units into worker-owned microenterprises that would offer subcontracting services to the newly formed private company, YPF SA. The YPFianos' change from public servants to independent business owners occurred so rapidly, Diego explained, that "you went to sleep at night with a baby bottle and the next day you got up with a tie and briefcase." With his Kafkaesque vision of metamorphosis, Diego captured an understanding, shared by his fellow YPFianos, that the formal conversion of state workers into small businessmen happened overnight. However, he later told me how their substantive transformation was a far more arduous and extended process. Bodies toughened by years of labor in the harsh Patagonian oilfields did not easily fit into business suits meant for deskwork, yet Diego learned to wear a businessman's clothing with poise.

The vast majority of state oil workers across Argentina lost their jobs during the privatization process, and many of these men, and a few women, became worker–owners in subcontracting microenterprises like Diego did. These subcontracting companies were known as *emprendimientos*, a word that could be rendered in English as "startups" if their owners were much younger, wealthier, and more formally educated.[2] The YPF emprendimientos were special oil service microenterprises collectively owned, managed, and staffed by former state workers. While many YPFianos joined these emprendimientos in the early 1990s, only a small percentage of them remained employed in the oil industry a decade later. The second half of this chapter examines how the remarkable ones who managed to stay in the industry were able to remake themselves into business owners and maintain their microenterprises for a dozen or more years against seemingly impossible odds. I was surprised to find that kinship was the key to comprehending their metamorphosis.

The conversion of YPF Estatal into a privately owned transnational oil corporation, first called YPF SA and later restructured as YPF-Repsol, was one of the most prominent pieces of the sweeping state and economic restructuring carried out by the Menem administration in the decade between 1989 and 1999.[3] YPF's privatization thus belongs to the ideas and actions that became "married" to form the global neoliberal "family" discussed in the Introduction. The midwives of this process stressed that the privatization of state enterprises and services was the panacea for multiple ills, including state debt, bureaucratic corruption, market inefficiency, and the failures of state development and welfare. President Menem in particular promised that privatizing state companies and services would allow Argentines to finally "join the First World," as they had been striving to do since the early twentieth century.[4]

The architects of Argentina's privatizations assumed that the legal and administrative changes that were reorganizing the state and the national economy would inevitably lead to modifications in people's dispositions and relationships. In particular, the privatization of state companies such as YPF was supposed to remake public servants into "entrepreneurs," the quintessential neoliberal actors.[5] That is, privatization was supposed to turn people who work for others into people who work for themselves, people who take orders into people who take risks, people who depend on the state into people who depend on themselves. This represents a significant change from the seventy years during which oil workers were supposed to be quintessential national actors, and thus public servants rather than entrepreneurs. The micro-enterprises were intended as a short-term tool to ease this transformation for the YPFianos, but there was no long-term plan for them. They were expected to become entrepreneurs on their own or to quietly disappear as they were replaced by young people with college degrees, computer skills, and an intuition for business. But the YPFianos did not quietly disappear.

Argentina's privatization process would not only alter how commodities and services are produced, distributed, and consumed, but would also transform the people who produce, distribute, and consume these products. However, it is wrong to assume that state projects or their representatives could determine these changes in subjectivity. This chapter elaborates my assertion that neoliberalismo is not a set of principles, a series of policies, or an ideology that is producing a new type of person: the autonomous, competitive, and calculative entrepreneur. Instead, neoliberalismo is a family of both novel and existing concepts, techniques, and discourses that is shaping personhood in unexpected ways. One of the unanticipated ways that the privatization of the Argentine oil industry has reshaped the YPFianos is by strengthening their longstanding kin relationships rather than replacing them with the short-term contractual agreements that neoliberal policies mandate.

The relationship between changes in state and economic institutions, on the one hand, and the transformation of social life and personhood, on the other hand, is never straightforward. There is no direct or predictable effect of the former upon the latter because, among other reasons, these processes cannot be untangled. As legal anthropologists have long pointed out, the law does not stand above society but is itself a social institution tightly imbricated with other aspects of social life. Chapter 2 examines how the legal and administrative aspects of the privatization of the Argentine oil industry intertwined with other processes of social transformation. This chapter focuses first on the development of a particular kind of person, family, and company that the national oil industry embodied and then on the intertwined reconfiguration of personhood, kinship, and labor that the privatization process entailed. What were the subjectivities, kinship formations, and social relationships that the privatization was intended to dismantle? How was the process of privatizing YPF and remaking YPFianos enacted on the ground? Why did it fail to generate the economic successes and autonomous individuals that it promised? What changes in personhood and social relations did the process of privatizing YPF produce? Conversely, what aspects of personhood and social life did not change despite the dramatic restructuring of the state and the oil industry?

Analyzing the interwoven lines of continuity and change between the state-led and privatized oil industry requires delving into the social history of petroleum production in Argentina. In the first part of this chapter, I chart the emergence of notions of YPF kinship including filial discourse and attendant practices of familial care in the oil towns in order to show, in the second part of the chapter, how YPFianos redeployed them during the privatization. Before I begin to tell the story of the YPFianos, however, I situate my analysis of it within scholarly debates about kinship and capitalism.

The Productive Power of Kinship Sentiments

Anthropologists long have criticized the assumption that kinship is a natural formation determined by seed, sperm, blood, or genes and have illustrated the varied grounds for generating kinship, from foods (Carsten 1997) to photographs (Bouquet 2001). This line of scholarship raises the possibility that kin relationships can be created through a substance as seemingly disconnected from biological reproduction, or the human body at all, as petroleum. This chapter joins contemporary kinship studies not only in demonstrating that countless materials are used to form kin relations, but also in showing that these relationships are based on intergenerational hierarchy and gendered discipline as much as on parental affection and sibling solidarity. Kinship sentiments and relationships are not a refuge from the world outside the home but are thoroughly part of it.[6] With the reinvigoration of the anthropological tradition of kinship studies, a burgeoning scholarship now focuses specifically on how science, technology, and capitalism have been deployed to reconfigure kin relations, familial reproduction, and the very concept of kinship itself. Anthropological studies of biomedical technology point to a collapse in the distinction between production and reproduction in the contemporary moment.[7] Furthermore, kinship sentiments now are recognized as both "resources that are used in production" and "cultural forces that incite, enable, constrain, and shape production" (Yanagisako 2002: 11). My examination of the formation and development of YPF, oil towns, and oil worker subjectivity builds on Sylvia Yanagisako's argument that kinship sentiments shape business enterprises as much as household dynamics. Affect, more generally, is not a force of reproduction trapped in the domestic domain, but a force of production that has important effects on the industrial and commercial processes of capitalism.

The rise and fall of YPF in Northwest Patagonia illustrates how company towns and their residents blur the assumed divides between kinship, labor, industry, and state. The history of the YPF town Plaza Huincul and neighboring Cutral Có shows how a particular kinship formed and attendant sentiments emerged in conjunction with the national oil industry and state rule over Patagonia. The intertwined paternalism of state and company has been central to this project. Paternalism undergirded the development of the oil industry but then came under attack during the neoliberal restructuring. Yet it hardly disappeared. Relationships among workers and between them and the state have continued to be understood and organized in terms of kinship, sometimes as brotherly dedication and intergenerational care and other times as filial constraint and paternal discipline. Yanagisako's analysis (2002) of struggles over inheritance and succession in Italian family firms shows how men's desires for filial continuity shape business strategy and the relationship between labor and capital. My analysis of YPF illustrates a similar dynamic, yet it also demonstrates that we cannot fully understand the productive power of kinship sentiments without paying attention to state institutions, their agents, and the national discourses they deploy. Kinship and nationalism come together to constitute a particularly powerful but unrecognized force in fueling oil production in Argentina and molding the people who have done the labor of producing petroleum, first for the state-owned company and then for the privately owned ones that succeeded them.

Paying attention to kinship sentiments is crucial not only for understanding the history of the national oil industry, but also for a robust analysis of its privatization as part of the larger project of neoliberalismo. The introduction identified several shortcomings in the bourgeoning literature on neoliberalism and suggested that attention to affect provides a fruitful path for addressing them and gaining a fuller understanding of neoliberal processes. There, I depicted neoliberalism as a family of discourses, techniques, and practices that resemble each other as kin do because of their shared genealogy, not because of a natural essence. Here, I highlight the crucial aspects of the Argentine branch of this family that would be overlooked without close attention to familial sentiments and kinship practices. These include both the lines of continuity between neoliberal and previous governing methods and the strategies used by those excluded from the privatized industry to regain a place within it. I demonstrate that, in short, YPF's privatization worked economically because it worked affectively.

Before elaborating the importance of kinship sentiments to the privatization of YPF, I turn to the history of the state oil company and the oil towns of Northwest Patagonia to explore the historical basis for the familial idiom and kinship practices that the YPFianos deployed in creating their emprendimientos. The history of Plaza Huincul and Cutral Có shows how YPF kinship emerged within the context of the extension of state governing, the development of oil extraction, and the advent of paternalism on the high desert plateau of Northwest Patagonia.

Fires in the Desert

The petroleum industry was established in Argentina within the context of the annihilation of native peoples, the encouragement of European immigration, and the incorporation of the southern territories into the nation and state. By the time of Argentina's independence from Spain in the first decade of the nineteenth century, missionaries had been working for almost two centuries to "civilize" the indigenous groups of the south, particularly to end their nomaticism, polygamy, and idolatry. While most native inhabitants did not take to sedentarism, they did to capitalism. They bought and sold livestock and frequently were accused of stealing them from the settlers who moved into the land that indigenous people had inhabited for centuries. Nearly all of the heterogeneous indigenous groups in Patagonia became incorporated into the Mapuche nation, whose *caciques* (chiefs) managed dealings with outsiders, including the livestock market and trade across the Andes (Nicoletti and Navarro 2000: 54–55). The military campaigns of the 1880s, however, exterminated most of the indigenous people, and state agents and Argentine *criollos* (people of Spanish descent) were able to assert control over Patagonia. The government in Buenos Aires attempted to repopulate the land with European settlers by rewarding soldiers with land grants and facilitating the creation of enormous farms and ranches. Contrary to the dominant national narrative, the Mapuche were not entirely wiped out, but the survivors joined poor criollos in becoming laborers on the new farms and ranches or *fiscaleros*, precarious occupants of the semi-arid grasslands and arid plains retained by the national state because they were undesirable for settlement (Nicoletti and Navarro 2002: 73–81, 90).[8]

The Argentine economy expanded tremendously as the country's farms and ranches increasingly fed the cities of Great Britain and Europe, but the growth was slow to reach the newly conquered Patagonian territories. The area that would become the Neuquén oil region was designated for grazing animals but was too dry for this use, so most settlers abandoned their allotments (Nicoletti and Navarro 2002: 81). The place called Huincul stood as an isolated way station for travelers across the Andes, purportedly run by a woman known as "the

Green Pasture" (*la Pasto Verde*) (Contreras n.d.). All this changed when the railroad was extended through the area in order to bring livestock and agricultural commodities from the interior of the Neuquén Territory to the Atlantic coast (Nicoletti and Navarro 2002: 89). At the same time that an enormous influx of immigrants arrived in Argentina, Huincul became a stop on the new southern train line. The railroad encouraged Italian and Spanish farmers to venture south from Buenos Aires in search of land and helped Syrian and Lebanese merchants to extend their filial trade networks across Patagonia. While official state discourse spoke of "Argentizing" the new settlements, it was not until oil was found near Huincul that the state's oil company took over the project of populating the region and governing it through biopolitical means.

After a state team found oil along the Patagonian coast at Comodoro Rivadavia in 1907, the federal state established a national oil reserve and founded the first state-owned oil company, within the Ministry of Agriculture, to produce and market the region's petroleum resources. A few years later, the Argentine Bureau of Mines, Geology, and Hydrology sent an exploration team to examine a promising spot in Northwest Patagonia. When the exploration team struck oil near Huincul, President Hipólito Yrigoyen designated a seventy-square-kilometer area centering on the first productive well as a second national oil reserve for exclusive exploitation by state agents (Favaro and Bucciarelli 1999: 230). Chapter 3 recounts with greater detail how battles between liberals who advocated "free-market" economic policies and nationalists who defended state-led industrialization have shaped the history of Argentina's oil industry ever since the founding of the first state oil enterprise. It is important to note here that the liberals restricted the growth of the state oil company in the first decades of the twentieth century, but energy shortages brought on by the two world wars allowed the nationalists to put in place the conditions for the state-managed oil regime that lasted from the 1920s until the 1990s. As will be explained below, it was military officers who spearheaded the founding of YPF Estatal in 1922 and invested it with a notion of national progress.

As oil exploration turned to oil extraction in the Neuquén Territory, the spot known as Huincul was transformed from a trade outpost into a work camp called "the Octagon" (Contreras n.d.). The state's hastily established camp soon grew into a company town, dotting the windy desert landscape with administration buildings, employee barracks, and other facilities. The population, which was highly mobile and mostly male, grew as the availability of jobs and the promise of above average salaries drew people to the oil enclave (Nicoletti and Navarro 2000: 126). Scores of Chilean, Syrian, Lebanese, and Argentine migrants came to capitalize on the effort to extract petroleum by selling goods and services to the state agents working in the Octagon and to the private oil companies working outside its boundaries. Men found jobs as manual laborers in the oilfields and women as domestic servants for the male geologists, engineers, and other professionals who stayed in the camp. Over the next two decades, administration buildings, sturdier barracks, a hospital, and other facilities were constructed in the northern part of the Octagon, while nonstate employees were permitted to build houses and operate small businesses in the southern part (Palacios and Paris 1993; Favaro and Bucciarelli 1999: 230). Luxuries such as electric lighting and heat, which were unheard of in Patagonia only a few years before, were now available in Plaza Huincul. The first residential area "was erected as an emblem of progress and prosperity in the midst of a landscape dominated by dryness, cold and wind" (Mombello 2005: 156).

YPF became not only the state's economic development agent, but also its medical and educational arm. The company operated the only hospital and school in the area until the rise of Peronism in the late 1940s. The oil camp thus enacted the state's "civilizing" mission in Patagonia and helped fulfill the liberal statesman Juan Bautista Alberdi's famous dictum "to govern is to populate."[9] The oil camp also embodied the emerging notion of petroleum nationalism.

General Mosconi's Petroleum Nationalism

The railways and meatpacking plants central to Argentina's economic growth in the early twentieth century depended on British capital investments and fuel imported by foreign companies. Military leaders, economists, and other nationalists argued that Argentina would not be able to industrialize, and thus never become the modern nation-state that they desired, without state control of the domestic oil supply. The military general who would become YPF's first director, Enrique Mosconi, articulated a vision of "petroleum nationalism" in which the state would supply energy, security, and sovereignty through its ownership and management of a vertically integrated national oil company (Solberg 1979). Mosconi credited his experience as director of the army's aeronautic service with showing him the problem with the military's reliance on a "foreign trust" for its fuel. He recounted a humiliating meeting with the director of Standard Oil of New Jersey's Latin American subsidiary in which he was forced to beg for jet fuel for the Argentine air force as an example of the country's foreign dependence (Pien 1999: 46–49). He saw an opportunity to address this injustice when Marcelo T. de Alvear succeeded Yrigoyen to the presidency in 1922. Mosconi became the director of the state oil company, which recently had been separated from the Ministry of Agriculture and renamed Yacimientos Petrolíferos Fiscales (YPF, literally "State Oil Deposits"), and he planned its reorganization and expansion. He argued that YPF must become a politically independent but state-owned company that controlled all aspects of the oil production process, from extraction to commercialization, if it was going to compete effectively with the foreign oil companies he liked to call "mammoth vampires" (Solberg 1982: 392). To help advance Mosconi's vision, President Alvear granted YPF administrative autonomy from the state, thus enabling its director to run the company without state approval for most business decisions (Solberg 1982: 385–86). Between 1922 and 1930, Mosconi led an ambitious program of building YPF's capacity to extract, transport, refine, and commercialize petroleum.

The historian Carl Solberg (1979) astutely asserts that Mosconi's greatest contribution was not the rigs, refineries, or gas stations he saw built, but his powerful articulation of "petroleum nationalism."[10] Mosconi belonged to a cohort of military officers who argued that industrialization was crucial for ensuring national security and political sovereignty. These military men joined nationalist economists and leaders of the burgeoning Radical Party (which included Presidents Yrigoyen and Alvear) who criticized former administrations' adoption of liberal economic policies that encouraged the export of agricultural products and the import of foreign commodities and capital (Belini 2006). Like many of their contemporaries across Latin America, these men asserted that Argentina could not throw off its dependence on Europe without developing its own industries, and industrialization was not possible without state support. In the years between the world wars, prominent figures—from economists such as Alejandro Bunge to writers such as Leopoldo Lugones—urged the federal government to enable Argentine industry to grow by protecting Argentine-owned companies from foreign competition and otherwise fostering Import Substitution Industrialization (Solberg 1979: 82–83; Belini 2006). Although they advocated increased state involvement in economic development, they hardly opposed privately owned, or even foreign owned, businesses. In fact, Mosconi initially argued that YPF should become a public-private partnership along the lines of the British Anglo-Persian Oil Company because he believed this form would best unite just ownership, fast growth, and maximum efficiency (Solberg 1982: 392). Only later did he come to see a state monopoly as the only effective vehicle for replacing foreign dependence with national independence.

While the U.S. administrations of the 1920s pushed an "open door policy," Mosconi traveled around Latin America encouraging states to "close the door" to foreign oil investment (Gibb and Knowlton 1956: 382; Solberg 1982: 392).

His adversaries portrayed foreign companies as bearers of progress, but he asserted that they were interested only in building reserves for future export and not in satisfying domestic consumption. Echoing an earlier description of Standard Oil as "a band of cruel, usurious pirates" and an "octopus . . . who has extended its tentacles everywhere," Mosconi equated Jersey Standard with a "hemp rope" and Royal Dutch Shell with a "silk rope," saying that "both might hang us"(Gibb and Knowlton 1956: 382; Solberg 1979: 19). These words resonated eighty years later during the national boycott of Shell and Exxon (see Chapter 3). Of importance here is that YPF differentiated itself from private oil companies by continually defining itself as embodying the nation. Not only did its pumps displaying the national colors serve as a reminder of the presence of the nation-state across the territory, but its policies and institutions attempted to embody national values. In speeches, books, and advertising campaigns, Mosconi asserted that the state-owned oil company would produce equally important "material and moral benefits" for the Argentine people. These material benefits would include the creation of state revenue, middle-class jobs, and a just fuel market across the country. YPF's moral benefits would include generating national pride in Argentina's "technical-administrative capacity" and thus bolstering the "national spirit" (Mosconi 1984: 167–75).

A 1934 poster captured the sentiment of petroleum nationalism when it proclaimed YPF as the vehicle that enabled the nation to propel itself forward (see Figure 4). YPF advertising presented the company, quite literally, as the motor for the improvement of the Argentine nation. Between the statements "the nation propelling itself forward" and "YPF the organ of power," the poster shows a monumental gear of progress, with each cog illustrating a different symbol of industrial motion: a bulldozer, a cargo truck, a barge, an airplane, a mine chute, a tractor, and a freight train. At the wheel's center sits an oil refinery, indicating that the whole operation is powered by YPF. Faintly in the background lies an image of oil rigs and a wharf leading to an oil tanker, which likely portray Comodoro Rivadavia, the major oil town on the Patagonian coast (see Map). The poster not only suggests that hydrocarbon-powered industrialization defines forward motion, but also that this progress will come from the oilfields of Patagonia and spread throughout the country as a whole. The state oil company is portrayed as combining the national territory—from subsurface minerals, to agricultural fields, to waterways, to the sky—into a single dehumanized machine. It is indicative of the historical moment that the nation which is "propelling itself forward" is represented as an industrial gear populated by vehicles,

Figure 4. This 1934 YPF poster states "The Nation Propelling Itself Forward. YPF The Organ of Power." Image courtesy of the University of Washington Libraries, Special Collections, UW 29646z.

not people. The poster captures a time when petroleum nationalism was popular among the growing number of urban consumers (Solberg 1979: 177–79) but before the rise of Peronism, when industrial workers would take center stage in depictions of the progress of the nation.

Housing Worker Families

YPF worker housing came to manifest the productive powers of Argentina's oil-rich territory in the name of personal and national improvement in a manner that was more resonant with Peronism than the 1934 poster. As one YPFiano put it, "YPF's purpose was not only that it had to extract petroleum, but also that it had to fittingly support its personnel." Petroleum national discourse contended that state oil workers were laboring for the well-being of the nation, and, in exchange, the state must care for them and their kin. Mosconi recounted, "The General Directorate proposed watching over and subsidizing, in the most complete manner possible, the general welfare of the organization's staff, so that the family head would not feel his energy or work capacity decreased by the worries inherent in the necessities of a home" (Mosconi 1984: 71–72). He advocated the construction of company housing to create what he called "a staff of strong men healthy in body and in spirit" and also to address concerns about their labor discipline amid increasing union militancy (Gorelik 1987).

Mosconi had a considerable effect on YPF, but he served as its director only for seven years before he was deposed by General José Uriburu following his overthrow of Yrigoyen in 1930. Mosconi refused to cooperate with the military dictatorship, and Uriburu feared that the admired "petroleum general" might lead opposition to his rule (Solberg 1979: 157). Yet after Mosconi left YPF, company architects began to design housing projects to realize his vision for YPF's "social mission." The dual project of generating national oil and national citizens advanced as the state responded to the anarchist and communist unions that emerged in the oilfields during the 1930s (Gorelik 1987). This project further accelerated when Juan Domingo Perón, who participated in Uriburu's coup, rose to national prominence under the military dictatorship of the early 1940s and after he gained the presidency in 1946. Perón helped found SUPE, the official state oil workers' union, as a measure to combat "social disorder" (see Chapter 3). While the military brutally repressed anarchist and communist movements, YPF more subtly tried to discipline the workforce by offering housing in exchange for "an inflexible discipline and an absolute rigidity in the completion of their duties and obligations" (Mosconi 1984: 71). Company housing provided material substantiation of the rewards of aligning with the emerging Peronist state. It also indicated how YPF represented a paternal company that was both nurturing and disciplining.

The housing they designed for oil towns like Plaza Huincul did not simply improve the barracks for single male workers that the state had been providing since the first oil well gushed in 1918. Instead, YPF built housing complexes around communal athletic and social facilities to promote both workers' "moral and physical health" and labor discipline (Gorelik 1987: 102). The company also built row homes and bungalows, which further differentiated employees by rank and family size. These residences were highly prized by YPF families because they were equipped with "modern conveniences" like electricity, heat, and indoor plumbing. Numerous YPFianos told of having a company employee come to their homes to do even minor repairs, such as replacing a light bulb when one burned out. YPFianos vied to gain access to this housing, which reaffirmed hierarchy, enforced discipline, and fostered a particular form of familial sociality in Plaza Huincul.

Housing was used to create YPF families in the double sense of workers positioned as children in relation to the state and of children raised to replace their parents' positions in the oil industry. An YPFiano named Franco Vincente explained to me that amid the chronic housing shortage that plagued Plaza Huincul and the surrounding area, company housing grew to have "a family logic." That is, YPFianos eased their sons into company jobs, bequeathed them their company housing, and thus were able to stay in their homes once they retired. Franco argued that this "recycling of the same house within the same family" was one of the reasons that many YPFiano families, including his own, were never able to live in company housing, despite Mosconi's emphasis on its practical and moral importance. Whereas Franco remarked on the inequitable distribution of resources, seen in another light, his comment indicates how a filial relation to an YPF worker gave a young man access to a job and a home and thus secured the continuity of both individual families and the state company. The state oil company's labor regime helped organize families along lines of patrilineal descent in which jobs in YPF and houses in Plaza Huincul were central forms of inheritance and tools of both familial and national continuity. They ensured conjugal fidelity, domestic stability, patrilineal inheritance, labor discipline, and state productivity in a region previously characterized by polygamy, nomadicism, unlawful land occupation, extralegal trade, and other enterprise unregulated by state institutions.

From the "Dangerous Neighborhood" to New Town

The state played a more ambivalent role in developing the familial settlements that grew outside of the official company town. After a 1932 fire in two oil tanks in Plaza Huincul was attributed to sabotage, the YPF director evicted the nonstate agents from the Octagon. Evictees described being thrown into an YPF truck and moved three kilometers away to an area that became known as Barrio Peligroso ("Dangerous Neighborhood," now part of Cutral Có), where approximately fifty households already resided (Palacios and Paris 1993: 321). Barrio Peligroso was one of several scattered settlements where manual laborers ineligible for company housing lived alongside domestic servants and peddlers in adobe and cardboard shacks around the few available water wells. There, an unpublished town history records, "these families lived, with their little ones, in an exceedingly miserable manner" (Contreras n.d.). Officials in Plaza Huincul feared that Barrio Peligroso was "breeding uncouth people," including gamblers and prostitutes who took advantage of the state workers for unsavory purposes. In response, some YPF administrators refused the settlers' requests for assistance and discouraged their employees from going there, while others wanted to normalize these settlements. Víctor Ezio Zanni, the director and doctor at the YPF hospital in Plaza Huincul, was among the latter. He set out to convert Barrio Peligroso from a haphazard encampment into a proper town, with the cooperation of another YPF professional, a state judge, and the chief of the civil registry stationed in Plaza Huincul, but without the consent of the YPF directorate or national land office in Buenos Aires.

On a few Sundays in June 1933, Dr. Zanni and his like-minded colleagues measured, sketched, and pegged a grid for a new town for oil workers in the sandy desert soil. They renamed it Barrio Nuevo ("New Settlement") and gave out lots to the men who lined up for them. When an YPF director, on a visit from the distant capital, objected that "it would have been better to attack the uncouth people who take shelter there than to give them benefits," Dr. Zanni countered that giving men landed property within a town grid was introducing "civilized" family structures into Patagonia (Contreras n.d.). Whether persuaded by Dr. Zanni's paternalist argument or not, the YPF director did not order the settlement razed as his predecessor had done to the one in the Octagon the year before.

This unofficial company town outgrew the official one next to it to become the second largest urban center in Neuquén Territory by the mid-1930s. Most of its more than twenty-five hundred inhabitants were newcomers and included numerous Argentines from other regions and immigrants from Italy, Spain, Syria, and Lebanon in addition to Chileans who had long inhabited Patagonia.

Several prominent Lebanese and Syrian families relocated their businesses there to supply the oil companies with equipment and to sell commodities to the oil workers and their kin (Favaro and Iuorno 1999: 64–66; Bandieri 2005). Although these families employed transatlantic kinship networks to achieve economic and then political success in Patagonia, they were never YPF employees and did not become integrated into YPF kinship. Yet they helped build a schoolhouse (Palacios and Paris 1993: 322)—amid the brothels and gambling halls at the site where a single woman previously managed a "green pasture" for the men who conducted trade across the Andes—in order to make the town into a better place for raising a family.

At the town's inauguration ceremony on the morning of October 22, 1933, officials recognized Barrio Nuevo as an official Argentine town. A short time later it was renamed Cutral Có, ostensibly an Araucanian (Mapuche) term meaning "firewater," thus discursively placing the region's indigenous occupation as the prehistory of the oil industry of the future. Although Dr. Zanni was credited as the town founder, he asserted that it was the hard-working laborers who reformed the settlement into a proper town in which a male worker could support his kin. In an interview conducted half a century later, Dr. Zanni recalled that the men who moved into the grid "erected their dwellings in only a few days, by stretching almost beyond their means, in order to relocate their families," and created a "very modest but at least decent and forward-looking town." In his speech at the inauguration, Dr. Zanni projected that "water, lights, heating, trees, aesthetics and much proper love: everything is possible when . . . the inhabitants of this new town, most of them humble soldiers of work, grab shovels and hoes to selflessly contribute to the general welfare." Neuquén Territory's military governor concurred with Dr. Zanni's idealized portrait of Barrio Nuevo as fulfilling a "civilizing mission." They both suggested that the labor of the town's male inhabitants not only made it possible to introduce "modern conveniences," but also to generate "selfless" sacrifice, "proper love," decency, and other romanticized signs of civilized kin relations (Contreras n.d.). While women's work went unmentioned at the inauguration, the event marked the initiation of a process through which marital desires were encouraged and women's remunerated labor as maids in Plaza Huincul barracks was replaced with their unremunerated labor as housewives in Cutral Có homes. The sentiments of dedication and sacrifice, and a gendered division of labor, became important aspects of the "YPF family" in Patagonia.

An article published in honor of the town's second anniversary in *La Prensa*, a leading Buenos Aires newspaper, on October 28, 1935, emphasized that

Cutral Có's development was the result of its residents' commitment to family and nation in a manner similar to Dr. Zanni's inauguration speech. The author, the established Argentine writer known as Fernán Félix de Amador, pointedly noted that state agents developed "the most valuable sources of petroleum deposits in the country" but failed to provide the "colonizing action of the state" to house those involved in petroleum production or to support their families. He argued that the "pertinacious existence of this remote urban center" represented "a valiant example of what can be done with goodwill, the spirit of colonization and love of the land." The town, he wrote, "has arisen from among the brush of the desert, by virtue of a social imperative: the institution of the family." When this Buenos Aires journalist named the family as a "social imperative," he hinted at how kinship sentiments, such as love, dedication, and the desire for family stability, merged with state and industrial forces of production to carry out the projects that enabled the creation of worker families on the Patagonian desert plateau. The doctor's, governor's, and journalist's narratives also combined military metaphors of discipline with a masculine settler ethos of hard work and love of the land to represent the nation on Argentina's remote southern frontier.

Both Dr. Zanni's statement about the connection between "proper love" and "the general welfare" and the Buenos Aires journalist's comments about the productive effects of "goodwill, the spirit of colonization and love of the land" drew on longstanding notions of the intimate connection between family and nation in Argentina. In literary and other representations of the nineteenth century, Latin America's nascent nations were portrayed in idealized kinship terms, sometimes as brotherhoods and other times as nuclear families (Sommer 1991; Plotkin 2003: 121; Anderson [1983] 1991). The Argentine nation was repeatedly envisioned as springing from the marital union of the strong gaucho and the fertile fields of the pampas. With increasing industrialization, the petroleum-rich territory on Argentina's southern periphery joined its agriculturally rich center as grounds for enacting this ideal of the nation as a marriage. The workers were encouraged, following the model of the gauchos, to embody the union of male labor with the natural riches of the land. The history of the oil towns illustrates how the mission of the state shifted from merely populating the frontier to encouraging "civilized" living arrangements and family structures there. While the former project was primarily expressed through a trope of the marriage of masculine labor and feminine land, the latter was expressed through one of marital desires and filial bonds between fathers and sons. Yet ideas of the nation as a brotherhood remained pervasive in both.

Peronism gave ideas about labor, family, and the nation new meaning as workers were positioned as dependent children in relation to a paternal state. At the same time that Peronism infantilized citizens, it promoted their rights to employment, commodity consumption, and public services. The promise of increased consumption and services depended on replacing an export-oriented economy with one centered on domestic production. This, in turn, rested on the production of sufficient and inexpensive energy from Argentine sources. As Mosconi articulated, relying on foreign fuels and companies placed the Argentine military and industries in a position of dependence on European powers. The extraction of oil in the southern reaches of the Argentine territory was thus framed as a project that would bring sovereignty to the nation as a whole.

Petroleum nationalism was manifest not only in presidential speeches and state policy, but also in the spaces of Patagonia and the lives of people in the oil towns. Public works related to oil extraction, such as roads, refineries, and water and gas lines, became symbols of national modernization (Nicoletti and Navarro 2000: 118). YPF workers and their spouses saw themselves as sacrificing for the advancement of the nation and thus deserving of the "goods" that corresponded to their roles in delivering modernity to their fellow citizens. However, the reality of everyday relationships—as one might expect—fell short of the ideal. On the one hand, the YPFianos served as harbingers of modernity when they installed natural gas heaters and stoves in their homes, bought cars and then quickly replaced them with the latest models, or traveled for leisure by plane or car. On the other hand, their lives revealed the ugly underbelly of this modernity when they experienced gas explosions, plane crashes, and the isolation of living far from family. Throughout the process of developing the national oil industry in Patagonia, kinship sentiment was both motivation and remedy for men's labor in the oilfields.

Creating YPF Families

Fernando Castillo's experience illustrates how "petroleum nationalism" and "the YPF family" together influenced the lives of ambitious young men who left their urban homes to work for YPF in the country's remote southern oilfields. Several other YPFianos described Fernando as the man who best knew YPF's social mission, as he had worked for many years in its social services division (*obra social*) before joining an emprendimiento called OptaNeu. In his late sixties when I met him in 2005, he was still strong and spry. He was also an exceedingly kind man. He insightfully explained how the YPF family developed through the combination of YPF policies and worker initiatives, using his own experience as an illustration.

Fernando was born and grew up in a tight-knit immigrant family in Buenos Aires. After finishing high school there, he sought one of the highly coveted positions in YPF. His mother's friend helped him land a job in the Neuquén oil-fields, but his parents opposed his leaving home to take it. Fernando was one of the many YPF workers who told me that although his parents took great pride in his working for the company, they disapproved of his moving to a place they saw as "the end of the earth." He recalled how hurt he had been that his father helped him prepare for his move but "didn't go to the send-off because for him it was not acceptable for sons to separate from the family." Soon, however, Fernando and his fellow workmates forged kin relations among themselves to supplement, or replace, their natal families living far from the oilfields.

Upon arriving in Plaza Huincul in 1964, Fernando traded filial kinship for brotherly and later marital relations, as YPFianos incorporated him within their web of kinship. He recounted that "the first thing that happened when it came out that you were from far away was that they invited you home to have an *asado* [barbeque] or some mate." His first Christmas exemplified his immediate incorporation within YPFianos' filial bonds. He always had cele-brated Christmas with his extended family in Buenos Aires, but, he explained, he started working for YPF just before the holiday and "therefore I didn't even think about going to Buenos Aires to be with my family." He rhetorically asked me, "Can you believe that there were *compañeros* [workmates] who invited me to celebrate Christmas with them, as if I was part of their family?" He ex-claimed, "I even became accustomed to the fact that someone would come up to me and say, 'Look, are you going to spend Christmas Eve alone? Come to my house!'" These "as if" kin relations were soon replaced by ones legitimated by their intersection with both the state's legal regime through marriage and its economic apparatus through YPF.

Fernando's incorporation into an YPF family was fully realized when he married Claudia, the daughter of a high-ranking YPFiano. Claudia was an of-fice intern at YPF's base in Plaza Huincul when she and Fernando met. More importantly, she belonged to one of the many families in which all of the men worked for the national oil company. Fernando recounted that his marriage to this daughter of a prominent YPF family was possible only because he spent his first eight years in Patagonia working at the Catriel oil camp rather than taking a job at the Plaza Huincul base after his obligatory rotation at the camp ended. YPFianos received a 10 percent bonus for working at places like Catriel because, Fernando explained, "it was removed from everything that was civilization; let's say it was the *Far West.*" The financial reward for suffering Catriel's "inconveniences" allowed Fernando to save money for marriage to an YPF daughter. When I asked him to explain his prescient planning, he instead told me about its results: "When I became engaged, with the years that I spent in Catriel, we bought the refrigerator, we bought the tiles . . . we bought out the whole commissary." YPF policy encouraged workers to purchase on credit and repay their debts through deductions from their future salary, thus further binding them to YPF. Fernando bought his house this way and, he continued, "When I had finished paying for everything, then I asked [Claudia] if she wanted to get married, and she said yes, and that was that." His marital desire thus necessitated his continued work for YPF but, once wed, he was well positioned to take a job at the Plaza Huincul base and spend more time in his new home. Many other YPFianos were not so fortunate and continued to spend long periods without their families in the distant oil camps in order to support them in the oil towns.

The importance of a house in the company town equipped with the comforts the petroleum industry brought to Patagonia became most clear to me when I mistakenly asked Fernando a question about the eight years he had lived at Catriel. Fernando interrupted me, explaining that although he spent fifteen days at a time at Catriel, he did not *live* there, only worked there. "We lived here," he said with a small laugh as he pointed out the window of the YPF-warehouse-turned-emprendimiento-office in which we were sitting. "Do you see that block of buildings, that house that has silver trim? Well, those two and also the one in front of it were for single men; they were bachelors' dormitories. I lived there until I got married; when I married I had my own little house." For Fernando, "living" meant having a residence in the company town where he engaged in familial practices such as holiday meals, first as the adoptive kin of already established YPF families and then as the head of his own household.

Beyond his personal experience living far from kin in Catriel (see Map, Inset B), Fernando dealt with these issues at work. His job in the social services division was to resolve the problems that arose because YPF required most of its workers to spend long intervals "removed from their family and far from their group of friends and others" in a place many YPFianos compared to the western United States that they saw portrayed in the cowboy and Indian movies they took their dates and then their wives to see at the YPF theater in Plaza Huincul (see Figure 5). Although state employment was often contingent on extended absence from one's family, this did not mean that YPF broke its employees' kinship bonds or even caused them to be neglected. State institutions can rework familial attachments to make them support national concerns (Stoler 2004: 17), as occurred on the Patagonian frontier.

Figure 5. Many YPFianos are nostalgic about "Petroleum Theater," the YPF movie theater in Plaza Huincul, which is now closed.

"Cradle-to-Grave"

Job inheritance, like company housing, was a crucial YPF practice that shaped the form of both worker families and industrial production. A man named Freddy (Alfredo) Garza, one of the very few YPFianos from Plaza Huincul who retained a position in YPF SA and then YPF-Repsol, told me that not only his father and mother, but also his two uncles, brother, father-in-law, and two brothers-in-law were all YPFianos. "Because of this," Freddy remarked, "everything revolved around YPF, everyone, all the families." Similarly, the first time I met an YPFiano named Octavio Marquez he too described his family as "all YP-Fiano" and listed each of his relatives who had held positions in the company. Octavio explained that working for YPF was a tradition that people in Neuquén handed down from generation to generation like a family heirloom.

The passing of positions in YPF from father to son was more than an informal practice; YPF policy gave hiring priority to children of employees and guaranteed positions to relatives of employees who were incapacitated or killed at work. Freddy Garza, for one, began working for YPF after his father died in a work-related accident when Freddy was a teenager. During one of our long conversations, Franco Vincente, another YPFiano mentioned above, expounded on the company's regulations regarding work accidents, providing the gory details of how much financial compensation one received for each kind of injury or dismemberment. In cases in which an employee could no longer work, he said, "they paid him a subsidy and life insurance payments for the family," emphasizing, "for those who had sons, they could enter YPF." This practice sometimes included daughters, as in the case of an YPFiano who died in a work accident when his only child, a girl, was eighteen years old. One of her friends explained to me, "The logical thing was that [she] inherited the job, not the same position, but employment." In addition to the official policies supporting the hiring of children of YPF employees, I heard numerous accounts of men who eased the way for their nephews, sons-in-law, and other relatives to take positions in YPF even though these kin bonds were not recognized by company job inheritance policy. Feelings of filial love, dedication to kin, and desire for family continuity motivated fathers to try to ensure the well-being of their children through both state-sanctioned and unsanctioned means. At the same time, these paternal sentiments constrained the career paths and personal lives of both parents and children.

YPF did not simply provide its largely male employees with the jobs, housing, and social services that allowed them to support a wife and children but also encouraged the formation of families in which labor was strictly gendered. As was typical at that time, YPF restricted women to a limited number of office jobs at the Plaza Huincul base, remunerating them far less than male workers. Women were expected to leave these positions when they married, although some continued to work until they gave birth to their first child. YPF pay scales, which increased a man's salary with the addition of each new family member, encouraged family structures in which women maintained homes, raised children, and cared for their worker husbands, so that these men could realize Mosconi's vision of not being distracted from their labors in the oilfields.

YPFianos derived both material and symbolic benefits from the package of "cradle-to-grave" services that YPF and its union SUPE provided to worker families in the oil towns. In addition to housing for some, YPFianos and their immediate families had access to high-quality health care, transportation, education, commissaries, sports and recreation clubs, and paid vacations to spend at SUPE-owned hotels. Many YPF men asserted that their wives and children were better able to take advantage of these social benefits than they were. One told me that each summer four or five hundred children would play sports at the YPF club in Plaza Huincul, and their mothers even learned to swim and play hockey; in contrast, their fathers had only a soccer ball with which to amuse themselves in the distant work camps. From the perspective of one of these women, "if you became engaged to someone from YPF, you had your life already settled . . . as far as your ability to construct a house, to have a family, to have children; all that was guaranteed." She was among many women and men her age whose experience with privatization made them nostalgic for the security that the state oil company had provided. Comments like hers emphasize how YPF made possible the fulfillment of filial desires, yet the enabling relation also worked in the other direction: kinship sentiments facilitated the production of oil.

The YPF Fallacy

Large numbers of YPF families without access to company housing formed cooperative housing complexes or constructed individual houses in Cutral Có. These houses had a slightly different "family logic" than those in Plaza Huincul, where YPF policies encouraged kin to continue living under the same roof for many years. For the YPFianos who were unable to reside in Plaza Huincul, the desire for a family composed of a bread-winner husband, a homemaker wife, and dependent children living in a single-family residence encouraged men to labor in distant oilfields for long periods. While many YPFianos boasted about the bonuses they had received when they married or had a new child, their labor histories indicate the necessity of working in the more isolated and dangerous positions in the oil fields in order to be able to have the kind of family that YPF promoted.

Franco and Maria Elena Vincente's experience exemplifies how familial sentiments enabled the production of oil by the state. The Vincentes were among the couples who founded an YPF worker neighborhood in the area between Plaza Huincul and Cutral Có in 1964. By 2003, their house sat on a paved street within the municipal boundaries of Cutral Có. During early periods of fieldwork, I lived with this family in their robust, two-story white stucco house, which had three bedrooms, a garage, a patio, and a large garden. In the evenings, as Maria Elena prepared meals for whichever of her three children, husband, and resident anthropologist were eating at home that day, she reminisced about single-handedly caring for children and house while her husband was away in the oilfields. She looked back with a mixture of satisfaction and regret at her labors, sometimes shaking her head in amazement that she had completed tasks such as hauling water alone. Franco tended toward the taciturn, but one winter afternoon as a storm raged outside, he and I sat at his sturdy wooden dining table while he recounted his life story. Maria Elena joined us, an hour or so later, after she had finished her household chores.

Franco remembered the exact date that he started working for YPF: December 21, 1961. He was born in another oil town where his father worked for a company that would later become part of Exxon. After Franco completed his formal education at age seventeen, he took a job with a U.S. seismology company. Three years later, Franco sought work at YPF, returning to the employment office each month to see where he stood on the hiring list. He had hoped to work in drilling, but when a position in transportation opened, he jumped at it. Like Fernando Castillo, the former YPF social services employee, Franco told me that YPF created the conditions that facilitated "a whole work plan so I could buy the materials, so I could build a house, so I could get married," like a perfectly arranged row of dominoes that only needed to be set in motion. Franco told me how he started to assemble the structure around us in order to house his wife and children. He began by negotiating with the landlord of his rented room to store building materials in the back of the lot. He then built "the essentials" needed to move Maria Elena and their newborn first daughter out of their rented quarters by skipping vacations to earn money more quickly. Thus, from the very beginning of their marriage, a desire for a familial residence motivated Franco to labor for long stretches far away from Maria Elena and their children.

As we spoke, the rain turned to hail, and one of Cutral Có's frequent blackouts plunged us into darkness. As we continued our conversation by candlelight, Franco described in great detail their neighborhood committee's efforts to obtain electricity, water, gas, and finally sewer service for their residential block. Maria Elena had cooked with kerosene canisters before utility lines were laid in the neighborhood. Supplying gas lines was emblematic of how Franco and his workmates partnered with YPF to transform their first cabins in Cutral Có into what they considered proper YPF worker houses. Their block committee first gathered and saved enough money to pay a laborer to dig ditches for pipelines, then they negotiated with Gas del Estado—then a division of YPF—to hook up lines to its network and asked the YPF management to "collaborate" by providing the necessary pipes. Once they put the infrastructure in place, these YPFianos began to be compensated for their work for YPF with the ability to use an unlimited but insignificant quantity of the product of their labor. Franco hesitantly pointed to the price of these utilities when he stated: "We were not given anything as a gift. It was because we obtained standing within YPF that we did not pay for gas; it and the water were free." While Franco asserted that he deserved gas as payment for his labor, his use of the word "free" indicates some ambivalence in his interpretation of how and why he obtained gas for his home. The Vincentes and their neighbors became consumers of petroleum before other Argentines of similar background and means, and they saw this as only fitting for an YPF family living in the "land of petroleum."

However, state-led petroleum production did not improve their lives in any simple sense because maintaining a home in Cutral Có required decades of working far away from it. Petroleum was, in other words, both a sentence and a reward for Franco.

When Franco took a position in YPF's transportation division as a single young man, he expected to trade dangerous and unpleasant work carrying explosives in a truck over the unpaved roads of the Patagonian desert for the ability to support a wife and children, and then to retire to the comfort and security of the home he built. Even though Franco benefited from the retirement incentives offered early in the privatization process, he was not as nostalgic about his years with YPF as many of his contemporaries. While most men I knew in his position celebrated YPF for "giving me everything," Franco looked back regretfully on his exchange of labor for family and house. On the one hand, Franco credited YPF with being "the mother of all creations," explaining, "the reality of these towns was born because YPF brought them all the conveniences, comforts, and everything else." On the other hand, this "mother" cruelly confiscated what she had created. Franco explained:

> I could have come here to the base but would have earned less than staying in the camp. For what was called uprooting [desarraigo], they paid you, you had a bonus. Well, that's logical [for] leaving your family. We were in a place where there was only sky and pampa, pampa and sky. There was nothing, you understand. One passed eighteen days looking in the faces of the very same people who were working there. If you had it good, let's say, you played soccer, what the hell. But it was very different from being able to be with family, being able to be with friends.

He concluded, "The most problematic for me always was the uprooting from family, that is, my wife alone here with my daughters, and me over there." He regretted that he was not able to accompany his children on their first days of school or attend their graduations, celebrate their birthdays, or hold their hands when they were sick. Franco resented that it took thirty years of being away from his wife and children to attain what he wanted for them. He felt it most acutely, he told me, in the missed moments with his children as they grew up; his youngest was already in secondary school by the time he was able to spend more time at home. With a quiver in his voice he repeated, "It's tough, it's hard when you are forming a good home but missing the enjoyment of it." This, he implied, was the fallacy that the state forced on those who worked for the state oil company.

As Fernando and Claudia Castillo's marriage suggested and Franco and Maria Elena Vincente's house corroborated, familial sentiments of love, dedication, decency, and a desire for continuity prompted and shaped the subjectification of YPF workers and their kin. These sentiments also helped generate domestic and industrial labor relations that were mutually dependent but starkly divorced. Yet, many years later when the privatization of YPF was well under way, most YPFianos looked back with nostalgia at the paternalism of the state company. YPFianos like Fernando and Franco depicted the state oil company as a loving and caring—if stern—father, or sometimes mother, and referred to YPF's "head," "heart," "bosom," and other corporal parts. They also frequently discussed their relationships to fellow workers through discourses of kinship as well as friendship. One YPFiano simply stated, "Everyone felt the company was a family." Speaking on behalf of his workmates from the YPF refinery in La Plata, another man explained: "We gave our youth to YPF, but YPF took care of us. We were very young when we entered, you see, recently married. I entered work one morning and that afternoon my first son was born. Do you realize? And when I left, I had grandchildren . . . Imagine that! How could one not love [*querer*] the company that offered [*brindaba*] you everything?" This man equated his labor history with his filial history and described both industrial and domestic relations as practices of giving and receiving care.[11] His account also represented a paternalist vision of the national state. YPFianos drew from the discourse about the nation as family as they reflected on the exchange of labor for welfare that YPF Estatal had offered them. Kinship is repeatedly framed as the antidote to the ills and hardships of frontier capitalism and thus a crucial ingredient in the recipe for national development in the twentieth century. Thus, kinship provided an important means for the YPFianos to deal with the newest capitalist frontier, euphemistically called "state reform," at the turn of the twenty-first century.

The Patagonian "Startups"

Of the forty-three thousand veteran oil workers across Argentina who left the state enterprise during the conversion of YPF Estatal to YPF SA, some were formally laid off, some accepted early retirement packages, and others were forcibly retired. Many were instructed by their YPF bosses and their union representatives to convert their work units into emprendimientos. The emprendimiento program was initially intended as a temporary measure to ease the transition to a privatized industry for state workers in isolated regions like Northwest Patagonia. The program promised these workers that they could retain their oil-sector jobs and "stake" in the industry, only now through subcontracting agreements between the emprendimientos they owned and the giant corporation they did not. In Plaza Huincul and Cutral Có, YPFianos founded forty-five different emprendimientos, some with as few as three worker–owners and others with as many as two hundred. Although a few of these ventures were organized as worker cooperatives similar to the auto-parts factory portrayed in the film *The Take* (2005), many more were organized along more normatively capitalist lines and reproduced the hierarchical structure of YPF Estatal's production units. The majority of these emprendimientos had closed by the end of 1993, but the ones discussed here survived until at least 2005.

As Diego Parmado indicated in the opening vignette, oil workers in Plaza Huincul and Cutral Có, as elsewhere, were expected to make the change from state employees to small-business owners just as quickly as President Menem signed the decree that privatized YPF. Toward the ostensible end of helping workers make this transition, YPF SA gave each emprendimiento a no-bid contract for a few years, sold each of them the far outdated equipment that the workers had used in YPF Estatal, and established schedules for repayment of debts from these sales with deductions from their earnings. Increased subcontracting was a technique employed worldwide by oil executives eager to decrease corporate costs and liabilities, but in Argentina it especially served to shift the responsibility for rising unemployment and falling welfare away from corporate and state actors and onto the shoulders of workers. The YPFianos observed with dismay as their health care was transferred from the company hospitals and clinics to the overburdened state system, company property was sold as private real estate, and the YPF clubs that housed social, sports, and entertainment programs were dismantled or left to fall to pieces. As we will see, subcontracting is a particularly neoliberal form of government that uses regulatory, disciplinary, and *affective* techniques to encourage people to govern themselves in the marketplace.[12]

The former state workers who became partners in emprendimientos continued to do almost everything necessary for petroleum production—from geological imaging and well drilling to pipeline cleaning and paper filing. Although they were doing for the private corporations essentially the same work they had done for YPF Estatal, they did these tasks without the guarantees of stable employment with middle-class status, predictable wages, and the numerous benefits they had had as state workers. The privatized oil company did not provide the salaries and welfare benefits to its subcontractors that the state had provided to its workers. Moreover, the ground under the YPFianos shifted, almost literally, because the vast majority of the public assets these workers had produced and used did not necessarily become their property. As a result, many lost their equipment, vehicles, and even their homes. The emprendimiento worker–owners also assumed complex new responsibilities for which they were unprepared, including negotiating contracts, managing large cash flows, providing insurance, obtaining credit, and paying business taxes. As the new emprendimiento partners struggled to figure out how to make the transition from state worker to business owner, they frequently turned for help to the small group of YPF Estatal bosses who had become managers in the privatized oil company.

Managing Mentality

The supervisors who worked for the privatized oil company asserted that they assisted the YPFianos–turned–emprendimiento owners in becoming independent "entrepreneurs" despite the obvious conflict of interest this entailed. At YPF-Repsol's posh high-tech office building in Neuquén City, an hour's drive from Plaza Huincul, an YPF-Repsol external-relations manager named Ricardo Alvarez explained that he and other corporate representatives "had to change the mentality of these people a little, because they were employees, not entrepreneurs." He explained the difference between these positions:

> To be an employee is to be dependent. For example, in a bar there is the owner, who is the entrepreneur, and the others are all employees. Here, the owner was the state and everybody was an employee, you understand. They didn't have the mentality to advance a business, because the business belonged to the state. And so when they became entrepreneurs they didn't know anything, they had no entrepreneurial mentality, and they were missing the *management.* An employee normally doesn't think, he receives orders. So, these people suddenly found themselves as owners of a company, and they didn't know how to manage it.

This corporate representative suggested that the YPFianos' difficulty in becoming successful business owners stemmed from their lack of entrepreneurial disposition as much as from their lack of financial and administrative skills. Ricardo assumed that business acumen is the result of a psychological process in which state employees rid themselves of their dependencies, the bane of entrepreneurship. Instead, he argued, emprendimiento owners must think for themselves, that is, think like the business consultants brought in to advise them. He did not mention either insufficient capital or the substantial debts to YPF SA that the emprendimiento owners stressed.

Ricardo and his colleagues' efforts to remake the YPFianos into business entrepreneurs was assisted by a well-known U.S.-based business consultancy, Morningside Advisors, that was hired to help privatize YPF. While its principal charge was to guide the rewriting of policy and procedure, after it became clear that the juridical privatization process had failed to remake the YPFianos into business entrepreneurs, the consulting company was charged with teaching the emprendimiento owners how to manage their businesses using calculative techniques of accounting, financial planning, and cash management. The transnational consultancy joined the privatized oil company in taking on an educational role usually assumed by state actors and tried to teach the YPFianos "global business culture."

During my visits to the Morningside offices overlooking the Buenos Aires skyline, I talked frequently with Gabriel Peretz, a sharp, hard-working, and thoughtful man with a master's degree in sociology from a highly respected Argentine university and a U.S. business school degree. Gabriel was the expert in human resources who led an interdisciplinary team of consultants that Neuquén Province and YPF-Repsol had jointly contracted to work with the emprendimientos in Northwest Patagonia. He took unaccustomed breaks from a job in which he billed every hour, reclined in one of the office's leather chairs, and patiently answered my questions. He asserted that YPF SA, and then YPF-Repsol, had tried to help "these people who fell outside of the market to insert themselves in companies," but they had failed to generate sustainable businesses. He explained:

> The strategic error is that for a workman from the former YPF Estatal, with its paternalistic culture in which it gave him everything, to become a businessman who is responsible for the management of finances, human resources, assets— this generated a very large *crack*. Also in the thinking of these people . . . One of the biggest problems that the emprendimientos possess has to do with their ignorance about business. They don't know what *a management* is. They don't know about the accounting issues, the financial issues, how to manage assets, manage machinery, manage people.

The "strategic error" to which Gabriel referred was the idea that the YPFianos would independently remake themselves from state workers into entrepreneurs who are able to form, maintain, and grow companies without being explicitly taught how. The task of Gabriel's team was to teach them to be entrepreneurs: "We wanted to generate a very important cultural change in the sense of, well, one has to understand now that one no longer depends on the state, on the paternal state, on 'Dad the State' as we say here. Instead, it depends a lot on you guys now, on great ingenuity, intuition, on being go-getters . . . on having the mentality of an entrepreneur, having a vision for business." Kinship, here in the form of "Dad the State," stood for an atavistic and juvenile dependence in contrast to the individualism, self-sufficiency, and competition of the market. Gabriel, like external-relations manager Ricardo Alvarez, associated the private domain with independence, initiative, and freedom but acknowledged that it did not arise simply from eliminating paternalism. They both suggested that the privatization of YPF did not automatically generate the independent oil entrepreneurs it was supposed to create. Instead, these new collective and individual subjects had to be actively generated by cultivating "the mentality of an entrepreneur." What is most surprising about how this process unfolded is how much it relied on extending paternal relationships.

Learning to Manage

Hernán de la Cruz's experience illustrates how YPFianos understood the difficulties of learning to manage an emprendimiento in terms distinct from those of the corporate representatives. When a mutual friend introduced us, I never would have guessed that Hernán was the managing director of a company with more than one hundred workers. He was a burly man who appeared older than his forty-eight years, with a head of salt-and-pepper hair and the leathery skin of someone who had spent most of his life outdoors. Despite his new management position, he continued to wear the sweater, jeans, and boots of the field foreman he previously had been. Between drags on a cigarette in a cold YPF warehouse-turned-office, he told me how he learned of YPF's privatization: "One day the shift director appeared and said, 'YPF Estatal is finished.' They just announced, 'Gentlemen, it is finished,'" Hernán repeated for emphasis. "YPF directly informed the management, and they informed all the employees that YPF was finished and that all of the sectors had to form companies." Mirroring Diego Parmado's experience discussed in the opening of this chapter, Hernán's pithy account of YPF's privatization shows that the dissolution of the state-owned petroleum enterprise was immediately translated into an imperative to create privately owned service companies. YPFianos were not simply dismissed but, instead, told to remake themselves from civil servants into business owners. Likewise, the social relations that bound these workers within the company were supposed to be transformed, with state dependence replaced by entrepreneurial independence.

Hernán spoke to me at length about his experience as we sat at his desk while construction workers knocked down the walls around us to transform a long-neglected YPF building into offices for his emprendimiento, POLIP. He lit a cigarette and told me how he tried to remake himself from an YPF unit head who inspected equipment into POLIP's managing director:

> I was the person [in my YPF unit] who went and checked the equipment so that it would work well. I was the one who spoke with the YPF inspectors, that is, with those highest up. Thus, when it fell to me to sit at a desk and look at the whole commercial part, it taxed me. I did not understand it, I did not understand it. Therefore, what did I have to do? I had to grab the accountant and say to him, "Explain this to me, explain what profit is, explain the value added tax, explain the 21 percent that we have to pay, explain what insurance is"—everything that I am learning. I had to go picking it up day by day. Nobody taught it to me. Look, no one explained to me, "When you assemble a company, when you are the head, you have the year-end bonus, you have the lawyers, you have the accounting practice." It was difficult.

As other studies of neoliberal projects suggest, YPF's privatization process encouraged the creation of corporate subjects who were responsible for their own education. A new businessman like Hernán had to actively seek business knowledge and skills. He described this learning process as being made up of a series of somatic practices: "sitting down at a desk," "looking at papers," and "grabbing an accountant." After stressing how taxing this learning process was, he concluded, "Now this is simple for me because I have lived it in my own body." Yet, Hernán did not reschool himself by increasing his autonomy or individualism but by strengthening his engagements with others. Hernán described his struggle, along with his partners, to build their emprendimiento as the "combined effort" of a family in which "everyone contributes and everyone helps." In establishing new affinities and collaborations, and in strengthening existing ones, Hernán and his partners drew on the twofold meaning of YPF kinship, as a set of closely interlinked domestic arrangements *and* industrial arrangements.

"Soup All Around!"

The YPFianos in emprendimientos reconfigured their affective attachments to YPF and to each other in order to deal with the oil industry's transformation and to generate associations largely removed from the purview of the state. They aimed to re-form YPF labor relations from bonds between a domineering father and his obedient, although sometimes rebellious, sons into bonds of familial cooperation to which all members equally contributed. They emphasized how they each converted the final benefit they received as state workers—their severance pay—into the foundation for their joint ventures as emprendimiento owners. Although only a few of the emprendimientos were worker cooperatives, most worker–owners placed great emphasis on their shared labor histories and similar financial situations to establish a parity in which the partners made equal investments, had an equal role in decision making, and contributed equal amounts of sweat to keep the oil rigs and refineries running. Their definition of business partnership as brotherhood was facilitated by the fact that the emprendimientos were composed of YPF workers within a narrow range of rankings, from laborers to skilled workers, but not upper-level managers or engineers, who were dismissed in lower numbers and had more employment opportunities than lower-level workers. In generating business partnerships as kinship bonds, the emprendimiento owners emphasized the mutual care within YPF families while deemphasizing or explicitly rejecting the unequal division of labor and hierarchical relations that were also crucial aspects of YPF Estatal.

YPFianos described their emprendimientos as products of kin solidarity in a manner that paralleled the way they spoke of YPF Estatal. For instance, when I asked Hernán de la Cruz why POLIP survived when so many other emprendimientos succumbed to bankruptcy, he turned off his cell phone so we would not be interrupted and narrated the story of how "a strong human group formed in the company." He recounted how the partners "put all the force that they had" and "suffered in the flesh some months" to make sure the company survived. Instead of paying their own salaries, they paid their debts to suppliers, insurance premiums, and taxes. He concluded: "It taxed us a great deal; therefore, it seems to me, our combined effort is like a family. If everyone contributes and everyone helps, I believe that you can move things forward." When Hernán asserted that POLIP endured the hardships because it was organized around familial bonds, he implied that his and his partners' unpaid labor was equivalent to parents working to ensure the survival of a child. He stressed that sustaining industrial relations within the privatized oil industry required as much shared sacrifice and mutual assistance as it had in YPF Estatal. "Moving the emprendimiento forward" involved combining affective labor, like building filial bonds, with calculative work, like managing the payroll and taxes.

The Lucano family provides a vivid illustration of how YPFianos reconciled familial and commercial obligations in developing emprendimientos. Theirs was a familiar story, a variant on a theme I heard repeatedly from YPFianos. Alberto Lucano came to northern Patagonia to take a job with YPF, as his brother had a few years before him. There, he met Teresa, who was the daughter in an YPFiano family and a secretary at the YPF offices in Plaza Huincul. They soon married. Alberto continued to work for YPF, but Teresa resigned when she was pregnant with their first child. The Lucanos' three children were born in the YPF hospital in Plaza Huincul, raised in a workers' cooperative housing complex in Cutral Có, and educated with YPF funding. Like most YPF employees, Alberto expected to work for the state company until he was ready to retire. But instead, he was dismissed at age fifty and found himself among the enormous number of YPFianos who were "too old to find a new job but too young to retire." With no other employment options, he joined a small group of skilled workers from YPF's exploration division to form Napalco, an emprendimiento offering oil well maintenance services to the privatized YPF.

Only a few years after Napalco was founded, Alberto's daughter, Carolina Lucano, returned from university to find her father's emprendimiento on the brink of bankruptcy. As a professional who credited her college education to her father's work at YPF, Carolina repaid her debt by assisting Napalco in facing its financial disaster. She managed the administrative aspects while her father and his partners conducted the work at the wells. As they labored to salvage Napalco, they translated the affective bonds that had existed in YPF to fit the meager possibilities available to subcontractors in the privatized oil industry. Carolina told me about the emprendimiento's May Day asado as an example of how her father and his partners "loved each other like a family and acted accordingly." The event was a small-scale adaptation of the May Day celebrations that YPF Estatal and the union SUPE had sponsored each year. In the photos Carolina showed me, the Napalco partners, their wives, and their children paused their festivities to put their arms around each other for the camera in a display of affection reminiscent of the earlier celebrations.

Alberto and Carolina Lucano, like Hernán de la Cruz, credited familial love with saving their company from the financial ruin to which numerous other emprendimientos succumbed, and then with helping them to expand. Once Napalco began to increase its business contracts and hire a few technicians, the owners drew on their experiences in YPF Estatal to strengthen their microenterprise, especially as they incorporated new employees who were not owners. During one of our long conversations over tea at her house, Carolina told me a story that demonstrated how her father took a role "as the bonding [*aglutinante*] element" in establishing kin relations within Napalco. A team of Napalco workers was staying in a hotel at Catriel. At dinnertime they would sit down together in the hotel's modest cafeteria. There, Carolina told me, Alberto "would ask for the food and would say, 'Soup for everyone!' Like the father of a family, that's how he was seated and [ordered] 'Soup for everyone, of course!'"

Alberto tried to provide some of the same benefits for Napalco's employees that the national oil company had given him. He could not afford to offer them as abundant a buffet as YPF had provided him when he was a junior assistant, but he saw soup with dinner as a fitting substitute. Carolina asserted that "the thing over there [in Catriel] is what generates belonging," thus interpreting her father's action as a calculated strategy to increase his employees' dedication to their jobs. Alberto, for his part, did not see himself as buying his employees' commitment; my conversations with him made evident that he was continuing YPF's tradition of nourishing those who gave their labor. Providing soup was a compromise that allowed Alberto to reconcile the paternal obligation he felt to care for his employees with the financial demands of the privatized oil industry.

When I asked Alberto to compare his feelings about his emprendimiento with what he had previously described to me as his loving attachment to YPF, he answered that property ownership made his affection for Napalco stronger than his love for YPF had been. This intensification occurred, he explained, because the company "is more our own," and then he repeated more emphatically, "because it is ours." Alberto credited YPF with having provided for him in almost every aspect of his life, including the unrequested opportunity to form his own business. Yet he stated that his care for company property increased when he formed Napalco and became a business owner. Like a house you own rather than rent, Alberto analogized, "you can do anything with what is yours, you do it and you are doing it for yourself." He, like many of his contemporaries, suggested that private property ownership was not only a more effective but also a more affective form of property relations than the national ownership that had previously existed in the Argentine oil industry. The privatization process had, quite unexpectedly, strengthened his affective attachments.

The affective kind of property ownership that Napalco embodied emerged most clearly as its owners attempted to extend care not only to their growing group of employees, but to their equipment as well. When Alberto's division of YPF Estatal was dissolved, his unit's trucks were converted from state to private property and sold to Napalco as part of its first contract with YPF SA. Carolina described how the emprendimiento partners carefully maintained these possessions, an example of their affective attachment to their microenterprise:

> [The Napalco partners] have an enormous love for their company, which does not occur in all [emprendimientos]. They take care of their things; they

love their things, but in a way that even the rest take note. If you get into one of their trucks, even though it is ten years old . . . everything is impeccable because they take care of it with an enormous consciousness that it is theirs . . . Therefore, it taxes us to get across the owners' mental model, who care for and love what is theirs, to the new people who simply carry out their duties.

When Alberto stopped by the house a few hours later, Carolina asked her father to explain to me himself why he and his partners loved Napalco with such intensity. Alberto immediately answered, "I have always said that our company was an adoptive son." Without having heard my previous conversation with Carolina, he too used the truck to portray his business as a web of loving kinship. He explained: "Because you love your son like a dad, you love him a lot. Also when you have an adoptive son that you raised from very small, you hold him with affection. For us, it taxes us very greatly to detach ourselves from things. Yesterday—we sold a truck . . ." As he said these last words, the voice of this burly oil worker broke, and he began to cry about the loss of this arm of his "adoptive son," which had accompanied him through all the trials of birthing Napalco and making the transition from state employee to small-business owner.

After Alberto recovered his composure, he told me how he and his partners realized that they could no longer use the truck in their business and had discussed building a pedestal mound and mounting the truck outside Napalco's main building so it could stand as a testament to how their emprendimiento had been born. In what Carolina called "the owners' mental model," the truck was not only a piece of private property whose benefits could be calculated in terms of financial risks and potential profits, but also a member of the Napalco family that was owed respect for its (his?) longevity and dedicated service. However, after a series of long discussions with Carolina and the consultants from Morningside Advisors, the Napalco partners realized that they had to "adapt to the times," try to replace their affective relationship with the truck with the detached perspective of businessmen, and sell this object of their love. Unlike his actions at dinner in Catriel, in this case, Alberto's effort to make himself into the company father was severely constrained by his legal agreement with YPF-Repsol. Napalco's service contract with the oil company stipulated the maximum age of trucks that could be driven into extraction sites, and, regardless of the partners' efforts to keep it in excellent condition, theirs was too old.

Events such as a May Day barbeque and quotidian practices like eating soup and repairing a truck illustrate how the emprendimiento owners expended a great deal of labor and capital reinforcing familial relations within their service companies at the same time that they were adopting calculative business methods. Carolina suggested that establishing intimate connections among Napalco's workers contributed to the emprendimiento's success but that maintaining loving attachments to material things blocked them from making proper business decisions. Alberto saw the same events from the perspective of a father who was attempting to keep his family united as they tried to overcome the challenges of their new situation. Alberto's business acumen emerged as he balanced his love for a truck and his need for cash. He and his fellow emprendimiento owners reconciled the historical labor relations of the Argentine oil industry with the realities of the corporate ownership of oil by creatively combining calculative and nurturing techniques into a new YPF family.

Driving Lessons

Whereas the YPFianos in emprendimientos employed kinship discourse and practices of familial care to construct, sustain, and expand their subcontracting businesses, the senior managers at the privatized oil company drew on the same notions of YPF kinship to establish patriarchical relationships between contractor and managing firm. At corporate headquarters in Neuquén City, the representatives of YPF-Repsol emphasized their efforts to help emprendimiento owners overcome their lack of "entrepreneurial mentality." Back in a rundown office with a broken window in Plaza Huincul, however, I heard a different version of this history. As we sat in front of an electric heater, Andrés Esposito, who never had been an YPFiano but who became the director of an emprendimiento named OptaNeu, offered an illuminating description of how, in the process of teaching managerial skills, the oil company managers presented themselves as fulfilling a parental or avuncular role to which the YPFianos were long accustomed:

> It is like there is someone who doesn't know how to drive and you say, "I will help you." Then, you sit next to him and you say, "Well, you have to—the steering wheel, the pedals—go faster, go faster." And when they go 120 [km/hour], you say, "Good, I'll get off here." Then, the other finds himself with a car that goes 120 and believes he knows how to drive, but in reality he learned a part of what he had to learn. And so it goes that he crashes on the first curve.

Andrés's simile implies that the company managers' instructions for steering the microenterprises gave their owners a false sense of their business aptitude and autonomy, which was destroyed soon after it was developed. Instead of teaching self-sufficiency, YPF SA's tutorials made the emprendimiento owners into "dependents" of the transnational company, providing lessons that Andrés and his partners in OptaNeu came to view quite critically. Andrés's comments highlight the astounding situation in which the emprendimientos found themselves: representatives of a company seeking profit through subcontracting production were charged with teaching their subcontractors how to do business with it.

The kind of relationship the corporate managers wanted to establish with the YPFianos first became evident to Andrés and several other emprendimiento directors in 1998, when YPF SA managers used a drop in the price of crude oil on global markets as justification to reduce the amount the oil company paid the subcontractors for their services. By this time, more than a third of the emprendimientos had already closed. Those that had survived the tumultuous first years depended on YPF SA as their sole client as well as their principal counselor.

Diego Parmado, whose story opens this chapter, comanaged the emprendimiento FESTA with a man named Edgar Mancini. Completing each other's sentences like an old married couple, Diego and Edgar recounted with more than a touch of sarcasm how an YPF SA accountant called them "strategic partners," when they were really partners "in the losses . . . but not in the profits." To further explicate the dynamic of FESTA's partnership with YPF SA at that time, Diego recounted that when the accountant came to talk to him about renegotiating FESTA's contract, the man sat down beside him like an old work buddy, patted him on the back, and used the informal second-person form (*vos*) to declare: "Look, you have to lower 10 percent for me because crude went down to nine dollars a barrel. And you, as our compañero, you see, as an ex-YPFiano, you have to support us in this. Take 10 percent off your costs and when the price of a barrel goes up, we will improve the prices [we are paying] you." This corporate manager coded his demands in the same language that the YPFianos used to portray the labor relations within the emprendimientos (although note the *ex* in front of YPFiano). The accountant and his colleagues attempted to strip away the emprendimiento owners' expectations of care while still presenting the privatized oil company as the "father" to the microenterprises. The private oil company's managers employed their shared history and affective ties in YPF Estatal to form an oil services market in which short-term legal contracts replaced lifelong commitments of mutual support. Here we see how contracting is a disciplinary, regulatory, and affective labor management technique.

The FESTA partners recognized the inequities of their contract, but they were in no position to either negotiate for better terms or walk away from the new arrangement. As Chapter 2 explains in greater detail, Diego saw that "the assassin was the same" for all the emprendimientos in the Neuquén region: when YPF SA lowered compensation rates for its local subcontractors, it "was the last smack to a drowning man." The emprendimiento owners realized that their loving father had become a bloodthirsty murderer. In response, Diego and his partners joined with the owners of several other emprendimientos that had survived to present their dire situation, and its threat of producing even greater unemployment in the region, to senior representatives of YPF-Repsol and Neuquén Province. The emprendimiento owners jointly negotiated with the transnational oil company and the state from a stronger position than any individual emprendimiento could. This tactic led to the formation of a formal corporate association of microenterprises, the Neuquén Unión Transitoria de Emprendimientos de Neuquén (Transitory Union of Emprendimientos in Neuquén, hereafter the UTE), discussed in the next chapter. The emprendimiento owners' relationship with YPF SA was only one of the many instances in which the tight-knit bonds of YPF kinship became a problem for their fledgling businesses.

When Family Becomes a Problem

Before privatization, YPFianos had envisioned oil industry employment as the most significant legacy that they could pass on to their children, an important assurance in the face of their dangerous, sometimes lethal, labor in the oilfields. Their expectations of filial inheritance remained strong, even in the face of the privatization of YPF, the elimination of familial benefits, and the reconfiguration of labor norms. Some children of YPFianos even felt that working for YPF was a duty they must fulfill. Veronica de Ramos explained that she and her two sisters were too young to take positions at YPF Estatal when their father died in a work accident at the age of forty-one, but "there was always the latent possibility of entering to work myself in the same sphere in which my dad had been." By the time she had finished her formal education and was looking for full-time employment, the privatization had begun and she did not receive a position at YPF. She sought work in the privatized petroleum industry, she explained, "as a debt, that is, as something pending from my dad." Veronica took a job with a foreign subcontracting company and then moved to a position at one of the emprendimientos, because it was "like an issue of continuing to inherit, let's say, leaving our surname within the petroleum field." Veronica translated job inheritance from the national company into the world of the privatized oil industry and creatively preserved her YPF legacy. She was thus able to remake herself from the daughter of an YPFiano into a private company employee.

Unlike Veronica, however, most YPFiano children were unable to find jobs in either the petroleum corporations or the emprendimientos. Employment was no longer the responsibility of the national state toward the families in the oil towns but instead became a concern of individual emprendimientos that was governed by their contracts with the transnational oil corporations.

Although emprendimiento partners continued to view kinship bonds as strengthening their companies, job inheritance became a serious challenge to the survival of their businesses. When the emprendimientos were first created, all YPFianos who wanted could join one. Soon, however, it became clear that these microenterprises were supporting many more people than their compensation from YPF SA could pay. Many of the emprendimiento partners were unwilling to thin their own ranks and borrowed money to pay salaries. This contributed to the bankruptcies that led several large emprendimientos to close and sparked those that remained to join the UTE. When, several years later, a few of the surviving emprendimientos began hiring people, their owners attempted to meld their employment practices with the YPF tradition of job inheritance. For instance, when I asked at the Lucanos' home about Napalco's hiring practices, Carolina explained that its partners prioritized "taking on the unemployed people who remained," because by doing this "we can resolve, although minimally, someone's problem by giving him work." Alberto underscored "the quantity of people who ask you for work because they know that you are in a company." Former workmates regularly stopped him in the street to ask him to "give me a hand," explaining that their sons could not afford to stay in school but had not found jobs.

The emprendimiento partners found it extremely difficult to deal with these pleas for employment. They could not create enough positions to give work to even a small fraction of the YPFianos whom the privatized corporation had let go but who continued to see employment as an inherited right, not to mention those teenagers who had grown up expecting to take over their fathers' positions and the children of workers killed on the job. In addition to the emprendimientos' decreased need for laborers, they faced pressure to restrict the age and educational backgrounds of their employees. Executives at YPF-Repsol and the other transnational oil companies working in the Neuquén oilfields wanted their subcontractors to hire only young workers with recent technical degrees, not YPFianos whose skills and knowledge came from work experience or children of YPFianos who had not completed their studies, like the ones Alberto mentioned. As the value placed on learning a trade from one's father had been replaced by Repsol's numerical employment matrix, emprendimiento owners found themselves in an increasingly tight bind. The transnational oil company executives, their consultants, and state allies used neoliberal discourses of competition, efficiency, and transparency to code job inheritance as a backwards practice. Yet children of YPFianos claimed they were the natural continuation of YPF kinship and appealed to the emprendimiento owners to fulfill this obligation and preserve the legacy of YPF.

The salience of the problem of filial job inheritance became evident to me when I conducted participant-observation in the spring of 2005 at OptaNeu, a medium-sized emprendimiento mentioned previously. The company's ambitious managing director, Andrés Esposito, had recently let go two partners' sons and warned the remaining ones that "their last name was their biggest problem." He reminded them that everyone was watching them especially closely to see whether they took their jobs for granted and did not work hard enough. As Andrés drove another OptaNeu employee and me from their base in Plaza Huincul to the remote extraction site of Rincón de los Sauces (see Map, Inset B), I asked them about job inheritance. Andrés said that OptaNeu's informal hiring policy gave partners' family members a chance but that he had no problem firing them if they did not work well in the company. Andrés's role may have been made easier by the fact that he was not an YPFiano himself, but firing the son of a partner in an emprendimiento was never easy.

This was clear when one of the most experienced partners at OptaNeu suddenly died, leaving his son Humberto in a low-status administrative position at the emprendimiento. The partner's death was a shock to the whole staff, who had looked to him as a role model, but it was especially difficult for Humberto, who had had an especially intimate kin–labor relationship with his father. In the months that followed, Humberto asked to be promoted to a technician position, but he fought with his coworkers and, according to many at OptaNeu, did not perform his duties well. Andrés was sympathetic to his situation and told me with great concern that Humberto carried his father's death "like a backpack that he could not take off." However, in addition to Humberto's poor performance, his technical degree was not in the right field for OptaNeu's services, which made him a weak candidate for promotion. After much discussion, the OptaNeu partners decided to give Humberto the new title of "administrative technician" and move him from the company's main office in Plaza Huincul to their smaller office at Rincón de los Sauces, where he would have additional responsibilities as an independent office manager. Andrés hoped Humberto would not be constantly reminded of his father's absence in new surroundings, would see this change of position as a promotion, and, therefore, would become a more productive employee. When last I heard, Humberto did not seem to be fulfilling these hopes, yet he had not been dismissed. As this example shows, the neoliberal process carried out in the Patagonian oilfields could neither neatly divorce familial and industrial domains nor make impersonal property ownership and other contractual relations eclipse the affective ones that preceded them. In the emprendimientos of northern Patagonia, as elsewhere, kinship sentiment continued to exert significant force, and everyone working in the privatized oil industry had to contend with the historical legacies of YPF.

Conclusion

This chapter charts the development of YPF kinship in the oil towns of Northwest Patagonia and illustrates how emprendimiento worker–owners selectively drew on this history as the state-owned oil company was being converted into a privately owned corporation and a series of subcontracting companies. The history of the Argentine oil industry, particularly the development of the Patagonian oil towns, illustrates the impossibility of separating the economic and familial domains, a distinction that is supposed to characterize modernity (Yanagisako 1979: 187; McKinnon and Cannell 2010). YPF kinship not only blurred boundaries between work and home, but also formed an important basis for constructing business, state, and nation. The establishment of kinship bonds made life on the Patagonian frontier bearable for migrants, facilitated the extension of state rule and feelings of national belonging to the southern territories, and enabled the extraction of oil by the state. Kinship was also the symbolic material used to imagine the nation and to promote the state oil company to its workforce.

Seven decades after the founding of the state oil company, kinship guided the YPFianos through the dismantling of the national oil industry and the construction of a transnational one. The YPFianos dealt with the neoliberal "reform" by strengthening the affective dimension of their labor relations, despite state and corporate policies that rejected familial privileges and encouraged dispassionate calculative business practices in their place. The state-workers-turned-small-business-owners envisioned their industrial relations in familial terms, preferentially hired and promoted their fellow YPFianos, and supported their kin. They also reconciled acts of familial care with calculative strategies for generating a dedicated workforce and a viable business. Kinship remained the ideal against which contractual and other relationships were judged. Yet the YPFianos' actions were severely constrained both by the neoliberal discourse of their supervisors and by their own kin obligations and the paternalism entrenched in the oilfields.

The history of the YPFianos not only illustrates the productive power of kinship sentiments, but also reveals that they can be as destructive as they are creative. At the same time that men deployed kinship to establish themselves as oil workers in the national industry, to build oil towns, and to create a legacy, their kinship sentiments constrained their life paths and those of their kin. At the same time that YPFianos used familial affect as an asset to develop their subcontracting businesses, kin-based obligations became a problem for the new business owners. In short, the national project of developing a state company and the neoliberal project of privatizing YPF were both enabled and troubled by kinship sentiments and familial relationships. Chapter 2 further illustrates how kinship not only was deployed to fortify small businesses in the face of economic challenges, but also to discipline former state workers and reinforce authority within subcontracting relationships.

An attention to kinship practices and sentiments reveals lines of continuity between neoliberal and previous regimes of rule that are not apparent when the introduction of new technical mechanisms is studied alone. Although privatization dismantled familial privileges in the oil industry and encouraged dispassionate calculations about equipment, employment, and benefits, it did not replace affective attachments with an imported model of disinterested rationality. Instead, YPFianos reconfigured their affective ties to YPF and to each other to fit the restructured oil industry. At the same time, corporate managers placed themselves in paternal or avuncular positions in relation to the emprendimiento owners with whom they contracted. As one emprendimiento director described it, the YPF SA representatives taught the emprendimiento partners to drive their vehicles in ways that bound them as "dependents" of the transnational company, much as YPF Estatal positioned workers as "children" of the paternalist company. Investigation of only the juridical and administrative changes would have made privatization seem a radical break with the preceding regime, but an examination of kinship and affect reveals a neoliberal project built on previous governing relations.

This chapter shows both how an actual neoliberal project reinforced affective governing techniques and how this project dissolved distinctions between affective and calculative methods. The YPFianos who were able to sustain emprendimientos through the privatization process did so by developing business practices that were at once generous nurturing acts and prudent financial computations. Napalco's ten-year-old truck stood as a testament to the investment—of capital, labor, and affect—that the worker–owners made in their new business ventures. The emprendimiento partners' relationships to vehicles, in particular, illustrate that private property ownership was grounded in affect as much as it was in law. The managers at the privatized oil company also blurred boundaries between nurturing and disciplining techniques as they managed the corporation's subcontractors by, for example, helping the emprendimiento owners learn financial budgeting while simultaneously reducing their compensation rates.

Kinship sentiments and practices of familial care carried YPFianos like Diego Parmado and his partners through the arduous process of remaking themselves from state workers into business owners. Their experience shows that an effective business strategy can include the maintenance, even the strengthening, of filial relationships. However, these YPFianos' desires to fulfill their debts to kin, to claim their inheritance, and to preserve their families' place in the oilfields also motivated them to work harder for less pay and fewer benefits than they had received while laboring for the state enterprise. Affective ties to YPF also led the emprendimiento owners to accept old equipment, exploitative contracts, arbitrary rules, and great financial and corporal risks. Thus, kinship sentiments and familial practices enabled state workers to reincorporate themselves within the transformed oil industry. In fact, maintaining preexisting kinship bonds was the technique that offered the YPFianos the best chance for survival in the reorganized circuits of the global oil industry. Yet these affective attachments incorporated YPFianos within a global regime in which a small number of giant corporations make enormous profits by subcontracting the production of oil to people who, as Diego and his partner aptly put it, share "in the losses . . . but not in the profits."

This chapter has examined how kinship sentiments and affective bonds among workers included the YPFianos in the restructuring of the oil industry; I now turn to how the juridical and technical mechanisms of the privatization process excluded them from it.

2 Creating a Privatized Public

NEW YORK CITY, JUNE 29, 1993, 9:30 A.M. A bell rings and trading starts for the day on the New York Stock Exchange. Brokers and traders begin the frantic business of selling and buying the rights to fractional ownership of corporations. For them, that Tuesday is no special day. For the citizens of Argentina, it is. It is the initial public offering of YPF SA on Wall Street—that is, the first day that shares of the country's most famous state-owned enterprise are sold to investors on the world's most famous trading floor. In a matter of a few weeks, the Argentine state will sell 45 percent of its holdings in YPF, making it the largest sale of Argentine assets to that point (Gerchunoff and Cánovas 1996: 210). The first day of trading thus publicly marks the legal transformation of Argentine petroleum from state to private property, from strategic to financial resource, from national to international asset. Now someone who has no connection to the country, its people, or its history can own a piece of its largest and most celebrated company. For someone like this, YPF represents only money, or more precisely, the risk of gaining or losing money. For the YPFianos back in Argentina, it means much more.

A month earlier, President Menem's economy minister Domingo Cavallo anticipated that "YPF will be Argentina's first truly publicly held company." Speaking to the press, he added, "We hope it will also open foreign markets for other Argentine firms wishing to venture out into the world" (*New York Times*, May, 31, 1993). What does Cavallo's statement that YPF would be the country's "first truly publicly held company" mean? What does it entail for YPF to be a "public" company? In the United States, a public corporation, or joint-stock company, is one that is owned by shareholders and whose shares are traded on stock markets so that, presumably, anyone can buy them. In Argentina, however, a public company is one that is owned by the state, ostensibly on behalf of the citizenry, whereas a private company is one that is fractionally owned by individuals. Cavallo, it seems, used the idea of "going public" to describe YPF's move away from what Argentines would consider a public company and into a private one.[1] Cavallo implied that ownership by the state no longer fit the definition of a public enterprise but that a company owned by an exclusive group of corporate and individual shareholders now fell squarely within the public domain. In other words, the privatization of the state-owned petroleum company was transforming the meaning of "public" to include what previously had been understood as a "private" business relationship. This act of selling shares to investors who had never stepped foot on Argentine soil also gave privateness a transnational dimension. In short, Cavallo's statement suggests that the process of privatizing the state oil company was creating a new public in Argentina—a privatized public that is both exclusive and transnational at the same time.

This chapter analyzes how the process of transforming YPF from a state-owned into a privately owned company generated what I call a privatized public in the Argentine oil industry. I first scrutinize the law-making process that transformed oil from state to private property and then examine how the privatized oil market was actualized in Northwest Patagonia. I analyze how state and nonstate actors, from the president to foreign-trained technocrats and business consultants to the YPFianos and other residents of the oil towns, participated in this process, but did so in different ways. As in Chapter 1, I focus on attempts to incorporate the Neuquén oil region within the global oil industry. I build on that chapter by examining how the former state oil workers and their families deployed notions of YPF kinship in their construction of civic and business associations to deal with YPF's privatization. In the second half of the chapter, I examine three groups in particular. The first is the re-created YPF family that emerged in the northern Patagonian oil region during the weeklong protest known as La Pueblada. The second is the Agrupación Patria de Ex Agentes de YPF y Gas del Estado (Patria Association of Former Employees of YPF and Gas del Estado, hereafter the Patria Association), the local chapter of a national network of workers dismissed from YPF who pursued legal strategies to claim their rights to stock in the privatized corporation. The third is the group of emprendimiento owners mentioned in Chapter 1 who united into the single oil service enterprise called the UTE (Unión Transitoria de Emprendimientos de Neuquén [Transitory Union of Emprendimientos in Neuquén]). Each group contested

Cavallo's conception of the public domain in a different way, but each also helped make the privatized public of the oil industry a reality on the ground.

Although YPFianos frequently described YPF's privatization as a process of "dismembering the YPF family," it was as much a process of putting together social relations as taking apart existing ones. How did that happen? Before addressing this question, I situate it within scholarly debates on privatization, publics, and neoliberalism.

Redefining Publics

The privatization of state enterprises and services occupies a prominent place in neoliberal theory and policy-oriented scholarship. In Latin America, Africa, Asia, and the former Soviet Union, privatization schemes have taken center stage in state reform programs because they purportedly solve the overlapping problems of the corruptibility of state agents, the irrationality of state economic regulation, and the poor quality of state services. Moreover, privatization has been seen as a strategy for implementing core neoliberal beliefs in the efficiency of private businesses and in the impartial judgment of the market (IMF 1998: 5–6). The stated goals of privatization policies have also included increasing economic efficiency and promoting private property ownership (Megginson and Netter 2001: 321). In Argentina, the rapid privatization of 90 percent of national enterprises and public services further aimed to thwart imminent political-economic collapse, to reduce state debt, and to "buy time" for more profound changes in the national economy. However, looking at neoliberalism as a list of policies with intended goals or as the ideology behind them mistakes a messy and inconsistent process for a coherent set of principles and subsequent course of action. Instead, Argentine neoliberalismo needs to be understood as a process that bundles together a set of complex and sometimes incongruous ideas, practices, and discourses that developed over more than a decade and whose effects are not yet fully realized.

I refer to the process of transforming the Argentine petroleum industry as its *privatization*, as other scholarly and popular sources do, yet I do not assume that this terminology has a stable meaning.[2] Although the term privatization seems self-evident in the policy literature, what does it really entail? How did oil shift from public to private property, from natural treasure to financial asset, and from a national resource to an international one? How has the process of privatizing YPF altered the emic distinction between public and private? What was the role of law in creating a privatized public in Argentina, and what are its limits? The common assumption that the legal privatization of state natural resources and financial assets moved petroleum from the public to the private domain misses the complex and contradictory process of generating, maintaining, and breaking the distinctions between public and private persons, objects, and relationships.

Feminist anthropologists long have argued that the division between the public and the private domains is a cultural creation of the Euro-American tradition that has been presented as a universal and natural division of human life. These scholars point out that the private domestic domain of the family is the practical result of specific social institutions, discourses, and practices that organize, and particularly divide, social life in some places but not in others (Yanagisako and Delaney 1995: 12). Building on David Schneider's insights into kinship, Sylvia Yanagisako and Carol Delaney (1995) have argued that the domains that long have been considered the foundational building blocks of modern society are themselves unstable. Property inheritance, for example, intersects kinship, economics, and, I would add, religion, thereby demonstrating that "it has never been clear where one cultural domain ends and another begins" (11). Marilyn Strathern (1988), among others, developed the critique of essential domains into an analytic that seeks to explain how some ideas, people, and objects come to be associated with the private domain while others are not. At English and American bed and breakfast inns, for instance, a female proprietor blurs assumed boundaries between capitalist labor (normatively public and male) and domestic labor (normatively private and female) when she offers the privacy of the domestic sphere as a product for consumption by people who are not her kin. While the private domain is made public through the sale of "traditional domestic comfort," the proprietor's profits, investments, and business acumen become "redomained" as private in this example (Bouquet 1985: 129–32; Strathern 1992: 128–292). An imperfectly analogous process of shifting domains is at work in Argentina when oil extracted from public lands becomes private property and available for ownership by corporations and individuals, including both Argentine citizens and foreigners. Inspired by the work of feminist anthropologists, I refer to this process as *redomaining*.

Anthropologists have called attention to the reconfiguration of the public domain as a particularly salient feature of the emergence of neoliberalism in Latin America. Chile was the first country in the region in which public services such as housing, education, and health care were transformed from rights allocated by the state into privileges distributed by private markets. Julia Paley (2001) has demonstrated that, in this process, nonstate actors took over roles previously occupied by public employees. The health and welfare of the citizenry thereby shifted from a public to a private responsibility. In Mexico, Cori Hayden (2003) has shown, at the same time that state services were being transferred to private hands, medicinal plants were redomained as belonging to the national public rather than to particular indigenous communities (119). Bioprospecting contracts among scientists, state representatives, and indigenous "communities" thereby reconstructed the public domain as a space without private property and thus erased indigenous claims to territory, natural resources, and knowledge, while enabling state and corporate claims to the profits from them. In Argentina, the redomaining of oil similarly shifted the responsibilities of state and nonstate actors, redefined natural resources as private property, and elevated some claims while foreclosing others.

Cavallo's comments about YPF's privatization hint at how the legal redomaining of oil also reworked definitions of democracy and citizenship. When Cavallo referred to the corporate actors who would soon own and manage the country's natural resources, he portrayed them as equivalent to public servants while refusing the YPFianos that role. YPF Estatal employees might have managed Argentina's petroleum reserves on behalf of the nation for many decades, but, he implied, that did not make YPF a "truly publicly held company" because it was controlled by a state that was monopolistic, inefficient, and irrational in distributing jobs and contracts. YPF SA, in contrast, promised a form of democratic participation and freedom in which ostensibly anyone could buy in and be represented as a "stakeholder." As Hayden (2003) noted, "Going public is a way to raise money, but this kind of capitalization also comes with multiple (and often illusory) promises attached," including inclusivity, accountability, representation, and compensation (7–8). Like many advocates of neoliberal reform at the time, Cavallo celebrated "going public" as deepening democracy. He did this in the context of still raw memories of a military dictatorship whose threats of violence persuaded Argentines not to make claims on public spaces, resources, or recognition for many years. The language of democracy and participation used to justify YPF's conversion into a privately owned corporation thus echoed popular demands for greater democracy but gave them a novel twist in terms of the global capitalist market. The conversion of oil from public to private property that Cavallo helped orchestrate replaced the claims of state workers and their families with those of corporate executives and shareholders, most of whom were historically, geographically, and socially removed from Argentina. It also more tightly integrated the national oil market into a global one (see Chapter 3). This process began with the executive and legislative acts that allowed state-owned companies and services to be transferred to corporate control.

The Law-Making Process

During most of the twentieth century, the Argentine state, led by its powerful executive branch, pursued national development by promoting and directing industrial production and service provision. This was part of a trend beginning in the 1930s in which Latin American states extensively regulated their national economies. Argentina stood out as a forerunner in this process, first when YPF was founded in 1922 and then again when it was granted sole right to explore and produce oil on state territory in 1932 (Solberg 1979: 160). As we have seen, YPF was envisioned as an engine that could uniquely propel the nation forward, economically and socially. The mission of the state-owned companies included creating jobs, enabling commodity consumption, raising revenue for the state, and generating economic opportunities in peripheral regions of the country—not maximizing efficiency, competition, or profit. Furthermore, state companies served as political instruments that could be used to secure Argentina's sovereignty and place in the "family of nations." Oil was understood in this context as a strategic resource, and state ownership of it was viewed as essential to achieving the country's political, economic, social, and foreign relations goals.

The pursuit of national economic development through state ownership of capitalist enterprises was practiced in one form or another for most of the twentieth century. By the 1980s, the Argentine state owned approximately one thousand enterprises, including monopolies in the telephone, railway, port, electricity, and natural gas industries, and owned controlling segments of the airline, banking, steel, chemicals, petroleum, and gas industries (Llanos 2002: 44–45). Then, in the decade before the turn of the twenty-first century, state-led development was seriously questioned and state practices drastically reconfigured amid prolonged economic decline. The history of YPF tells this story vividly. Yet the changes wrought during the 1990s were not unprecedented. As I argue throughout this book, the privatization of YPF illustrates important lines of continuity as much as significant departures from the previous political, economic, and social configuration of Argentine society and the global oil industry. Here, I emphasize that state actors continued to play crucial roles in shaping economic activities and relationships. Novel to the 1990s, however, was how they did so.

Groundwork for the sweeping privatization of state enterprises and services during Menem's presidency was laid during the military dictatorship that ruled Argentina from 1976 to 1983. A series of dictators implemented economic "liberalization" policies that dismantled some Import Substitution Industrialization efforts, eased the movement of foreign capital in and out of the country, and reduced state welfare provisioning. The first military dictatorship that replaced Perón's widow in the late 1970s increased its control over the oil industry by converting YPF from a largely autonomous state enterprise into a joint-stock corporation in which the state owned all of the stock (Solberg 1979: 174). This opened the way for the dictators to use YPF as collateral for the foreign loans that enabled their repressive regime. Subsequent military rulers also executed a policy of "peripheral privatization" that encouraged state-owned enterprises such as YPF to subcontract some services to private companies. While the military rulers endorsed the emerging discourse of neoliberalismo, they continued to envision petroleum as a strategic national resource rather than a primarily economic asset. Their privatization measures were quite limited compared with what was to come in the next decade.

At the same time that the dictatorship began limited privatization projects, the state's involvement in the business ventures of the political elite grew. During the seven years of dictatorship, the state provided numerous Argentine-owned private companies with state contracts, subsidies, tax credits, and protection from foreign competition. When the easy availability of foreign loans ceased after Mexico defaulted on its loans in 1982 and an "economic crisis" erupted across Latin America, the military rulers rescued many of these debt-ridden companies from bankruptcy by nationalizing their foreign debt obligations (Canitrot 1994: 76, 80). The state also accumulated an enormous foreign debt from the military expenditures that sustained the dictatorship's control. This debt was largely held by public enterprises because they were uniquely able to offer collateral to lenders. YPF possessed the largest foreign debt, holding $5.6 billion in 1989 (Manzetti 1999: 82).[3] The "debt crisis" contributed to the fall of the last military ruler and the effective mobilization for democratic elections in 1983.

The first post-dictatorship government, led by Raúl Alfonsín, promised to reconstruct the democratic institutions destroyed by military rule. It thus framed its economic program in terms of undoing the illegitimate distribution of wealth that the dictatorship had created. Yet when Argentina faced persistent inflation, the Alfonsín administration switched to economic policies similar to those of the military regime before it. These included proposing limited privatization measures for state enterprises that the government deemed not to be of "national interest" or to provide no "social benefits" to the population, as well as a few others that were declared "inefficient" and "noncompetitive." An Alfonsín representative explained that the administration's proposed 1986 privatization bill was designed with the aims of "eliminating the monopolistic features that hinder competitiveness, winning flexibility to operate in a very demanding market, and obtaining greater efficiency to make the enterprise's competitive appearance in the world possible" (Llanos 2002: 52). This statement indicates how a transnational neoliberal discourse of competition and efficiency was used to challenge ideas that Argentina's state enterprises should ensure national sovereignty and create economic opportunities for the country as a whole. However, the Alfonsín administration did not signal a diminished role for the state, only a shift in its strategy. When it submitted its bill to Congress, it made clear that "the state had to continue to play its leading role in the economy, and privatization was the right means to do this" (Llanos 2002: 53). Despite its limited character, this first privatization bill did not win congressional approval.

The privatization of state enterprises was effectively opposed during Alfonsín's presidency by an unprecedented coalition among congressional representatives from the Peronist Party (Partido Justicialista) and some members of the centrist Radical Party (Unión Cívica Radical) to which Alfonsín belonged. They were joined by labor unions, state bureaucrats, the military, and business associations (Llanos 2002: 57–66). The powerful conglomeration of unions belonging to the Peronist-affiliated Confederación General de Trabajo (General Labor Confederation [CGT], discussed further in Chapter 3) were particularly militant in their opposition and mounted thirteen general strikes during Alfonsín's presidency. His program disintegrated as the economic situation in Argentina precipitously declined. The situation was not helped by the U.S. withdrawal of support for Alfonsín's economic strategy and the World Bank's denial of Argentina's requests for loans (Llanos 2002: 73). Unemployment skyrocketed, hyperinflation set in, the state faced insolvency, and capital flight reached extraordinary levels. Alfonsín turned over the executive office to Carlos Menem six months ahead of schedule amid food riots in several cities and fears of imminent political and economic collapse across the country.

Alfonsín was a reluctant promoter of neoliberalismo, and his privatization program was largely unsuccessful. Yet his presidency, particularly his political discourse about national change, created the conditions that made possible the more dramatic transformations that would later reshape Argentina. Alfonsín's presidency also represented a crucial moment in neoliberalismo because it established a connection between the re-creation of a democratic polity and the privatization of state resources. Links between democracy and private property were hardly new in this moment; their mutual imbrication had roots in the liberal tradition of the nineteenth century (see Chapter 3). However, early

Peronism had effectively challenged the idea that democracy means the legal guarantee of individual rights, such as private property, and not economic ones, such as employment. This changed in the post-dictatorship period when the private ownership of natural and other resources was once again understood as key to the creation of a democratic polity. This history underlies the subsequent process of redomaining oil from strategic asset to economic good, and from public resource to private property.

The Menem Factor

The Peronist Menem took over the presidency from the Radical Alfonsín in 1989—the first change in ruling party without military intervention in Argentine history. Menem had campaigned for the presidency as a popular savior who would return Argentina to the "traditional" Peronist commitment to social justice through state-led economic management and development, a promise in clear contrast to Alfonsín's failed privatization plans. As governor of La Rioja Province during Alfonsín's presidency, Menem had directed provincial affairs in expected Peronist fashion, increasing state employment and creating new social welfare programs. He thus surprised many Argentines, especially his Peronist base, by immediately and fervently pursuing a neoliberal "reform" program that prominently featured the transition to corporate ownership and management of Argentine industry, commerce, and banking. Menem held the presidency for an unprecedented ten years, during which he initiated fundamental changes in Argentina's political, economic, and social organization.

Menem effectively deployed the imminent national economic collapse to gain wide authority to restructure the state and national economy along neoliberal lines. Before taking over the presidency from Alfonsín prematurely, Menem secured a covert agreement in which the Radical Party promised to support his proposals for addressing the political-economic situation through drastic state restructuring. He soon filled his administration with prominent businessmen and U.S.-trained economists rather than the expected Peronist union leaders. His economic team gave high prominence to the privatization of state-owned enterprises and services within their proposed "market-oriented reforms." In the first six weeks of Menem's term, Congress passed two laws, the State Reform Law and the Economic Emergency Law, that enabled Menem to initiate this process of transforming the state from the executor of development projects to the facilitator of the activities of private corporations. These laws cleared a path for a series of regulatory and administrative steps that led to the sale of YPF stock on Wall Street.

The State Reform and Economic Emergency laws expanded the executive branch's already extensive authority and granted the president the legal means to restructure the state by using decrees of "urgency and necessity" that did not require congressional approval.[4] In particular, these laws enabled the legal conversion of state assets into corporate ones. The State Reform Law pronounced a "state of emergency" for all state-owned enterprises, declared many of them "subject to privatization," and authorized the president to put their management in the hands of corporate trustees who would prepare them for their transformation to private ownership. It also allowed the president to disregard existing regulations, to dismantle trade protections, and to suspend legal restrictions on foreign investment. When Domingo Cavallo, the economist quoted in the beginning of this chapter, took over the Ministry of the Economy in 1991, he furthered the privatization process by spearheading a law, known as the Convertibility Law, that pegged the Argentine peso to the U.S. dollar. This law indirectly advanced the privatizations because it required the state to enact spending policies that were attainable only with the funds from the sale of state companies and service contracts. This law facilitated the transfer of ownership and control of Argentina's state enterprises and public services to corporate entities. Together, these laws represented the first legal actions in a privatization process that has been called "one of the broadest and most rapid in the Western Hemisphere," if not the world (Alexander, Corti, and World Bank 1993: ix).

The Legal Conversion of YPF

Menem pursued the privatization of the oil industry through the presidential decrees of urgency and necessity that the State Reform Law sanctioned. Using executive methods akin to those of the military rulers, he rapidly ended state control of prices and production levels in the oil industry, terminated YPF's monopoly on the sale of crude oil within Argentina, eliminated tariffs on importing and exporting fuels, suspended industrial and mining subsidies and tax breaks to Argentine companies, and instituted 200 to 600 percent price hikes for fuels and utilities. His administration additionally suspended the collective-bargaining agreement with the state oil workers union SUPE, froze state hiring, and reduced public employees' job security (Acuña 1994: 65–66; Manzetti 1999: 72). The new agreement with SUPE decreased worker benefits, increased work hours, and reduced the number and categories of employees covered by its contract (Murillo 2001: 153). In accordance with guidelines from multilateral lending agencies, Menem appointed corporate trustees for YPF Estatal who transformed the company's service contracts with private companies into generous concessions that granted them ownership of the oil they extracted or refined. The trustees also established new joint ventures (Etchemendy 2001: 11–12). This reduction in the national government's control of YPF was reinforced by the 1994 constitutional reforms that featured a series of "decentralization" measures, including one that transferred ownership of subsoil resources from the federal state to the provincial governments. Although these changes were carried out in the name of greater democratic participation and local control, they gave the representatives of oil companies the upper hand in dealing with both provincial officials who lacked experience and knowledge in negotiating concessions and joint ventures, and workers who no longer had the backing of a national union structure.

Executive action effectively privatized the oil industry in many respects; still, the YPF trustees could not legally sell the company stock outright without congressional approval. Congress authorized the completion of the formal privatization of the state oil company when it passed the Privatization of Hydrocarbons and YPF Law in 1992 (Llanos 2002: 137–52). This law sanctioned the reconstitution of YPF Estatal as YPF SA; that is, it sanctioned the conversion of the state oil enterprise into a privately owned corporation, a change that was already well under way in many respects. The law also enabled the transfer of $5.6 billion in foreign debt from the company to the state, a vast reduction of YPF's labor force, and the formation of the emprendimientos. As a result, the company's finances passed quickly from a deficit of $576 million in 1990 to a profit of $400 million two years later (Manzetti 1999: 115). The 1992 law seemed to complete the process of moving oil from the public to the private domain, but as we will see, it took considerably more work by both state and nonstate actors to create a viable private oil industry than it did to enact it legally. Yet, the legal history demonstrates that state actors played an important role in generating a lucrative private market in the oil industry.

It is important to note that it was not until after YPF's profitability was established and thus the state's "goods" had become more enticing to investors that the administration began selling the company's stock to corporations, banks, and individual shareholders. The YPF stock that the state sold on the New York Stock Exchange in June 1993 generated approximately $3 billion for state coffers in a matter of weeks (Gerchunoff and Cánovas 1996: 210–11). Although this represents a large sum to gain in such a short period of time, it is small when compared with the state's deficit and debt. Moreover, the Argentine state did not benefit from the sale of YPF in the long term. Although the Menem administration used the revenue from the sale to reduce some of its debts, the private owners have used these assets to make enormous profits ever since. Whereas the state oil company had a mandate to increase the prosperity of Argentine workers and consumers and to provide resources for the national state, the private oil company is supposed to enrich the transnational elite who constitute its shareholders. This is, in fact, a legal requirement of corporations (Bakan 2005). The majority of this wealth has not remained in Argentina. The conversion of YPF from public to private property thus replaced the claims of Argentine oil workers and other citizens with those of corporate executives and shareholders.

The process of selling shares of stock to investors living around the world not only illustrates how a public resource was redomained as a private one, but also draws attention to how the notion of privateness that is usually associated with the domestic domain acquired a transnational dimension. The 1992 privatization law required that the state retain ownership of more than half of YPF SA's shares; however, the state eventually sold more and more of its shares in the company until the stake of private shareholders eclipsed that of the state. The privatized Spanish national petroleum company Repsol bought the Argentine state's remaining shares of stock in 1999 and renamed the company YPF-Repsol SA. This form of ownership at a distance more completely divorced the oil company's proprietors from its day-to-day operations. The separation of ownership from control is a defining feature of the corporate form (Berle and Means 1932; see also Westbrook 2007), but Repsol's purchase of shares further distanced the owners in terms of geographic location and, with it, political, economic, and social context of the practices of the company. The Spanish executives and foreign shareholders did not share the Argentine history of petroleum nationalism, the Peronist commitment to workers' political and economic rights, or a feeling of debt to the YPFianos who "fueled the nation."

A Transforming Idea

Privatization was not a new idea in the early 1990s, but it had yet to gain political traction in Argentina. Menem's position as a Peronist leader made it politically and ethically viable for him to make the move from state-led to business-led development in a country where nationalism had long signified state ownership of key industries. His charismatic style of populism and ability to deploy the economic crisis to his advantage allowed him to secure support across class divides for ideas that many Argentines had previously opposed (Llanos 2002; Treisman 2003). Menem was particularly effective in thwarting opposition to his privatization project within the labor movement by disaggregating the national union structure and pitting formerly allied unions against each other. For instance, the privatization laws left crucial policy details to be negotiated between state and union representatives for each company, thus offering an opportunity for state representatives to reward cooperative unions and punish uncooperative ones. SUPE was among those that organized strikes against minimal foreign investment during the Alfonsín administration but that cooperated with the Menem administration's far more drastic privatization measures. In exchange for its cooperation, SUPE received health-care subsidies and severance pay for the "voluntary" retirement of large numbers of its members, while its leaders gained lucrative positions as administrators for the workers' shares of stock in the privatized company. The consequence of fractured negotiations like these was that the national CGT, which had staunchly opposed Alfonsín's privatization attempts, divided over Menem's similar measures.[5]

Union participation in the development of neoliberalismo was aided by the changes occurring within the Peronist movement as it was being rebuilt after a decade of repression during the military dictatorship. The shift away from manufacturing and the weakening of industrial unions across Latin America during the 1970s and 1980s both reduced and fragmented Peronism's traditional working-class base. The Peronists thus emerged from the dictatorship severely weakened and lost the 1983 presidential election to the Radical Party. The Peronist leadership rebuilt the party and movement by replacing its traditional union-centered organization with what Javier Auyero (2000) has described as "personalized political mediation" through patron–client networks. As Part II discusses, Peronist neighborhood bosses, called *punteros*, and their allied block captains, called *manzaneras*, provided food, medical care, construction materials, and other items to some among the vast population of nonunionized and unemployed workers in exchange for party loyalty at election time. Therefore, at the same time that state companies were being transferred to corporate control, state services were distributed through personal networks that encouraged alignment with the governing party. This move from workplace-based organizing to personalized gifting relations helped defuse opposition to neoliberalismo among the Peronists' working- and lower-class constituents. The deunionization of the national party structure also created the conditions that made neoliberalismo possible by eliminating the strongest promoters of trade barriers and restrictions on private investment. This reorganization of Peronism helps explain the appearance of popular support for the privatization of state enterprises such as YPF.

The growth of neoliberalismo was further aided by the widespread enthusiasm for the inexpensive foreign commodities that flooded the country after the elimination of trade barriers. Among middle- and upper-class Argentines, especially those in the capital region, the celebration of imported commodities restored the preexisting narrative in which they represented the First World within Latin America and claimed to be more "modern" than those around them (Guano 2002: 184). The declining quality and availability of products and services provided by state enterprises, which partially resulted from the dictatorship's previous appropriations of the state enterprises' revenue and debt capacity, further generated consumers' interest in privatization. While the consensus in favor of privatization was not as firm as it at first seemed, Menem enacted the decrees of urgency and necessity within a context of an outward display of popular support.

Multilateral financial institutions and foreign state agencies also played an important role in the privatization of state enterprises and services in Argentina. Institutions such as the World Bank, the IMF, the Inter-American Development Bank, and the U.S. Treasury had long been involved in shaping Latin American economies. In the 1980s and 1990s, the economists and policy wonks who were affiliated with these institutions promoted a single set of economic goals across the world, including the removal of barriers to transnational trade and direct foreign investment, the strengthening of national private property laws, and the privatization of state enterprises (Babb 2004: 10–11). They were able to support their vision for neoliberalism with mounting evidence that the state developmentalism of the 1960s and 1970s had failed to extend prosperity across Latin America.[6] Though they promoted their policies with a celebratory discourse about how the free market would strengthen democracy, officials at these institutions were highly suspicious of democratic governing techniques and preferred rule by an elite cohort of economic experts (Harvey 2005: 66). Their ideas came with powerful financial incentives in the form of loans for "specific and circumscribed purposes" that motivated heavily indebted states such as Mexico and Argentina to adopt them (Babb 2004: 9). Argentina's privatization program was particularly crafted to demonstrate the country's cooperation with the multilateral financial institutions (Alexander, Corti, and World Bank 1993). For instance, Menem's economic team wrote the congressional bill for the privatization of Gas del Estado, the natural gas entity tied to YPF, under the close supervision of the World Bank and then submitted it to Congress amidst important negotiations with the IMF (Llanos 2001: 87; 2002: 98).

It is important to underscore that Menem hardly acted alone. The transnational and foreign financial institutions promoting privatization were aided by a cadre of foreign-trained Argentine technocrats and business executives who occupied crucial positions in state institutions during the Menem years and played important roles in designing, directing, and executing the privatization projects. Menem's appointment of Domingo Cavallo as economy minister in 1991 marked the pinnacle of Argentine technocrats with advanced degrees from U.S. universities displacing Peronist Party agents in key state entities. This appointment also signaled a shift in the kind of actors involved in crafting legislation. Even if Menem could persuasively claim a popular mandate, the legislation enacted during his presidency was not written by elected officials who represented the national polity, but by an exclusive group of economic experts, most of whom were sympathetic to the desires of large private businesses.

Foreign-trained Argentines also became private consultants whom state agencies and corporate entities hired for specific projects, such as the Morningside Advisors group introduced in Chapter 1. The role of business consultants in transforming Argentina's public enterprises into private corporations has been far less noted and analyzed than the much discussed roles of the multilateral financial institutions and President Menem, but they were no less important. Both the business consultants and the government technocrats were overwhelmingly Argentine citizens; thus, as Sarah Babb (2004) has argued for the case of Mexico, "in many respects, neoliberalism looks much more like an inside job than an external imposition" (174).[7]

The sale of YPF on Wall Street may seem, in hindsight, the culmination of a coherent neoliberal policy, but it is better understood as a result of a process full of missteps, back steps, and sidesteps.[8] Privatization was not a fully formed policy pushed by either foreigners or elite Argentines onto an unwilling population, but a protean process shaped by differently positioned participants to different degrees at different moments. Menem, his economic advisors, and his legislative staff led the legal conversion of oil from state to private property, but other actors also shaped the privatization process, especially after the first two years. Congressional representatives and provincial governors ensured that particular provisions were included in the privatization legislation (Llanos 2002), and union leaders played a significant role in establishing privatization on the ground. The chronicle of events given above only begins to illustrate how actors who had previously managed the state ownership of petroleum did not fade from view but actively facilitated the shift to corporate ownership and control. The YPFianos, their corporate managers, and business consultants all played a crucial but overlooked role in the process of creating a privatized public domain.

Existing studies of the privatization of Argentina's state companies and services conclude with the legal changes explored above, but ending the story of YPF's privatization here is deceptive. Doing so gives a false sense of the efficacy of legal discourse and bureaucratic practices to remake social worlds, and it ignores the far messier process by which corporate enterprises were carved from the remains of a state company, corporate actors were molded out of state workers, and the public and private domains were redefined. The legal changes are only a starting point for illustrating how the privatization process involved remaking public entities and their subjects, in addition to reconfiguring property and other social relations in the oil industry. The law was an important instrument used to redomain oil, oil companies, and oil workers, but it was hardly the only one. For instance, even before the Privatization of Hydrocarbons and YPF Law was passed, the corporate trustees who took over the company's management from state administrators used financial techniques to transform the state company into a privately owned corporation. These executives set out to reduce expenses by introducing labor-replacing technologies and by otherwise shrinking the number of workers and their benefits. The labor force was largely cut through coercive and sometimes illegal methods of pressuring workers to leave, a theme to which I will return.

I now beyond the realm of legal discourse to the conflict-ridden process by which a state-centered public domain was transformed into the privatized public of the global oil industry. Were the YPF workers and other people in Northwest Patagonia who were largely unable to influence the law-making process able to shape its actualization on the ground? To what extent did they contest the exclusive and transnational character of the private oil market? How did they participate in shaping the privatized public domain? Did they also oppose it? I begin with La Pueblada's contestation of the distribution of resources in the private oil industry. I then focus on the Patria Association's effort to reclaim the YPFianos' shares of stock in YPF-Repsol and the UTE's attempt to form a viable business association among the emprendimientos in the Neuquén region.

La Pueblada

YPFianos bitterly recall that at the same time that the private company's profits began to soar, they arrived for their shifts to find long lists pinned to the fence outside the refinery naming those who had been dismissed. The conversion of the state company into a privately owned corporation had little effect on the everyday lives of the investors who bought its stock, but the process of remaking YPF Estatal into YPF SA and then YPF-Repsol dramatically reconfigured the lives of the tens of thousands of YPFianos across Argentina. YPF personnel dropped from fifty-one thousand in December 1990 to eight thousand in December 1993.[9] The isolated oil towns in the north and south of the country bore the brunt of this "downsizing." After YPF-Repsol moved its regional headquarters from Plaza Huincul to the capital of Neuquén Province, Plaza Huincul and Cutral Có lost their special status as the towns that fueled the nation. Their unemployment rates rose to higher than 20 percent (Costallat 1997: 5). Before this process had fully unfolded, the YPFianos' dedication to kin and desire for familial stability turned to frustration and anger because they, and the other oil town residents whose livelihoods also depended on the petroleum industry, were no longer able to support their families.

In June 1996, tens of thousands of people blocked the local, provincial, and national roads in Northwest Patagonia in a protest that was a forerunner of the mobilizations to come across the country. This protest arose almost three years to the day after YPF stock was first sold on Wall Street but three years before the state's last shares were sold to Repsol. The immediate trigger for the protest was the cancellation of an agreement between Neuquén Province and a Canadian company to build a petrochemical plant in Plaza Huincul, a project that had promised residents who had lost their livelihoods during the privatization a chance to reenter the oil industry. As news of the cancellation was broadcast on the radio, and at the urging of the announcer, YPFianos and other residents of the oil towns expressed their anger and frustration in the streets. This event became known as La Pueblada, literally the uprising, as it was the first social mobilization of its size and kind during the Menem years (Svampa and Pereyra 2003).

The participants in La Pueblada were the first to call themselves piqueteros, a term that united people to protest injustices in a manner that explicitly rejected their representation by political parties and labor unions and undercut distinctions between unemployed, underemployed, and marginally employed workers. Although politicians facilitated the protest from behind the scenes, the piqueteros organized resident commissions that were led by people without formal party or union affiliation and little if any prior political experience. These commissions set up blockades of the highways that pass through the oil towns, recruiting groups of teenagers to guard piles of burning tires and old machinery to obstruct the roads day and night for a week. Others joined them in shifts. Older people who could not withstand the cold and wind of the

Patagonian plateau brought food, drink, and clothing to those who guarded the road blockades. At the height of the protest, more than twenty thousand people stood behind the barricade. They united with cries of *"No entra ni sale nadie"* (Nobody enters or leaves) and *"Queremos trabajo"* (We want jobs). The national guard was called in to open the highway, but the troops turned back upon seeing the enormous numbers of people in the road.

La Pueblada has been widely celebrated as an expression of resistance to neoliberalismo, yet numerous YPFianos reminded me that it was not until several years after YPF's privatization was legally effected that this event broke the eerie quiet in Cutral Có and Plaza Huincul. The protest is better understood as the public expression of the YPFianos' desire to be included in the privatized public domain carved out by the private oil companies and the state that supported them, than as opposition to it. The protests disrupted the circulation of people, petroleum, and other commodities through Argentina's largest oil-producing region in an attempt to compel state and corporate actors to reallocate some of the wealth generated by the privatized industry to employment and social services for those who had dedicated their lives to producing energy for the nation. While this uprising was partially rooted in longstanding provincial and municipal political disputes (Auyero 2005), it gained wide political traction by focusing protest at Torre Uno, the oil-rig-turned-monument celebrating the discovery of oil, which stands at the point where the national highway Route 22 passes into Plaza Huincul (see Map, Inset B). Torre Uno recalled oil's significance for political sovereignty and economic nationalism, in opposition to the idea that natural resources were merely a form of capital. Though La Pueblada invoked this history, the uprising was not delayed resistance to neoliberalismo; it was an attempt by workers and other residents to reconstitute YPF's social mission within the private oil industry.

YPF kinship was evoked throughout La Pueblada and in the participants' subsequent reflections on it. Laura Padilla, the thirty-six-year-old underemployed tutor who negotiated with the governor on behalf of the protesters, described the event in words full of nostalgia for YPF kinship. She explained her motivation to lead the protesters in terms of her strong sense of the dignity of labor, care for kin, and understanding of YPF as a family of families. For instance, two weeks after the end of the protest, she was the guest on a popular national television program and, surrounded by her daughter and two sons, she stated, "As the days went by, the suffering united us." She continued: "I think that all of a sudden, we learned to love each other. We didn't know each other, we didn't recognize each other's faces, but the love we felt for each other was great" (Auyero 2003: 23). By framing the protest as "an act of love," Laura's account evoked the notion that La Pueblada bonded the population of the twin oil towns around the simultaneous death of "Father YPF" and emotional reunion of "the YPF family." This understanding of the event in terms of familial affect was encouraged by the local radio announcer, who called for people to express their anger over "unemployment, 'Father YPF' was gone, hunger, nothing to do" (Auyero 2003: 32). Numerous other participants implied that La Pueblada was the consummate funeral for the YPF family; yet the protest did not represent the demise of the affective bonds of YPF kinship, but rather their revitalization in a novel privatized public form.

As we have seen, many of the state oil workers did not passively accept their exclusion from the privatized oil industry but actively pursued reentry into it. Fernando Castillo, one of the YPFianos introduced in the previous chapter, provides an example of how YPFianos fought to maintain the YPF family alongside their vocation. He was among those who portrayed the process of privatizing the state oil company as the "dismemberment of the YPF body." He described the privatization as abolishing YPFianos' source of livelihood and eliminating the inheritance they expected to pass on to their children, thereby transforming the kinship relations they had established and maintained through state petroleum production and destroying the affective bonds within YPF. Fernando was fortunate because he became a co-owner of one of the emprendimientos discussed in Chapter 1. Although he recognized that he was better off than many of his workmates, he still described how difficult it was for him to depend on his wife's financial support for the several years it took his emprendimiento to earn enough money to pay him a salary. This situation clearly violated the YPF norm of a family composed of a breadwinner husband and a homemaker wife.

Fernando also told me about numerous fellow YPFianos who were unable to retain jobs in the emprendimientos. Their situations were much worse because they had been "living off relatives' help" for more than a decade. He told me that when YPF was privatized, "we all became harder; that is, [we each felt] 'I have to defend my family,' and everyone else, well, they will handle things as they can, because here the priority is my family and my job." The violence of his familial metaphor highlights how kinship sentiments are "both emotional orientations and embodied dispositions" that are destructive as well as creative forces (Yanagisako 2002: 10). In recounting the YPFianos' plight, Fernando stated that it went against their "human nature" to shift from being supporters of kin to being supported by them. "One is paid to fund one's family, to keep it well, so that they can eat," he said. Defending YPF's maligned social mission, he added "and yes, it is also necessary for them to have the money to go to the theater or a movie, or a dance if they are young." Thus, Fernando and other YPFianos with jobs joined their unemployed friends and kin at the road blockades out of a sense of solidarity. The legal conversion of YPF did not destroy the kinship sentiments and practices that grew up in the oil towns over the course of the twentieth century, and YPFianos redeployed these ties to organize a protest that was not against the privatization but for their inclusion in the reconfigured domain of the exclusive yet transnational oil industry.

The understanding that La Pueblada re-created the YPF family as a privatized form of the state-centered community that once existed in the oil towns is apparent in participants' descriptions of it, both immediately after the event and several years later. When La Pueblada first came up during one of my conversations with Fernando, his face dropped in sorrow.[10] He described how he saw everyone he knew, except the elderly and small children, at the road blockade. He and other protesters used the term *el pueblo* to talk about the participants as a broader group of people than the YPFianos or even other members of the working class. "El pueblo finally reacted then," he said, "and then was when we most realized the loss of the father that we had in YPF." A father, he added, "who resolved everything for us, who paid for everything." He compared the mood during La Pueblada to the feeling in the oil towns at the time of the crash of an YPF airplane bringing workers back for Holy Week:

> In that moment [after the crash], I saw what the community was, what people here are, because the whole town poured out. The whole town felt the pain that they suffered because their cousins, siblings, in-laws are here. Everyone lives here; perhaps they didn't get along but they know that his cousin lives over there, you see . . . [At La Pueblada] I again saw the whole town here. There were blocks where there was no one at home because it was leave your house and go [to the road blockades] because you had to or we will die.

He concluded, "Those two occasions were when I saw el pueblo totally united [and] everyone very, very shocked." The two moments thus represented the strengthening of YPF kinship in the face of death.

The YPF family was reconstituted as a privatized public in the sense that it created a political community bound by the sharing of domestic sentiments of loss and love, and of domestic resources such as food and drink, rather than one united by the region's role as oil producer, a common state worker identity, or a union or party structure. The protesters united around a common attachment to place and a feeling of anger at their abandonment by both state and company. La Pueblada was thus both a reaction to the disintegration of a state-centered public domain and an attempt to create a new one by mobilizing kinship sentiments and household resources. The event indicates how the privatization process led to a revitalization of the notion of the YPF family outside of traditional state institutions, such as the union and the company, yet it did not restrict kinship to the domestic domain. While YPFianos like Fernando might have prioritized their immediate families, kinship still remained part of the "public."

The piqueteros' rearticulation of the YPF family as a privatized public reveals an ambivalent relationship to the state. The protesters refused representation by their municipal officials but demanded that the longtime governor of Neuquén Province, Felipe Sapag, come and talk directly with them. The elderly governor Sapag represented the lost figure of the paternal state that guaranteed a comfortable life to residents of the oil-rich region and that defended them against those who wanted to transfer the oil wealth to other places. After the roads had been closed for a week, Sapag arrived to negotiate an end to the blockade. He signed an agreement to improve the welfare of the area residents by, in the short term, addressing the hunger and utility shutoffs and, in the longer term, increasing state jobs through public works projects. The state did not fulfill its side of the agreement, and residents carried out further protests, including a second Pueblada in 1997 that turned deadly when police shot an uninvolved woman on her way to the store. The community that the protesters created did not persist after the roadblocks were dismantled. Yet, despite its unsurprising failures, La Pueblada was the harbinger of the 2001 protests that ousted Menem's successor, Fernando de la Rúa, and led to the election of Néstor Kirchner.

While La Pueblada added another reference to Plaza Huincul and Cutral Có in Argentine history books, two other organizations formed by YPFianos—the Patria Association and the UTE—were both more populous and influential movements that more significantly shaped the privatization process and challenged Cavallo's definition of the public domain than did the extensively commented upon Pueblada. Despite being largely overlooked by the news media and academics alike, in 2004 approximately ten thousand YPFianos were pursuing legal actions through the national Federación de Ex Agentes de YPF y Gas del Estado, to which the Patria Association belonged. In addition, more than five hundred people were employed by the emprendimientos in the UTE in the Neuquén oilfield. Like La Pueblada, the actions of these associations did not contest YPF's privatization but instead challenged the YPFianos' exclusion from the private oil industry. In doing so, they attempted to re-form the privatized oil market along lines unexpected by the architects of the privatization legislation.

Participatory Property

The neoliberal goals of expanding the reach of the market, promoting private property relations, and ending citizens' dependence on the state were embodied in the Participatory Property Program, a provision of the 1989 State Reform Law that remade state workers into shareholders who would own pieces of the soon-to-be-privatized companies. It was intended to incorporate those who labored for the state into the privatized industry by granting them a financial stake in its future, but it was not a guarantee of jobs or benefits. The inclusion of this provision in the law implied that workers would no longer be an inherent part of the company by virtue of their employment, but instead would be included through the form of property ownership distinctive to the corporate form: shares of stock. This form of property does not give owners rights to (or responsibility for) the company itself, only a right to a percentage of its profits. Adolf Berle and Gardiner Means wrote in their influential 1932 study of corporations that while owners of nonliquid property such as farms are "married to it," shareholders "have no direct personal relation" to the property they own because a corporation's ownership is separated from its management (284–85). Karen Ho (2009) has built on Berle and Means's argument to show that even though the value of shares bought and sold on Wall Street is practically unrelated to the activities of corporations, Wall Street investment banks are reshaping corporations in their image. She has asserted that "stocks, then, are not little pieces of corporations, mirror representations, or a faithful repository of all that a corporation does and says," nor are they "culturally or historically connected to the practices of the corporation"; nonetheless, stocks have significant influence over corporations because their success of corporations is measured in terms of the stocks' value (185, 187). In Argentina, like in the United States, shareholders are now recognized as the "true owners" of a corporation and "employees, located *outside* the corporation's central purpose, are readily liquidated in the pursuit of stock price appreciation" (Ho 2009: 3). Stock ownership is therefore a potentially powerful but indirect, impersonal, and temporary connection to a company compared with employment. The difference between these two relationships is particularly evident in a case like YPF, where jobs were once long-term, even intergenerational commitments, with a strongly affective dimension. The YPFianos' shift from workers to shareholders, and then to plaintiffs, reveals much about the creation and form of the privatized public domain that emerged along with neoliberalismo.

The actualization of privatization on the ground in Northwest Patagonia demonstrates that the YPFianos' property relationship was more attenuated than either the theory of stock ownership or the text of the law implies. In the name of increasing participation, the Participatory Property Program tried to replace a substantive and integral form of worker involvement with a far more limited and indirect one. Former state workers received a minuscule percentage of the new corporations' stock at the same time that they were dispossessed of their entitlements to state employment and benefits, including housing, health care, and livable retirement pensions. As noted earlier, crucial program details were established through negotiations between state and union representatives for each privatized company. The State Reform Law, for instance, did not specify what percentage of the stock of each company would be designated for its employees. The state oil workers union SUPE won its members a smaller than average share compared to other privitized companies, but its leadership gained a lucrative role in administering this and other benefits. Worse yet, even though all employees who still worked for YPF at the time of its conversion into a private company were due shares in stock, not all YPFianos received or retained them. Many of the YPFianos who were not old enough to retire were forced to take what was called "voluntary withdrawal" and were informed that they must give back any stock they received without payment for it.

The Participatory Property Program was intended to preempt larger claims by former state workers. The Morningside Advisor consultant Gabriel Peretz brightly asserted that YPF employees "obviously participated in the revenues and the profits" of the new oil corporation, but even he cautioned against seeing this property ownership as an opportunity for YPFianos' substantial incorporation into the privatized oil industry. Gabriel repeated an understanding I had heard from numerous others when he commented that the program was one of the ways that state and union officials "masked" the detrimental effects of the privatizations for state workers and prevented protest against the dramatic reduction of the YPF labor force. The dismissed YPFianos were supposed to use their corporate stock and severance pay to start entrepreneurial ventures like the emprendimientos. Many of those who did not join emprendimientos opened individual businesses, such as kiosks or taxi services. As there was no one to buy their products and services, however, their newly acquired financial resources were quickly exhausted and they went bankrupt. While the

Participatory Property Program sat well with neoliberal notions of freedom, participation, and representation, the process of creating private ownership did not meet its promises of greater opportunity, prosperity, or equity for YPFianos.

The architects of the privatization program envisioned stock ownership as a tool for generating workers' independence from the state; however, the YPFianos who received stock understood it as a continuation of YPF's practice of giving workers a share of its profits as a bonus at the end of each year. YPF Estatal had provided its workers and their kin with benefits for their entire lives and offered an inheritance to pass on to their children. YPFianos thus understood their industrial labor relations as bonds of lifelong care. In contrast, YPF SA presented the relationship between a worker/shareholder and the company as a temporary contractual association and transient form of ownership that terminated with employment. Most YPFianos thus lost their shares of stock when they lost their jobs with YPF.

YPFianos in Cutral Có and Plaza Huincul decried the dispossession from their economic rights and benefits, but most were at a loss for what to do because the union that had previously advocated on their behalf did not support their demands. Franco Vincente, one of the YPFianos introduced in Chapter 1, expressed a widely shared sentiment: "From one day to the next they said, well, YPF is finished. We were going to make a fuss, we were going to strike. But it was all already handed over, let's say, everything was already all taken apart. The union was also already arranged with the government to move forward all the privatizations that were to come, which was very unlucky [*nefastas*] for many people." The Participatory Property Program was more effective in providing an avenue for the unions to become involved in the privatization process than it was in incorporating workers into the privatized oil industry. As Franco suggested, this led to a great deal of resentment among YPFianos.

Franco's comment also hints at the overwhelming feeling of inevitability among YPFianos about the privatization. Despite this, a small group of them used the skills and experience they had learned from their previous union involvement to begin to reunite the former state oil workers in Northwest Patagonia. They organized a sort of shadow union in several of the oil towns, which later became part of the Federación de Ex Agentes de YPF y Gas del Estado. These YPFianos wanted to contest their disassociation from the oil industry with nonviolent means, but they had little recourse to address their problems in any substantive sense until the state attempted to sell its last shares to Repsol.

Battles for Shares of the Oil Wealth

The Participatory Property Program offered an unexpected legal avenue for YPFianos to contest both the distribution of goods that resulted from the privatization laws and their exclusion from the privatized oil industry. A group of about one hundred YPF sailors who had worked on the state oil tankers consulted Cellis and Associates, a small Buenos Aires law firm that specialized in labor law, because they believed that their severance pay was incorrectly calculated when they were dismissed in September 1992.[11] The lawyers combed through the details of the privatization law and found that these workers not only were deprived of their full severance pay, but also were denied the corporate stock to which they were entitled through the Participatory Property Program.

Pablo Peña, a soft-spoken but ambitious man in his late forties, was one of the two Cellis lawyers who worked on this case over the course of several years. In the Cellis partners' cramped, dark, and shabby office in downtown Buenos Aires, he told me how they realized the YPFianos' illegal dispossession:

> We might have the bad habit that when a client comes in . . . and says "I have come to claim this that belongs to me, and this that belongs to me," we do not restrict ourselves to this. Instead, we do it in reverse. It is like a patient who goes to a doctor and says, "Doctor, look at what I have and cure me of it." Well, here the client comes [and says] "They dismissed me. Look, what rights do I have?" From this we set out to look at what rights they have and we find three claims, for example.

Through their doctorlike examination of the law, Pablo and his partner discovered that YPF workers were entitled to sell back their corporate stock if they left YPF SA after January 1, 1991. They also realized that the sailors who consulted them represented only a tiny fraction of those who were due compensation for having to give back the stock without recompense. Pablo concluded, "This [matter] of the stocks is the one that has had the greatest political and economic repercussions on a general level."

YPFianos described to me the legal actions that followed the Cellis lawyers' discovery as a contemporary David and Goliath story. Argentine law did not allow the lawyers to present the YPFianos as a class, and so they began with independent cases. These seemingly individual disputes took on national importance after Repsol won its bid to buy the Argentine state's remaining stake in YPF SA in January 1999. The *Wall Street Journal* declared that Repsol had "pulled off one of the best deals in its history, and perhaps in the recent history of the industry" (January, 21, 1999).[12] For the YPFianos, this deal meant an opportunity to reclaim their stake in the company. The initial group of YPFianos and their Cellis lawyers froze the sale of YPF SA stock to Repsol for two days with their legal claim that the state could not sell shares that really belonged to YPFianos. Despite the strong opposition of numerous state and company officials, the Argentine court recognized that the Cellis lawyers' argument had enough merit to adjudicate, and the sale was delayed.

As the press coverage of these events spread across the country, YPFianos in Plaza Huincul and Cutral Có began to wonder whether they too were owed stock. Néstor Pietro, who became one of the central figures in the Patria Association, explained to me that he was shocked when he learned that he was owed money for his YPF stock when he was "thrown out" of YPF SA. He was quickly motivated to do something about it. Some of those who had begun mobilizing YPFianos into a shadow union invited the Cellis lawyers to a community meeting in Cutral Có. In front of the large crowd that gathered that day, Pablo Peña explained what rights the former state workers had, how the legal system functioned, and the possibilities for filing suit to regain their stock. About twenty attendees began to envision a partnership between the dispossessed YPFianos and the two gutsy lawyers willing to stake their reputations and financial solvency on this issue. This meeting prompted YPFianos in Cutral Có and Plaza Huincul to begin organizing themselves and led to the formation of the Patria Association. Meanwhile, the embryonic national Federación de Ex Agentes de YPF y Gas del Estado hired the Cellis law firm to study the possibility of conducting group suits on behalf of YPFianos in the same position, rather than continuing to handle individual clients.

The case of one small group of YPFianos reached the Argentine Supreme Court after six years of legal battles. In what has been called one of the most important cases of the past twenty years, in 2001 the state legal apparatus recognized that YPFianos' property could not be simply rescinded with their dismissal as employees.[13] The justices acknowledged the former state oil workers' right to stock but ruled that they were due financial compensation for their lost property, not shares of stock in YPF-Repsol. Faced with the possibility of thousands of individual trials, the Argentine Congress passed a law stating that all those who were forced to return their YPF SA stock without being paid for it could receive government bonds as compensation by going to the National Bank with the proper documentation. The Patria Association joined a national network of groups to mobilize YPFianos around translating the legal statute into the complex set of bureaucratic practices required to obtain these bonds. YPFianos contested their exclusion from corporate stock ownership through juridical techniques, but instituting an alternative vision for inclusion in the privatized public domain presented additional challenges.

The Bonds That Did Not Bond

We sat on rickety chairs around the small space heater stationed in the Patria Association's cramped front room in June 2003. The office was closed for the day, and we drank mate as we talked, passing the warm gourd slowly among the five of us. Néstor Pietro, the association's president Mariana Roccio, and the two less loquacious leaders who were with us described the situation of those who were dismissed from YPF when they were too young to retire and too old to gain other employment. They narrated a history of material and social decline in which workers who once bought a new car each year were forced to sell their possessions in order to feed themselves and their families. Néstor emphasized how many dismissed YPFianos had committed suicide. Their stories underscored the YPFianos' shared experiences and sentiments.

The Patria leaders attempted to reestablish an affectively bound community of YPFianos in Plaza Huincul and Cutral Có, like the one momentarily created by La Pueblada, through their long struggle to seek financial compensation for former state oil workers. They envisioned sustaining their association through the contribution of all YPFianos toward a collective resolution to their shared problem. Like the piquetero leaders, those who ran the Patria Association tried to re-create the public domain carved out by YPF Estatal, and then threatened by YPF SA, through an association that interacted with the national state but was no longer part of it. They too tried to draw on notions of YPF solidarity to form a new kind of community. For instance, the Patria leaders did not charge a fee to the YPFianos who consulted them, but, Mariana explained, they asked each member to make a monthly "donation" to cover the association's costs. One day, when only the four leaders and I remained in the office, Néstor, with an exaggerated frown, shook the wooden contribution box that sat on the desk in the front room and showed me the record book that indicated how few of the members had made a monthly contribution. The leaders were disappointed, even angry, at their fellow members' failure to supply funds or labor to the Patria Association. They felt that this community did not live up to the solidarity of the YPF community on which it was based. The Patria Association inspired neither the economic commitment nor the emotional intensity that La Pueblada's effort to re-create the YPF family had been able to inspire. Why?

The lack of affective attachment to the Patria Association cannot be disentangled from its members' lack of financial recompense for their stock. Nearly every YPFiano with whom I spoke lamented that almost a decade after the lawsuits began only a few plaintiffs had received the money due them. And when they did receive a financial reward, no one could satisfactorily explain why they received the amount that they did. The details of the legal battles that ensued after the Supreme Court case were extremely complex, and the Cellis lawyers have been busy ever since contesting how much compensation each YPFiano should receive. After Pablo Peña patiently explained to me the intricacies of this legal process, he concluded:

> Today one can say that everyone . . . should have "won" the trial in terms of his right. The only thing that remains to resolve . . . is an issue of the criteria for how the amount of the compensation is fixed. Here opens the great paradox. Maybe it is a difficulty on the part of the people who say, "Why did my neighbor get a pile X amount higher, and I got one a lot shorter, in the same situation?" Well, that's how it is.

Pablo identified a "great paradox" in the situation in which all YPFianos employed by YPF SA on January 1, 1991, were denied the same right, but they were receiving different amounts of compensation for their loss. The YPFianos' exclusion from the petroleum industry was compensated by a quantity of money that did not relate to their experience of taking part in petroleum production or YPF kinship because the legal process generated financial differences that were not based on their labor position, family size, or other criteria with which YPFianos were familiar. In Pablo's words, the amount of compensation was "an individual question in each case . . . because there are no standards, laws, or constitutional guarantees in play." A decade after the illegal dismissals from YPF SA, judges used their own formulas to assess the quantity of government bonds each YPFiano was owed. Subsequently, a fluctuating global bond market determined their monetary worth at any given moment. After the dismissed YPFianos' property rights were domained a public concern and adjudicated in the highest national court, their compensation was quickly redomained as a private matter. Moreover, their juridical victory did not provide them with YPF-Repsol stock and thereby did not help them join the public domain now occupied by shareholders that Menem, Cavallo, and their supporters extolled.

While Pablo accepted this situation as "how it is," many members of the Patria Association did not and disassociated themselves from the organization because of its failure to provide an avenue for them to reenter the oil industry. Few came to the office to report that they had received notice of the outcome of their case and to record how much they were going to receive, as they were supposed to do. Furthermore, Néstor told me that many people who collected their settlements not only failed to contribute to the Patria Association, but also did not pay the lawyers their contractually obligated fee. However, from these YPFianos' perspectives, the bonds they received through the trials neither counteracted their dispossession from the job, house, and other sources of security they had expected to pass on to their children nor accurately reflected their participation in YPF. Many of them exhausted their funds repaying outstanding debts from their failed business ventures, leaving nothing for new entrepreneurial endeavors or as a legacy for the next generation.

Néstor lamented the Patria Association's failure to establish the kind of community that he envisioned. He told me that while Karl Marx had written that religion was the workers' opiate, for YPFianos the trials were their drug. He suggested that the legal process might have constituted the YPFianos who were denied stock as a legal class, but it also created an expectation that the court process would solve their problems and therefore paralyzed YPFianos from pursuing other actions. What Néstor saw as renewed dependence was, I argue, the effective if unintended production of the very kind of privatized public domain that the Participatory Property Program encouraged. The joint-stock company is a historically unique kind of corporation because its members pool a delimited quantity of financial assets but do not share affective ties or obligations of mutual aid (Moore [1978] 2000: 116). Likewise, participation in the association came to consist of giving and receiving financial payment, not the mutual exchange of labor, sentiment, or resources. Stock ownership is a form of community in which relations are only based on shared financial desires and not on more substantive kinds of bonds, not to mention brotherly solidarity. As in a joint-stock corporation, ownership and management in the Patria Association were starkly divided between a large number of constituents who had little control and a few representatives who managed everything. In this way, the process of substantiating the YPFianos' private property rights continued their exclusion from the privatized and globalized oil industry. Moreover, the process of adjudicating the lost property had further divided the YPFianos, despite the Patria leaders' efforts to create solidarity. The Patria Association thus reinforced the replacement of a national public domain composed of corporatist groups like unions (see Chapter 3) and the affective bonds of YPF kinship with a privatized public domain composed of individuated property owners. This strenghtened the redomaining of oil and oil companies as belonging to the privatized public domain and YPFianos as decidedly excluded from it.

From Nostalgic Solidarity to a Transitory Union

At the same time that YPFianos were kept ignorant of their right to keep their corporate stock, they were actively encouraged to form emprendimientos. Like the Participatory Property Program, the formation of emprendimientos was an attempt to translate dependence into independence and remake workers who took orders into entrepreneurs who actively participated in shaping business ventures. To effect this change, YPF SA promised the former state workers that they could retain oil-sector jobs through agreements between the emprendimientos they owned and the giant corporation they did not. But as we have seen, subcontracting served to shift responsibility for rising unemployment and declining welfare away from business and state actors and toward individual workers. Like the lawsuits described above, this transformation demonstrates that YPF's privatization did not represent a direct translation from the public to the private domain, but a messy redomaining of property, labor, and welfare into a reconfigured public—in this case the highly concentrated global oil industry.

Chapter 1 recounts how the emprendimiento owners employed kinship discourse and practices of familial care to develop their subcontracting businesses, while the senior managers at the privatized oil company drew on the same notions of YPF kinship to establish patriarchical relationships with their subcontractors. Before a contentious relationship developed between the emprendimientos and YPF SA, the owners of thirty-five emprendimientos formed a business association called the Cámara Empresarial Industria Petrolera y Afines (Chamber of Petroleum and Allied Businesses, hereafter CEIPA) to unite the oilfield subcontractors in the Neuquén region. Edgar Mancini, one of the partners in the emprendimiento FESTA, discussed its founding:

> CEIPA was born in '92 from the desire of everyone who was going to be privatized to group themselves together . . . I have old photos from CEIPA when it was meeting where the old YPF power plant was. [The members] were meeting without having a political vision, only for the fact of joining together, like a club of the ex-YPFianos who had companies, with very little commercial vision . . . It was a social group—for eating asado, for chatting—to the point of hypocrisy, because they did not put the existing realities on the table. It was an

issue of not demonstrating to the compañero next to me that I am incapable [of running a business]. He who had been working with me for twenty years should not see that things were going badly for me. Therefore, I had to lie, to create a situation, a *belief.*

Edgar's statement illustrates how the emprendimientos organized themselves around affective attachments that resembled the ones described in Chapter 1 but with some important differences. They established their association as a continuation of the YPF family by meeting in an YPF landmark and resuming YPF traditions, like company barbeques, but divorced social events from business matters in a way YPF Estatal did not. At first, the CEIPA members saw their emprendimientos' failures as individual shortcomings. Only later did they counter the corporate definition of "strategic partnership," by converting their bonds of shared achievements into an alliance in which participants also shared their difficulties.

CEIPA members began to come together around a common problem after YPF SA awarded a series of contracts to a transnational oil services corporation instead of to the emprendimientos that had previously provided the services. Diego Parmado, whose story opened Chapter 1, told me about this change among CEIPA members:

The spark was the fall of the giant [emprendimiento] that invoiced the most, with a very large quantity of assets. All of a sudden, from one day to the next, it was in bankruptcy. What happened? That was the way in which many of them started to face reality and recognize their own problems. There was one reality that was killing us all, and the assassin was the same. "Yes, YPF [SA] hit me with a [belt] tightening and I lowered my price 10 percent." Therefore, it was the last smack to a drowning man. The only thing that remained was to speak the truth.

Once one of the emprendimientos had unequivocally demonstrated its problems, the members of CEIPA quickly recognized a common cause for what they had previously seen as individual failings. In Diego's terms, their loving father had turned into a bloodthirsty murderer.

This bankruptcy led the CEIPA members to more clearly articulate their vision for maintaining a regional oil industry that would not be swallowed up by the global market and to develop a business association to advance it. Andrés Esposito of OptaNeu recounted how representatives from twenty emprendimientos began "to throw ideas on the table about asking the [Neuquén] provincial government for help." Fearing a repeat of La Pueblada's spectacular form of YPF solidarity, the provincial representatives listened to the CEIPA members describe the possibility of an enormous rise in joblessness if more emprendimientos went bankrupt. Andrés explained that these joint meetings with provincial authorities reinforced CEIPA's efforts to unite the emprendimientos in a larger entity because state representatives told them they would recognize a "serious problem" and concomitant "necessity" to assist them only if the Neuquén emprendimientos were "all together" in the same dire situation. Andrés emphasized that the idea of forming an association among the emprendimientos did not spring from some sort of spontaneous recognition of need. Instead, it was a gradual process of defining common interests. Many leaders initially resisted forming a union amid the repeated calls for YPFianos to renounce their dependence on others and take individual responsibility for their problems. Andrés hinted at his continuing doubts when, at the conclusion of his passionate explanation of these events, he hesitantly requested my approval, asking, "Isn't it better if we unite, no?"

Because the constitutional changes of 1994 made the provinces sovereign over the oilfields within their subterritories and granted them the right to negotiate extraction contracts with corporate entities, Neuquén Province officials raised the emprendimientos' problems with YPF-Repsol executives with an authority that the emprendimientos could not muster. The provincial representatives expressed concern over YPF-Repsol's subcontracting practices during the renegotiation of the concession for Loma de la Lata, the oilfield that contained the largest proven natural gas reserve in Argentina at the time. The provincial authorities extended YPF-Repsol's contract to exploit the field and right to own any petroleum extracted from it for an additional seventeen years in exchange for the company providing 30 million pesos (then equivalent to $30 million) to pay the emprendimientos' debts and help them regain profitability. To this end, representatives from YPF-Repsol, Neuquén Province, and CEIPA agreed to form a formal corporate association of emprendimientos. This is how the UTE was born.

Of the forty-five emprendimientos formed early in the privatization process, the largest eighteen remaining became part of the UTE in May 2001. YPF-Repsol agreed to finance the association for four years but placed it under the control of an outside administrator. The administrator, which the agreement granted YPF-Repsol free rein to select, was a team from a transnational oil service corporation, similar to Halliburton but headquartered in Europe, called the Muller-Lange Group. The UTE agreement thereby elaborated a novel experiment to re-form the links among state entities (national, provincial, and municipal), transnational corporations, subcontractors, and oil workers. It attempted to reshape the regional oil industry within the global one, and, in my terms, to help constitute the privatized public in Argentina.

A Transitory Union

The emprendimiento owners who entered the UTE believed that they had reached a solution to the emprendimientos' woes that benefited all of the partners in the joint venture and generated a collective entity that merged principles of YPF kinship with corporate independence. However, the company executives interpreted these notions quite differently from the way the YPFianos did, and tensions between the competing definitions of partnership and understandings of a corporate association became the central theme in the UTE's brief history. Over the course of the four years the UTE lasted, the emprendimiento owners attempted to foster mutual long-term support and what one member called "associativity" (*la asociatividad*), while the company managers instituted temporary contractual relationships. By the time of the UTE's formal dissolution in 2004, it was evident to everyone involved that what was initiated as a creative experiment in regional association had come to resemble the rest of the transnational oil industry, in which an exclusive group of giant transnational companies dominate. In other words, the UTE demonstrated how an exclusive private market was created by linking certain corporate actors and barring others.

The emprendimiento owners' understanding of the aims of the UTE is evident in the press release Andrés Esposito prepared at its formal conclusion in 2004:

> The expectation created by the parties that actively intervened in this process
> . . . was that they would give these companies the necessary push so that at the
> end of four years they would be *PyMEs de servicio* [small and medium-sized
> service companies] that could manage themselves alone in the market. They
> were to do this so that at the end of this period [the emprendimientos] would
> be reequipped, economically healthy, financially established, and their man-
> agement picture would be enabled with the assets necessary to be in control
> of their situation.

This statement suggested that the corporate and state actors shared the emprendimiento partners' aim to develop their companies in a way that would eliminate their dependence on either YPF-Repsol or the state and allow them to become full participants in the privatized oilfield services market. When he handed me this press release, Andrés told me in more personal terms the difficult compromise the OptaNeu owners were obliged to make in order to rejoin the industry: "We handed over our company to them, and they managed it," he said regretfully. In the view of emprendimiento leaders like Andrés, each member of the UTE made sacrifices and provided resources to develop the region's place in the global market, much like each YPFiano provided skills, experience, labor, and severance pay to start the emprendimientos. However, they found that their corporate partners did not share their view of what the oil services market would look like. Whereas the YPFianos envisioned a public based on the equal participation of all its members, the corporate executives imagined integrating the emprendimientos into the global market by absorbing them into larger corporate entities.

Evidence that the association was not benefiting the emprendimientos began building from the initiation of the UTE. In one of the most egregious violations of their agreement, YPF-Repsol had not yet begun to fulfill the stipulation that it would provide the emprendimientos with formal training in entrepreneurial business management by the time the final year of the UTE had begun. The emprendimiento partners contested YPF-Repsol's contract violation and successfully pressured the company to hire the business consultancy Morningside Advisors to teach a "mini-MBA" course to the managing partners who directed the emprendimientos in the UTE. Gabriel Peretz led the team of economists, accountants, human resources experts, engineers, lawyers, and a psychologist who spent more than a year traveling back and forth between Buenos Aires and Neuquén to work closely with the emprendimiento directors. The team first assessed each of the emprendimientos' situations and needs, then designed a series of classes to teach them the management skills and entrepreneurial attitudes that they felt they lacked, and finally helped them write business plans to develop their emprendimientos into independent PyMEs de servicio, that is, members of the legally constituted class of small- and medium-sized service companies.[14]

Among the materials presented in the Morningside "mini-MBA" course was a 1998 *Harvard Business Review* article that argued, in contrast to the prevailing wisdom of globalization, that "the enduring competitive advantages in a global economy lie increasingly in local things—knowledge, relationships, motivation—that distant rivals cannot match" (Porter 1998: 78). The article advocated the construction of "clusters" of related businesses and institutions in a concentrated geography because "a cluster allows each member to benefit *as if* it had greater scale or *as if* it had joined with others formally—without requiring it to sacrifice its flexibility" (80, emphasis in original). The emprendimiento directors' discussion of this article led most of them to join Andrés in concluding that "associativity" was the "crux of the future." Speaking on behalf of the members of the UTE, he explained:

> What is the problem that we have? We have a contract, we are working very well with Repsol, we are not complaining. We have many outside clients. However, we have a problem with the size of the companies. As a policy on the global level—this is not my invention, nor YPF-Repsol's whim—the petroleum industry is tending to immediately hand over oilfields to large service companies that conglomerate the largest quantity of services possible . . . Therefore, when our competitors are companies that are international and have lots of economic power, we face a problem if we do not join together. What I have proposed is that if we join together the moment the UTE ends, then we can make a *cluster*, or a large service company, without the need to associate ourselves with other companies.

The association that the emprendimiento owners envisioned would extend the UTE beyond the initial four years and, like the emprendimientos themselves, would be based on the partners having equal roles in labor management, organizational decision making, and financial investment. With assistance from the Morningside consultants, Andrés and a few of his colleagues composed a business plan for this "cluster" in which each emprendimiento would manage its own affairs but they would offer their services as a conglomerate so that they could compete with transnational corporations like Muller-Lange.

When YPF-Repsol endorsed Andrés's proposal, it seemed that the emprendimiento leaders had succeeded in instituting a form of partnership that resembled their idealized notion of brotherhood. Then suddenly, in June 2004, the Morningside consultant who was most critical of Muller-Lange was removed from the project, and the remaining consultants, under pressure from the YPF-Repsol executives who hired them, began giving the emprendimiento leaders conflicting messages about the feasibility of their business plan. The project to extend the UTE was halted, and instead, the Morningside consultants attempted to persuade each of the emprendimientos to find a foreign corporation, or alternately an established Argentine one, with which to form an individual partnership. To the anger of many participants in the UTE, several of the emprendimientos quickly became subsidiaries of Muller-Lange. Diego

Parmado explained these "buyouts" that were being "envisioned for many of the emprendimientos that were born during the privatization":

> The particular character of the associations that are being generated is now showing . . . they are between a giant, you see, and a little emprendimiento . . . In the relatively short term, the emprendimiento stops existing as an emprendimiento, and not through a management decision but through the giant's commercial strategy of going out and looking for individual [emprendimiento] partners and offering them . . . 25,000 pesos . . . Already we can say from the existing contracts that the capitalist partners that are doing the acquiring have the deciding power, the operational power, the administrative power. That is to say, nothing remains for you as an emprendimiento, down to having to hand over your contract . . . you end up being an employee once more . . . the only difference is that before one was a YPF employee and now one is going to be the employee of a multinational, to which you end up giving your contract, your van, your equipment, with only the aim of continuing to have work.

Diego later said that the emprendimientos were becoming "one finger on the two hands" of the corporation's "giant" body. Here, as in the previous chapter, an emprendimiento is envisioned as a web that binds human hands and trucks through labor and property relations. And here, as we will also see in Chapter 4, a transnational oil company is described as possessing a somatic and affective form of corporate personhood. In contrast to this enormous corporation, Diego and his partners at FESTA sought to find a company that would support their vision of associativity. When Diego and Edgar began tentative negotiations with one company in late 2005, FESTA was one of the very few emprendimientos whose owners were still attempting to form a partnership based on egalitarian brotherly bonds, rather than on either parental dependence or bodily absorption.

Carolina Lucano, who stepped in to help save her father's emprendimiento Napalco from bankruptcy, explained to me how she came to realize that Napalco's relationship with YPF-Repsol and Muller-Lange was not what it seemed at first. She recounted how the YPF-Repsol representative with whom she most closely dealt promised that the UTE would "train" the emprendimientos to manage their own affairs at the same time that he told her, "I am going to donate [money] for doing this, this, and this, and in this way." Furthermore, Muller-Lange offered many of the same services as the emprendimientos did and secretly planned to incorporate the strongest of them as subsidiaries. The Morningside consultant, Gabriel Peretz, concurred:

> Carolina was the girl [*sic*] who defended [the Muller-Lange guys] to the death, and then ended up realizing that they almost melted down, almost broke, her father's company (because in reality it's her father's company). We had disputes with Carolina, I swear, we stayed up arguing with her until 11, 12 at night in the Hotel Isola drinking coffee ... The team showed her the numbers. "Look, look at what they are doing to you!" And she defended them to the death, and then at the end realized that the administrator was not so good because it let go of her hand. It is like your father gives you a hand, takes your hand and leads you to the park, takes you to the zoo, and then lets go of your hand and you are left alone. She realized this.

Like Andrés Esposito's metaphor about learning to drive in Chapter 1, Gabriel's paternal metaphor indicates that the emprendimiento traded one filial dependence for another. The father-child relationship serves here, as John Borneman (2004) has illustrated elsewhere, to perform political authority. Chapter 1 shows how the YPF SA and then the YPF-Repsol executives employed the same discourse of partnership as the emprendimiento owners did but pursued practices that disabled the emprendimientos from managing their current businesses or ensuring their future existence. Similarly, while the executive architects of YPF's privatization imagined a privatized public domain as the site of independence and freedom, they also reinscribed it as the place of patriarchical bonds.

The UTE did not incorporate the emprendimientos into an association resembling the *Harvard Business Review* article's model of a "local cluster." Neither did it generate the neoliberal advocates' ideal of "the free market," nor the YPFianos' vision of "the YPF family." It created a highly concentrated private oil industry in which YPFianos could only be the most expendable workers, if that. By 2005, several of Alberto Lucanos's Napalco partners had retired, and those who remained with the emprendimiento had purchased some computer imaging equipment and hired young technicians who had learned to use it in school, rather than drawing new employees from the large pool of YPFianos with years of experience in the Neuquén oilfields. The prohibitive cost of this new equipment had forced the partners to begin negotiating a merger with a translocal oil service company that had the capital to frequently update its technology. Alberto told me of his retirement in his always poetic way, saying that those who remained "will have to attend to the future; I am headed for my winter quarters."

After the UTE was formally dissolved, Andrés and his partners at Opta-Neu retained the hope of re-forming a business association, despite the small number of emprendimientos that had not become subsidiaries of larger companies. In my last meeting with Andrés in 2005, he corrected my reference to OptaNeu as an emprendimiento, stating that it was really a PyME now. In that moment, I realized that the term *emprendimiento* had ceased to represent a business partnership based on parity and mutual care among YPFianos and had become a demeaning term for what Diego Parmado described as a single digit on the monstrous corporate body. In other words, the private oil sector that emerged in Northwest Patagonia through the privatization process was increasingly incorporated into a transnational petroleum industry in which a small number of "oil giants" managed a vast network of subcontracted micro-enterprises that carried out the work of producing oil and its derivatives. Like the "community" of corporate shareholders, the oil services sector was provisionally tied together by short-term legal contracts. The history of the UTE illustrated that although the YPFianos in emprendimientos contested the meaning and practice of the privatized public that Cavallo embraced, they were excluded from this public as long as they remained YPFianos and asserted their kinship bonds and expectations for long-term relationships of mutual care.

Conclusion

The oil services sector was not the only arena that introduced obstacles to the inclusion of YPFianos and their kin into the privatized public of the petroleum industry. When I returned to the Patria Association office after several months' absence, Néstor told me that the only thing that had changed since I had been there last was that they were all older now. He pointed to a piece of paper taped to the office wall with the names of members who had died before receiving their court-ordered compensation. He said, "It's all men, next to their names are their widows." Néstor explained that there is no provision for automatic inheritance in Argentine law, adding that a court must decide how to divide a man's property and money, although usually his spouse gets half and the children divide the other half. Though trials were too costly for most YPFianos, without one an YPFiano's spouse and children could not receive compensation for his (or infrequently her) dispossessed stock. Néstor bemoaned the number of men who had died waiting to receive the payment they deserved and the fact that they could not pass it on posthumously either. As he noted, the privatization process did not simply eliminate familial benefits, but introduced in their place a kind of property—shares of stock—that proved difficult to transfer to kin but all too easy to transfer to foreign investors.

The creation of a privatized public subjected YPFianos and their kin to dependencies that circumscribed their actions as much as the state-based public had. While advocates of neoliberalismo proclaimed that YPF's privatization would produce "Argentina's first truly publicly held company" and would allow its members greater participation, independence, and freedom, the public domain that was created by the privatization process was just as restrictive and patriarchal as the one that preceded it. The redomaining of property and people had not created the democratic polity that many in Argentina envisioned as the site of substantive and equal citizen participation. Instead, the privatization of the national oil market turned a state-centered public into a privatized public. It was private in the double sense of being made up of privately owned businesses and being part of a realm largely beyond the control of the state. This is not to say that the state "pulled back" from the oil industry. State actors—including senior government officials, laborers employed by the state, and many in positions of authority somewhere between them—were crucial in creating a privatized public that was at the same time exclusive and transnational. It is to say that the public that emerged through the privatization process was decidedly not state-centered.

Like Cavallo and his team of economic experts in Buenos Aires, the men and women in the oil towns of Northwest Patagonia engaged in practices of redomaining, that is, of reconfiguring the private, the public, and the boundary between them. They did so not by arguing that YPF Estatal was Argentina's only truly public oil company or that oil was really public property, but by establishing associations that challenged their exclusion from the private oil industry. La Pueblada was not a protest against the conversion of the state oil company into a private one—as it was several years too late for that—or a demand for its renationalization, but a call for the residents of the oil towns to receive some benefits from the private oil industry. The Patria Association likewise demanded recompense for the YPFianos' exclusion from stock ownership, while the UTE attempted to make a way for the emprendimientos to remain worker-owned businesses but still be involved in oil production. Their histories show that privatization was not a policy imposed on unwilling people but a protean process carried out by myriad actors who were variously positioned in relation to both the oil industry and the state.

II   Petroleum Citizenship

3 Fueling Consumer Citizenship

THE SUNSHINE COMMUNITY CENTER is a rickety shack made of broken cinder blocks, scrap wood, corrugated sheet metal, and cardboard, with no running water. It was here that I began my fieldwork in the neighborhood surrounding the Polo Petroquímico Dock Sud (Dock Sud Petrochemical Complex) on the outskirts of Buenos Aires. The Sunshine Center sits on the main drag in Goldendas, a shanty settlement fewer than five miles from the presidential palace in the Plaza de Mayo and even closer to one of the largest complexes of oil refineries in Argentina (see Map, Inset A). I went there because I was curious about the relationship between those Argentines hardest hit by neoliberalismo and the private corporations that now occupied the petrochemical complex and managed the national oil market. How did people who had little direct connection to the oil industry experience the privatization in ways similar to and different from that of the YPFianos, whose lives were so intimately tied to it?

My entrée into life in the shanty settlements came as an "ally" (colaboradora) at the Sunshine Center. Each day, I joined some of the area's most impoverished residents in making stew for the collective kitchen that served a daily hot meal to approximately one hundred children and a number of adults whose families did not have enough money for food. One Friday afternoon was exemplary of my early experiences there: I was helping to break up wooden cartons from fruits and vegetables that we used as kindling to light the cooking fire outside the shack when a young boy appeared in the alley. Sara Santos, the center's head coordinator, paused her work to listen to the boy explain that his mother had sent him because she had found a large piece of wood that the Sunshine Center could use to make fires. Sara dispatched Pato, one of the few men closely involved with daily activities at the center, and a few of the older boys who ate at the communal kitchen to retrieve the wood. Pato and the boys returned shortly with a rotten electricity post. Pato started breaking it up with his hands, then fetched a handleless ax to finish the job. In the meantime, Ramona Costanera, who often took charge of preparing meals, carefully carried a five-gallon pot from the shack and gingerly balanced it on a bent piece of metal grating over the fire pit. The pot was full of water and the potatoes, onions, carrots, and scraps of meat we had spent the past few hours cutting up. Sara, her sister-in-law Carmen, Ramona, and two or three other women gathered around the fire, taking turns stirring the stew with a metal fork bound to a long wooden stick (see Figure 6). The sun was already setting by the time the stew started boiling, so Pato paused his chopping to thread an electrical cord through a small glassless window hole in the shack's wall. He attached the light

Figure 6. Two women stand outside the Sunshine Community Center as stew boils on a fire. The woman on the left holds a fork tied to a stick that serves as a multipurpose utensil, and the one on the right holds a plastic pitcher used to carry water into the center, which has no running water.

bulb outside so that we could see what we were cooking. As the women took turns bending over the hot fire on that evening to stir, talk turned to personal, municipal, and national politics, as they often did.

A month later we would be cooking the daily stew inside the Sunshine Center on a gas stove connected to a propane canister. How and why did this move to using hydrocarbon fuel happen? Answering this question requires understanding the importance of oil consumption for citizenship and social class in Argentina. It also requires looking more closely at the history of liberalism and Peronism, as well as the current place of private oil companies within Argentine society.

Several of the people I knew from the Sunshine Center took time away from their daily provisioning to join the march and rally in support of the national boycott of Shell and Exxon (described in the introduction) as members of a piquetero movement called FUNDA.[1] I open this book with a scene from the boycott because it highlights the intersection of my two central concerns: it is evocative of the ways that petroleum matters in a country that is not an "oil nation," and it shows what neoliberalismo looks like more than two decades after it first emerged. The boycott also illustrates that oil and its politics are consequential to the lives of people who consume very little of it. Why, given their extremely limited means, did the participants of the Sunshine Center's communal kitchen begin to use more hydrocarbon fuel at the time of the boycott? I connect these two events—the national boycott of Shell and Exxon and cooking at a community center in a shanty settlement—in order to examine how hydrocarbon fuel consumption became a method of political subjectification and national imagination. In this chapter I analyze the symbolic and material deployments of petroleum in the streets of Buenos Aires, the national press, and the Sunshine Center to investigate how Argentines pursued petroleum consumption as a citizenship entitlement following the country's transition from state-led to corporate-led industrial development.

Consumer Citizenship

Numerous anthropologists have proposed that citizenship is being radically reconfigured in the contemporary moment. They have suggested a range of new forms of citizenship beyond state-centered political membership, including cultural, flexible, biological, indigenous, insurgent, consumer, and corporate citizenship.[2] This scholarship builds on work that shows that citizenship is not an identity category that trumps other ones with its legal codification of rights within the state, but a set of claims to resources and recognition within a political community (Somers 1993; Somers 1994; Holston and Appadurai 1996).

Many of the new forms of citizenship that anthropologists have identified fit well with neoliberal discourses about entrepreneurship, competition, and self-responsibility. For instance, Nancy Postero (2007) insightfully has demonstrated that in order for indigenous people to gain something approaching full citizenship in Bolivia, they must fit themselves within globalized capitalism and make sure that their representative organizations adopt bureaucratic practices of transparency and accountability and engage in rational self-government. They must also conform to a limiting notion of permissible cultural difference, such as speaking an indigenous language, not more profound differences in ways of thinking and acting.

Other anthropologists have argued that the transnational emergence of neoliberalism is delinking citizenship from states and sometimes from national frames altogether. These scholars assert that many people, instead of seeing their country as the principal site of social membership and political recognition, now unite by constructing transnational commonalities, for instance, around sexual identities that crosscut geopolitical lines. However, Lisa Rofel's study of postsocialist China (2007) shows that "gayness" has emerged as a cultural identity, social allegiance, and political commitment that is constructed out of transnational dialogues but does not contribute to the construction of a global identity. "Gayness" is generating and organizing belonging in China in a manner that replaces class-based struggle and state-based definitions of political citizenship but still asserts a desire for inclusion in the Chinese nation.

Recent elaborations of "consumer citizenship" similarly illustrate how people express *national* belonging through their purchase and display of commodities that are produced through *transnational* networks.[3] Citizens use clearly symbolic objects such as flags and figurines of national heroes, and even mundane things like soft drinks, to reassert the importance of their nation amid globalized commodity circuits (Özyürek 2004; Özkan and Foster 2005). In these instances, commodity consumption is a political act that identifies one as a citizen who seeks recognition by a polity. In examining consumer citizenship in Argentina, I follow Fernando Coronil (1997) in focusing attention on the simultaneously symbolic and material uses of petroleum to link state and nation and to bind (sub)territorial space to the body politic.

There are also more subtle ways that the purchase and use of mundane commodities encourage people to see themselves as national citizens and enable them to be recognized both by state institutions and by other citizens. Robert J. Foster (1995, 1996, 2002) has argued that the legal regulation of advertising in Papua New Guinea has constructed proper citizenship as conforming to a "possessive individualism" in which people are supposed to make their own identities by choosing commodities that express their lifestyles and commitments, including both a desire to be unique and a sense of national belonging. Advertisements for soda, gasoline, and other everyday items present a conception of personhood far more similar to Euro-American notions of individualism, self-determination, and the rights-bearing citizen than to a Melanesian understanding of relational personhood, that is, as a "node" in a web of relationships among people and things.[4] A Shell advertisement acclaiming the company's state-sanctioned sponsorship of Papua New Guinean athletes exemplifies the ideal citizen as the "uniforms of the athletes double as national flags and corporate logos, the vestments *par excellence* of standardized consumer-citizenship" (1996: 6). Here, athletic competition is the sign of individual achievement, brand loyalty, and national belonging at the same time. The consumption of transnational commodities can thus signal a person's conformity with the state's expectations of citizen behavior and thereby incorporate that person into the nation and state.

A comparison of the cultural meanings of gasoline in Papua New Guinea and Argentina, however, illustrates the contingencies of consumer citizenship, particularly highlighting the uses of the same commodities to represent different forms of collective belonging and political participation. Whereas the consumption of Shell gasoline represented state-sanctioned citizenship in Papua New Guinea (Foster 1996), it represented national betrayal in Argentina. This distinction demonstrates that although national citizenship may be asserted through the purchase and display of identically branded "goods," commodities are neither vessels holding inherent or stable meanings nor free-floating signifiers. I join Foster in emphasizing the complex ties among commodity consumption, national belonging, and state institutions but question equating contemporary citizenship with the rise of individualization, competition, and the ideal of the self-sovereign actor. Argentine consumer citizenship combined preexisting collective and individualized notions of personhood in a manner that strengthened citizens' identification with both their nation and their class.

Like several aspects of neoliberalismo already discussed, contemporary consumer citizenship grew out of earlier manifestations of citizenship that are specific to the country. The cultural meanings and practices of oil consumption in Argentina have been significantly shaped by the genealogies of liberalism and Peronism. Yet, it also is important to point out that recent events there resemble political struggles in other places that also have taken commodities and markets as crucial sites for contesting state governing practices and the definition of legitimate and illegitimate economic regulation. To take one well-known example, E. P. Thompson ([1971] 1991) illustrated how, in eighteenth-century England, poor people's grievances over changes in grain laws, market practices, and bread prices grew into uprisings. These popular revolts drew on widely shared social norms and ideas about the common good that together constituted a "moral economy of the poor" (318). This particular moral economy included a "consumer-consciousness" that rested on the assumptions that the poor should be ensured the ability to purchase bread, local desires should be sated before distant ones, profits should be moderated by custom, and emergency measures should be taken when scarcity threatens to produce widespread hunger. When this consumer consciousness was disregarded, poor people used the tools at their disposal to reinstate it. Thompson's incisive history indicates that even when a laissez-faire political economy was overthrowing the moral economy of the poor, the latter did not disappear, and the poor were able to forcefully reassert it in moments of crisis.

There are several parallels between the protests over bread in eighteenth-century England and those over oil in contemporary Argentina. In both cases, price increases prompted popular protest, but price alone cannot explain the strategies, meanings, and consequences of people's actions. Many Argentines were angered that, while more crude oil was being produced at lower cost in Argentina in 2005 than ever before, the price of gasoline at service stations was rising to reflect its price in foreign markets. More importantly, events in 2005 demonstrated that a neoliberal market economy did not entirely replace the moral economy that developed with Peronism during the 1940s. The Peronist moral economy suggested that Argentine industries should create good jobs for citizens, consumer prices should fit workers' financial means and consumptive desires, and industrialists and workers alike should support the economic development of the nation. When neoliberal ideas about economic efficiency and market freedom rose to prominence in the 1990s, they neither faithfully reproduced the liberal tradition developed during the early years of the Argentine Republic nor fully replaced the Peronist notions of economic justice that emerged after 1940. I extend Thompson's argument that new economic norms do not fully erase preceding ones, but that the latter reemerge in moments of crisis. However, rather than describe a struggle between a singular moral economy and another immoral one, I identify competing moral economies that differently drew from Peronist and liberal ideas about citizenship, morality, and the common good. The boycott and the communal kitchen brought these traditions together in distinct but complementary ways.

Metamorphoses of Argentine Citizenship

As the colonial order crumbled in the Americas, many among the elite read Enlightenment, and later Romantic, treatises and envisioned strategies to establish nation-states that could both remake South America's social and political institutions and alter the region's position in global capitalist circuits. The statesmen who imagined the initial legal structures for the Argentine Republic tried to reconcile the liberal discourses about freedom and equality with the historical experience of colonialism.[5] The tradition of liberalism that they developed advocated ending the trade restrictions that the Spanish had put in place and developing a state that would actively engage in market formation and expansion. The first Argentine statesmen aimed to create a national community together with a state but established hierarchical paternalist links rather than "deep horizontal comradeship" (Anderson [1983] 1991: 6; but see Sommer 1990).

The revolutionary leaders in the River Plate region asserted that the abstract rights of European liberal theory should form the foundation for constructing political institutions in the region; however, the next generation of political elite countered that equality was not a natural feature of humanity but a historical achievement that had to be earned through education and hard work. As civil wars raged and economic prosperity failed to materialize, these men, known as the "Generation of 1837," blamed the failure to fulfill the promises of liberalism in the River Plate on the masses' incapacity to properly exercise the rights and responsibilities of citizenship.[6] An influential member of this group, Juan Bautista Alberdi, claimed that popular representation jeopardized the ability of the state to preserve the social order that was necessary for the advancement of the republic. He argued that if the state promoted economic growth rather than merely granting property rights, it would lead citizens to realize their individual potentials and also to acquire the civic virtues necessary for them to properly contribute to the common good. Alberdi therefore contended that a legal framework based on a contract, not an abstract declaration of rights, was the foundation of a society that could teach people to be upstanding citizens (Adelman 1999: 203–5, 13–14). The Generation of 1837's vision of citizenship as a privilege to be achieved, rather than a natural right to be extended, significantly shaped the text of the Argentine constitution and the practices of state officials until the rise of Peronism.

The constitutional framers granted individual citizens several of the emblematic liberal freedoms and property rights but envisioned them as necessary measures to attract European capital and settlers and thus to fulfill the state's economic purpose, rather than seeing abstract citizenship rights as ends in themselves. Furthermore, individual rights and entitlements were understood as secondary to the collective rights to order and stability that, the constitutional framers asserted, were necessary for commerce to function. The members of the constitutional convention thus ratified a constitution that diminished political enfranchisement and vested the federal government with the authority to intervene in the ostensibly sovereign provinces in order to "stabilize provincial affairs in the name of national unity and prevent civil strife that would imperil property" (Adelman 1999: 207). The constitution emphasized the rights of the state over those of its citizens and privileged their commercial liberties over their juridical ones. The legal constraints on citizenship have varied since then, and not consistently in the direction of greater inclusion.[7] What has remained fairly consistent is that the president, more than any other state authority, has been conceived as legitimately representing popular sovereignty (see Chapter 2 for discussion of how Menem used this legitimacy to powerful effect).

Anthropologists and social historians have repeatedly shown that the practice of citizenship significantly differs from its textual elaboration in constitutions and the like. The Argentine constitution established voting as the legitimate means of political representation, yet only a small segment of the population participated in this political rite. Even among those men who were eligible to vote, most found the practice either impossible or ineffective and used other strategies to participate in state and provincial politics. Armed insurrection was among the most powerful of their techniques in the early days of the republic, as citizens who were required to join the national guard used their military experience to discipline political leaders who abused their authority and became seen as "tyrants" (Sábato [1998] 2001: 9). After 1862, armed insurrections were increasingly replaced by the usually nonviolent activities of the civic associations that bloomed in the urban centers of the River Plate region.[8] Hilda Sábato ([1998] 2001) has shown that in the mid-nineteenth century, civic associations, not voting, came to represent "the most genuine expression of the common will of the nation" (12). These institutions mediated between citizens and their political representatives and together became an important force in the configuration, the legitimation, and sometimes the contestation of political rule. Yet these associations, no less than the constitution, reflected the liberal assumption that citizens are individuals who are equally free to sell their labor, to defend their interests, and to express their views in "the public sphere." It was not until the 1940s that Peronism thoroughly challenged the landed elite who had governed Argentina since the 1860s, the notions of individual citizenship that they had promoted, and the economic system based on agricultural exports that they had fostered. Peronism shattered the hegemony of the statesmen who proudly professed their liberalism, and with it the assumed natural link between liberalism and democracy (Laclau 1979).

The Peronist Reconfiguration of Citizenship

The rise of Peronism as a political party, a social movement, and a personal identification for millions of Argentines was a watershed event that profoundly altered the political landscape of the country.[9] Though Argentina experienced economic growth and came to rival Europe in several economic measures during the first decades of the twentieth century, the majority of the population was excluded both from formal political participation and from the fruits of the export boom. The little-known military officer Juan Domingo Perón deftly drew on challenges to the ruling regime coming from several sides in order to shift the terms of political debate, to incorporate excluded segments of the population into the polity, and to spearhead a major transformation in Argentine society.[10]

Perón first emerged on the national stage through his participation in the nationalists' 1930 coup that overthrew the Radical president Hipólito Yrigoyen (see Chapter 1). Perón went on to become an important player in the military dictatorship that ruled from 1943 until 1946. His rhetorical skill captured the attention of the working people who were contributing to, but not benefiting from, Argentina's rapid industrialization and dramatic economic expansion. As he forged the positions of secretary of labor, vice president, and minister of war in the military government of the early 1940s, he developed a loyal following among industrial workers by assisting the trade unions that supported his program of state-managed labor relations and by censuring those he found disloyal, as Menem would again five decades later.

The petroleum industry provides a prominent example of Perón's praxis. In the oilfields of Patagonia, the Communist Party and anarchist groups had organized strikes during the 1930s even though unions were officially banned and violently prosecuted. Perón permitted the state oil workers to unionize but carefully fostered the development of SUPE as the sole union that could legitimately represent them to the state. SUPE won wage increases and improvements to labor and living conditions in exchange for abandoning its hostile stance against YPF. It became one of the unions that helped win Perón the presidency in 1946 and formed part of the Peronists' popular base during his first administration (Solberg 1979: 163).

A crucial aspect of Peronism's appeal to urban workers, the rural poor, soldiers, and small-business owners alike was its expansion of the notion of citizenship to encompass entitlement to social and economic inclusion as well as the realization of formal political rights. Peronist discourse absorbed the liberals' language of universal democratic enfranchisement and the Radical Party's endeavor to oust the traditional oligarchy but deployed their words to show the hypocrisy of those who had controlled the state. According to historian Daniel James (1988), "Perón explicitly challenged the legitimacy of a notion of democracy which limited itself to participation in formal political rights, and he extended it to include participation in the social and economic life of the nation" (16). In other words, Perón did not simply offer liberal democratic rights to those previously denied them; he infused citizenship with a social and economic component framed in terms of social justice and what today would be called "participatory democracy."

Perón promoted equal citizenship for all Argentines by substituting the liberal notion of citizenship as the protection of the autonomous rights-bearing individual with a class-based conception of citizenship entitlements. He and his supporters criticized the liberal concern with merchants' market freedoms and property rights and instead emphasized workers' freedom from exploitation and rights to a "dignified life" and a minimal standard of living. They repeatedly denounced the oligarchs, *vendepatria* (literally the "fatherland sellers"), and other "enemies of the people" who gave away Argentina's resources to foreigners and sustained economic colonialism for their own gain. Peronist discourse asserted, for instance, that employment was a fundamental right in itself and necessary for fulfilling most other rights. It suggested, more strongly, that citizens' rights, obligations, and entitlements were defined in terms of those citizens' class position in society. Peronism thus implied a moral economy framed around the rights, entitlements, and duties of workers rather than around owners of capital. He and his followers further argued that workers should be collectively recognized as having a distinctive role as the motor of national prosperity, and thus they deserved privileged representation within the state as a class, not simply the rights granted to them as individuals.

Perón shared with other nationalists in the military and beyond a vision of an ordered society organized around corporatist institutions representing distinct interest groups but all held together by a "spiritual unity" (Plotkin 2003). Like many of his contemporaries across the political spectrum, he believed the state should prevent imminent social disorder by improving the economic situation of those people who might be attracted to the anarchist and communist movements. To fulfill this vision of corporatist citizenship in which workers were privileged as a group, the Peronist administration established a highly centralized and hierarchical national confederation of unions. Under Perón's tutelage, local trade unions were organized into national networks, and these national federations into a single confederation, the Confederatión General de Trabajo (General Labor Confederation, hereafter, CGT). Through the CGT's coordination of collective bargaining, workers gained higher wages, improved working conditions, and benefits such as medical care and paid vacation time. Union leaders became congressional representatives and mediated between citizen-workers and the state. In this way, the Peronist unions both molded and represented Argentines much more actively than the civic associations of previous generations did.

Despite a considerable rise in unionization that took place under Perón's guiding hand, more than half of Argentina's urban and rural workers still were not part of this union apparatus in 1954 (Plotkin 2003: 143). While unaffiliated workers received some vicarious benefits from the gains of the CGT, there was a growing divide between unionized and nonunionized workers. The Peronist effort to extend citizenship beyond the unions was carried out through two key institutions: the Ministry of Labor and the Eva Perón Foundation. Like the Peronist unions, these institutions provided social services and material benefits to those who previously had not been served by the state. In the process, they created a loyal base for the Peronist movement among women who worked in the home, children, the elderly, the disabled, and other poor people.[11] The Peronist Party stepped in to mobilize this population at election time. Moreover, while the Peronists discursively framed the distribution of state benefits in terms of social justice, they also established paternalistic relationships that promised that the state would take care of the male breadwinners and female homemakers who labored for the good of the nation. Peronism, like the Eastern European regimes that Katherine Verdery (1996) has described, "posited a moral tie linking subjects with the state through their rights to a share in the redistributed social product," in which subjects "were presumed to be grateful recipients—like small children in a family—of benefits their rulers decided upon for them" (63; see also Borneman 2004). Conversely, those citizens who did not appreciate what Perón had done for them and properly show their support for the Peronist cause faced discipline or violent repression.

Several of the tensions within the Peronist configuration of workers as ideal citizens were revealed by the rapid growth in commodity consumption. Perón called on Argentine workers, as both producers and consumers, to support his vision for the "New Argentina" by replacing imports with items made in the country. By the end of his first term, domestic production of consumer products had increased considerably, and workers had been rewarded with significant increases in their real wages. However, these new consumers encountered long lines and numerous shortages when they went to purchase the commodities that were now ostensibly made accessible to them. Already by 1949 an inflationary spiral significantly cut into Argentines' purchasing power despite increasing state regulation of wages, rents, and the prices of commodities considered necessities. In short, commodity consumption had passed from a central goal of Peronism to become a challenge to it. The Peronist administration responded to the inflation, shortages, and other economic ills with programs that required all citizens to increase their labor efficiency, to reduce their commodity consumption, and to augment their savings for the "advancement of the nation." Yet as these new programs were carried out, the burden was not distributed evenly. While Peronist discourse and institutions privileged workers, Perón singled out two other segments of the population for special citizen roles: housewives and owners of capital.[12]

Argentine statesmen long had held women responsible for rearing citizens for the nation, and the Peronists specially charged them with the task of raising soldiers for the Peronist cause. Peronism implied that the state's responsibility was to ensure just wages and set fair prices, while the citizens' duty was to actively defend their families' purchasing power. As the economic situation soured during the early 1950s, housewives were assigned the latter task in part because they were envisioned as more naturally devoted to household economy than their profligate husbands (Milanesio 2006: 93–94). Furthermore, Perón suggested that because he granted women the right to vote in 1947, they owed him cooperation when the national economy took a dive a few years later. To fulfill their debt to Perón and to prove that they were worthy citizens, women had to be frugal, calculating, and assertive housewives.

Although it was usually Eva Perón who sustained her husband's pledge to maintain direct contact with el pueblo, Perón led the campaign to enlist housewives in his 1953 economic recovery program. He took on the role of shopping consultant, speaking personally to housewives as feminized consumer citizens. He expressed dismay at the amount of food that Argentines wasted, frequently citing the meat he saw in trash cans along his walk to his office (Milanesio 2006: 100). He advocated shopping at municipal markets, consumer cooperatives, and grocery stores run by unions or the Eva Perón Foundation instead of frequenting neighborhood shops, where the Peronists claimed proprietors overcharged their clients. Wherever they shopped, housewives were instructed to keep track of official prices, look out for ill-weighted scales, and boycott stores that violated the law or the Peronist moral economy. State agencies and the women's branch of the Peronist Party launched "consumer education" programs to teach housewives these techniques for being responsible female citizens. The Peronists also utilized the press to spread their message. A full-page ad in one women's magazine commanded "Don't pay a cent more" (Elena 2007: 125). An article in another magazine exhorted its readers: "Do not be passive. React . . . Reporting done with justice is noble work. If you hand over 'just one coin' [a bribe], it is because your sense of morality has expired" (Milanesio 2006: 98). As Eduardo Elena (2007) observed, when commodity consumption became the focal point of Perón's first economic recovery campaign, "mundane objects—a hunk of cheese, a square of cloth, a loaf of bread—became contested symbols of the achievements and failures of Peronist social justice" (113). They also became symbols of the achievements and failures of a markedly gendered form of citizenship.

While the Peronists envisioned housewives as becoming ideal female citizens, they saw owners of capital as potentially threatening the nation. Perón gently reprimanded housewives for being irresponsible consumers, but he vigorously attacked the owners of capital as "oligarchs" and "vendepatria." He asserted that wealthy industrialists and agricultural estate owners were not inherently bad citizens; they only became so when they failed to work for the national good. An ordered society and corporatist democracy, in fact, depended on the participation of the economic elite. However, he argued, the liberal notions of freedom and equality had permitted a small group of Argentines to cooperate with foreign capitalists and exploit Argentina's physical and human resources to grow their personal wealth and political power. Perón stated in a speech responding to demands for elections two years after the 1943 military coup, "if some ask for liberty we too demand it . . . but not the liberty of fraud . . . nor the liberty to sell the country out, nor to exploit the working people" (James 1988: 16–17). Peronism hardly implied the overthrow of capitalism. Instead, it called for a "third position" between capitalism and communism. To execute this vision, the Peronist state asked for capitalists' cooperation with Import Substitution Industrialization and other economic development projects. Those who supported Peronism were generously rewarded for their contributions to "the common good."[13]

Fifty years later, President Néstor Kirchner echoed many of Perón's words when he called for the boycott of Shell and Exxon. Kirchner reasserted that Argentines' rights and duties as citizens depended on their position within global capitalist circuits. He, like Perón, positioned himself as the consumer's advisor and suggested that consumer citizens owed him allegiance for having renegotiated the enormous foreign debt on which a previous administration had defaulted. For their part, foreign oil companies had an obligation to provide fuel at reasonable cost, especially during the season when greater quantities are needed for the harvest. As will be evident from the discussion below, citizenship was as clearly defined in gendered terms and as unmistakably differentiated by class in 2005 as it had been in the 1940s and 1950s. In both moments, commodity consumption was invested with moral as well as political-economic importance for the nation. Yet despite these similarities, what held Peronism together over the several decades between Perón's and Kirchner's presidencies was not a consistent ideology or a set of policies, but the combination of a historical identification with el pueblo, the development of a working class with particular interests and passions, and the integration of this class into the nation and state, all under the aegis of charismatic leadership.

While I have emphasized the Peronist reformulation of citizenship around class, it is also important to stress that even at the height of Perón's rule, corporatist citizenship did not completely erase forms of individual citizenship. For example, individual citizenship continued in the judiciary domain of the state, which recognizes only individual claims to injury and does not permit class-action lawsuits (see Chapter 2 for how this legal tradition was consequential for the YPFianos who used the courts to claim property rights in the privatized oil industry). The emergence of Argentine neoliberalismo during the military dictatorship of the late 1970s and early 1980s and its elaboration during the Menem administration (1989–1999) show the falsity of strictly dividing liberalism from Peronism. The Shell and Exxon boycott and the Sunshine Community Center demonstrate how both the middle-class residents of Buenos Aires and the impoverished residents of the shanty settlements on its periphery understood and practiced petroleum consumption in ways that recombined Peronist and neoliberal discourses and techniques into a novel form of consumer citizenship.

Argentine Energy, Inc.

"Neoliberalismo" was a dirty word in Argentina in 2005. For many across Latin America, it signified a foreign economic model and set of policies that had severely harmed the welfare of the population and the sovereignty of the nation. In Argentina, neoliberalismo was widely blamed for the severe economic decline that began during the Menem presidency and came to a head during the de la Rúa administration in 2001. In the tumultuous times that followed the resignation of de la Rúa, Néstor Kirchner, who was then the little-known governor of Santa Cruz Province, challenged Menem, who was running for a third term, as the Peronist candidate for the presidency. The Peronists split, and three candidates ran without official party endorsement. None obtained a majority of votes in the first election, but Kirchner won the presidency after Menem dropped out of the race amid predictions of a landslide victory in the runoff with Kirchner. By 2003, Menem stood for the continuation of "neoliberal structural adjustment," while Kirchner positioned himself as joining Brazil's Luiz Ignacio da Silva (Lula) and other Latin American leaders in fighting against it.

Kirchner vowed that his administration would continue to eliminate the vestiges of neoliberalismo from Argentina. In a speech to Congress only days before calling for the boycott of Shell and Exxon stations, he described Argentina in the previous decade as "a meticulous student of the Washington Consensus" who "rigorously applied its advice for opening [the national economy]" to disastrous effect. He explained that the economists' lessons taught "neoliberal models that pushed the country to develop a model of 'spurious competitiveness' based on the over-exploitation of its labor force, the deterioration of its natural resources, and financial speculation." With the expected pomp for such an occasion, Kirchner proposed an alternative "model of genuine competitiveness" based on homegrown technology, knowledge, and labor, led by the state (Kirchner 2005). The oil industry would soon become a crucial site for attempts to materialize these ideas.

To enact Kirchner's vision for an "alternative to neoliberalismo" twelve years after YPF's conversion from state-owned enterprise into privately owned corporation, his administration founded a new state oil company, formally named Energía Argentina SA and known as ENARSA. This company was created as a corporate joint venture in which the national state would own 53 percent of the shares of stock, provincial states another 12 percent, and private investors could buy and sell the remaining shares. It was not a re-creation of YPF Estatal, yet Kirchner was still accused of advocating the return to failed programs of state-led development. In fact, his administration encouraged the development of transnational enterprises and markets and prioritized the export of Argentine commodities. Kirchner wanted Argentines to show foreigners, who had rapidly invested in and then divested from Argentine business ventures during the 1990s, that Argentine companies could (re)gain positions as players in the global economy without foreign assistance but with the help of the state. As the law creating ENARSA declared, the new state company was intended to support this vision by reintroducing a state entity "to intervene in the market for the purpose of avoiding situations in which the abuse of a dominant position is caused by the structure of monopolies or oligarchies" (ENARSA, 2004). The state thus promoted ENARSA as a vehicle to provide an alternative to neoliberal modes of production, consumption, and citizenship. However, it was granted only 50 million pesos of state funds (little more than $15 million) at its incorporation in November 2004—nowhere near the amount necessary to buy existing concessions or to develop new off-shore oilfields. Someone closely involved in the privatized petroleum industry described ENARSA to me as a "Potemkin village" that could never carry out what it appeared to do. However, the discursive and spatial representations of the new state oil company had the powerful effect of marking a shift in the relationship between the state and oil companies.

The new vision for the oil industry was clearly expressed on February 1, 2005, when ENARSA's first gas station was dedicated. This station on Buenos Aires's elegant Avenida Libertador was, in fact, jointly owned with the Venezuelan national oil company Petróleos de Venezuela, SA (PDVSA). The eagerness of Venezuelan President Hugo Chávez to collaborate with other Latin American governments provided a possibility for ENARSA to take material form despite its severe financial limitations. The opening event was full of carefully planned symbolism to summon the renewal of the Argentine nation. The station's fuels were called Tango, Super Tango, and Eco Tango, after the popular dance style that has come to represent Argentine culture around the world.[14] The first vehicles filled with this fuel were a Porsche manufactured by an Argentine state-owned company in the 1950s and the Chevrolet coupe that five-time world champion Formula One racer Juan Manuel Fangio drove from Buenos Aires to Caracas in 1948. Echoing the concept of "petroleum nationalism," the minister representing the Argentine state that day declared, "Every liter of fuel that is sold will be part of the patrimony of all Argentines."

ENARSA was supposed to represent a re-formed national oil industry, but Kirchner's nationally framed vision stood in some tension with Chávez's pan-national one. In his usual exuberant style, Chávez announced that ENARSA and PDVSA would open six hundred more jointly owned and operated service stations in Argentina within the year. He declared that these gas stations not only would provide an alternative to the transnational corporations that sold most of the fuel consumed in Argentina but also would begin "to Latin-Americanize petroleum." Chávez's pledge made only slightly veiled reference to PDVSA's bid to buy Shell's chain of nearly one thousand gas stations in Argentina and its refineries in the Polo Petroquímico Dock Sud. Though the Venezuelan minister of energy who accompanied Chávez announced to the press that their negotiations with Shell were advancing rapidly, the next day a Shell representative abruptly declared that the company was not exiting Argentina or selling any of its installations. With this, the most expedient vehicle for swiftly realizing Kirchner's vision for ENARSA broke down. However, another avenue for reshaping the Argentine petroleum market soon came into view.

"Not Even a Single Can of Oil"

On the heels of his wildly popular renegotiation of Argentina's defaulted debt with the IMF, President Kirchner announced an anti-inflation campaign that aimed to increase the "purchasing power" of the Argentine citizenry. Like Perón's campaigns in the 1950s, this one centered on agreements with key industries to maintain consumer prices in the face of a 4 percent increase in the domestic consumer price index during the first quarter of 2005, a steep rise in the price of crude oil on transnational markets, and growing fear of a return to the spiraling inflation of years past. Oil was once again among the key industries targeted by the state, but in defiance of the ongoing state-industry negotiations, Shell raised its gasoline and diesel fuel prices between 2.6 and 4.2 percent. This move came less than a month after the Shell executive's unexpected declaration that the company would not sell its service stations to PDVSA.

On the day after Shell service stations raised their prices, President Kirchner reacted with these words: "Let's take a stand and make common cause against them. We will not buy anything of theirs—not even a single can of oil—so that they realize that we Argentines will no longer support this type of action. Against those who take advantage of el pueblo, there is nothing better than waging a 'national boycott.' El pueblo will be mobilized in the right and proper way, without violence." At the same time that Kirchner called for a national boycott of all Shell products from the presidential mansion, more than a dozen consumer organizations and piquetero movements announced rallies at Shell's national headquarters in downtown Buenos Aires and occupations of Shell gas stations around the country. Members of the youth wing of the president's Peronist organization plastered the city overnight with posters stating: "From those who raise prices, do not buy. Buy from others. Defend your purse and your country" (see Figure 7). These swift demonstrations by state and nonstate actors were carefully coordinated to communicate widespread disapproval of

Figure 7. Buenos Aires was plastered overnight with posters like the ones on this closed kiosk downtown. The poster states "From those who raise prices, do not buy. Buy from others. Defend your purse and your country." On the right is an "X" in the celestial blue of the national flag across Shell's signature yellow-and-red logo.

Shell's market activity. They claimed that consumer citizens held a nonviolent weapon that would defend both citizen and nation.

When I visited the Shell station near my apartment on the first day of the boycott, I found only one man fueling a car, but the YPF-Repsol station across the street was full of vehicles. The Shell attendant thought that the other oil companies would raise their prices to meet Shell's in the next few days. As she and most experts predicted, Exxon increased its prices to Shell's level, but YPF-Repsol and Petrobras did not follow suit as expected. Kirchner called for the extension of the national boycott to Exxon, and the actions against Shell continued to escalate. Several commentators subsequently implied that the difference in strategy between Shell and Exxon, on the one hand, and YPF-Repsol and Petrobras, on the other hand, was not surprising since the former were decidedly "foreign" corporations and the latter were at least somewhat "local."[15] This ignored the fact that all four were transnational corporations chartered and headquartered outside of Argentina that engaged in fully globalized petroleum production and trade. As we will see, a great deal of discursive work was needed to make the consumption of certain brands of gasoline into an act of national treason and consumption of other brands into "good citizenship."

The demonstrations outside Shell headquarters and occupations of gas stations carried out during the first days of the boycott culminated in the march and rally in downtown Buenos Aires described in the introduction. Reinforcing my ethnographic evidence that the boycott almost completely halted Shell sales, the Federación de Empresarios de Combustibles (Federation of Fuel Businessmen) recorded more than a 50 percent decline in the retail of Shell products (*La Nación*, March 14, 2005). Yet despite the dramatic plunge in both sales and corporate image, neither Shell nor Exxon budged for four tense weeks. Then, in the beginning of April, both companies reduced their consumer prices to below what they had been a month earlier.[16] This marked the first time in recent memory that fuel prices had decreased.

Kirchner celebrated this lowering of prices as "a clear victory for the Argentine people." But what exactly had the boycott accomplished? Did it do anything more than temporarily lower fuel prices and humiliate a few corporate executives? The answer, I believe, is that the hydrocarbon fuel market provided a site for Argentines to define what neoliberalismo meant and articulate why they opposed it. As a prominent columnist for the left-leaning newspaper *Página/12* commented at the time, Shell's actions provided a convenient opportunity to realize a "redefinition of the standard role of the largest private companies in the country," especially "those that provide public services, which until the previous decade were in the hands of the state" (March, 13, 2005). It did not hurt that Shell was already widely recognized as a giant foreign corporation worthy of condemnation. Kirchner pointed out that it had been named one of the "Ten Worst Corporations in 2002" by the *Multinational Monitor*. Finally, as we have seen, petroleum had long been a powerful symbol of capitalist dreams that crossed scales from the person to the nation. Yet despite the anti-neoliberal rhetoric, the boycott did not attempt to eliminate neoliberal ideas and institutions but to reconfigure them. The month-long boycott of Shell and Exxon was itself profoundly neoliberal. It recombined Peronist notions of citizenship with liberal ones in a way that was compatible with the globalized and privatized oil industry of the twenty-first century.

A New Citizenship Curriculum

On most days during the boycott, the Shell stations and the street in front of Shell headquarters stood quiet, their emptiness the only sign that anything was unusual. In contrast, the newspapers and radio and television stations were abuzz with discussion of all matters relating to the petroleum industry.[17] The boycott was thus sustained as much by the discursive and visual practices of the media as by the material and spatial practices of the gasoline purchases and street protests. The boycott's simultaneous enactment in gas stations, city streets, and news media reinforces Néstor García Canclini's point that people today are "brought together as consumers even when we are being addressed as citizens" ([1995] 2001: 15–16). The boycott used petroleum's powerful symbolism to portray the nation as a democratic community of oil consumers in which citizens collectively acted as classed subjects to fight neoliberalismo and its privileging of corporate actors. At the same time, the boycott subtly but powerfully interpolated citizens as individual consumers who chose to participate in the global market in hydrocarbon fuels.

One could argue that the boycott worked not through imagination and rhetorical persuasion, as I suggest, but through a simple economic logic. Shell and Exxon's fuels were more expensive than those of their competitors, so no one bought them until the companies lowered their prices to win back customers. It seems that the boycott advocates simply asked citizens to do what was in their rational economic interest, and the companies (eventually) did what was in theirs. But, if economic interests followed a natural rationality, then a boycott would not have been necessary in the first place. But it *was* necessary. The Shell attendant I spoke with on the first day of the boycott recounted that the previous day, when Shell had first raised its gasoline prices, was just like any other day, even though the station where she worked sat directly across the street from a less expensive YPF-Repsol station. It was not until after President Kirchner called for the boycott that, she reported, "you noticed a difference" at the pumps. Argentines needed to be instructed in their personal desires and national interests, a point that Kirchner did not miss an opportunity to emphasize. Most crucial here, Kirchner used discursive techniques to encourage Argentines to choose certain transnationally produced commodities over others, rather than legal techniques to set prices or restrict imports.[18]

As President Perón had presented himself as an advisor for housewives who needed to become responsible consumers, President Kirchner portrayed himself as the school principal and set a new citizenship curriculum for the nation. He argued that because Argentines had been diligent students of neoliberal economics in previous years, they needed to be reeducated before they could practice citizenship through their market choices. For instance, in his speech after Shell and Exxon lowered their prices, Kirchner portrayed Argentines as bright students who now taught their former economics teachers about the moral economy of petroleum:

> I believe that the people have given us a lesson at this essential moment because they are starting to use the tremendous power they have with rationality ... We in the government could have said this, but it was people who then took the step of saying "*I* do not buy where they charge me more." People are continuing to take this type of attitude, and they are going to win the battle for justice, for logical profitability, the battle to defend purchasing power ... This kind of conduct is the attitude people should take. (Kirchner 2005)

Kirchner's speech emphasized the correct "attitude" and the specific "conduct" that embodied economic "rationality" and also stated that Shell and Exxon's price decreases signified a victory in a "battle for justice." The combination of these statements illustrates a tension between principles drawn from liberal political economy and from the Peronist workers' struggle for economic justice. There is a slippage from the collective subject of "the people" (in this case *la gente*, not el pueblo) to the individualized "I" of the normative consumer. There was also a threat of violence lurking behind Kirchner's battlefield metaphors. If the oil companies had not responded to the citizenry's peaceful defense of their "purchasing power," they might have turned to more aggressive means— and would have received the backing of the state. The imagined community of consumer citizens ambiguously blended the individualization of consumers in commodity markets with the collective incorporation of the working class as a powerful force within both the state and the market.

Patricia Vaca Narvaja, the sub-secretary of consumer defense in 2005, further articulated to middle-class citizens the Kirchner administration's understanding of consumer citizenship. She argued that the president was "blazing a trail" for Argentines to improve themselves and their nation, but the responsibility for concrete action fell on these citizens to recognize the collective effect of their consumer actions. In an extended interview with *Página/12* (March, 13, 2005), she explained: "As citizens we have to think about our purchasing decisions not as something individual, but instead know that they produce an impact in the market. What we do as consumers has consequences." She asserted that citizens had a responsibility to use their purchases as "votes" to discipline the transnational corporations' "unilateral" actions. She further stated that the boycott served "to raise the awareness of the citizenry in order to involve them in their own consumption decisions. And we helped them to modify their conduct and punish those who raised prices in an unjustified manner." Once again, individual and collective action, education and the threat of violence, choice and compulsion sat tensely next to each other. State representatives suggested that while electing government officials was a periodic rite of democratic participation and filling up at the ENARSA station was possible only for the miniscule fraction of the population who lived near its swanky location, *not* purchasing fuel at Shell and Exxon stations was an everyday technique that many Argentines could employ to express national belonging and support the democratization of the polity.

Consumer advocacy organizations similarly depicted the boycott as a democratic action in which car-owning citizens wielded the legitimate power to govern the petroleum market. When Sandra González, the president of the Asociación de Defensa de los Consumidores y Usuarios de la Argentina (Argentine Association of Consumers and Subscribers [ADECUA]), argued "people have to realize that today they have the power to choose what best suits them," she equated Argentine citizens' right to choose between candidates to represent them in the state and the ability to choose between service stations to purchase gasoline. A representative of another consumer advocacy organization stated that a boycott "is a legal tool that we as consumers have facing an abusive [price] increase across the world." When corporations behaved in an "unjustified" and "abusive" manner, she suggested, then consumers should express "a responsible attitude" by not buying from them. These statements exemplified the boycott supporters' view that commodity consumption could unite citizens who share a common interest despite the competing tendency to differentiate themselves according to branded identities.

While consumer citizens were being celebrated as democratic market regulators, Shell and Exxon were characterized as foreign tyrants and national traitors. Kirchner made this point clear at the award ceremony for recipients of a Ministry of Social Development project, which fell on the day that Shell first raised its fuel prices. He divided Argentines into the people who were "carrying out tasks that move [us] forward" and those "sectors that do not desire the gradual improvement of the purchasing power of society." He further proclaimed: "On one side we have the struggle for [advancing] the process of social inclusion . . . But on the other side are those interests that continue to believe that they can continue to have special privileges, and can continue to determine the Argentine economy." Shell provided a perfect example of the latter's "absolute lack of collaboration with Argentine society." He explained, "They are trying to raise costs, trying to damage the processes of productive development and social inclusion in Argentina." Here, Shell was a foil to "the people" and took advantage of its powerful position in transnational economic relations in order to shape the national economy to its benefit. Kirchner asserted that by raising its prices, the company selfishly refused to cooperate with the citizenry's effort to help their nation recover from the economic crisis caused by Menem's neoliberal structural adjustment programs. The next day, Kirchner reinforced his point by calling Shell a bully that "believes that it is its own boss" (Kirchner 2005). Shell's price increase not only represented a discredited paradigm in which transnational corporations were granted a privileged position in reshaping and controlling the national economy, but Shell also personified the vendepatria who sold national wealth for individual gain (see Chapter 4).

At the same time that the discursive and material practices of consumer citizenship were connected to state institutions and a national frame, Argentines' use of the English-derived term boicot linked them to an extensive genealogy of transnational struggles over il/legitimate economic practices across the world. The term boycott came from an English land agent in Ireland, Captain Charles Cunningham Boycott, who in 1880 was ruthless in his eviction of impoverished tenants. The Irish Land League organized Captain Boycott's employees to refuse all contact with him in an attempt to force him to return the land to its former tenants. During the same period, Argentines were turning away from armed insurrections and toward street demonstrations as a more effective means of political participation (Sábato [1998] 2001). More than a century later, leaders of the Shell and Exxon boycott argued that the country did not return to democracy when the military dictatorship fell in 1983, claiming instead that economic relations remained ruled by an oligarchy of national capitalists and foreign corporations. They suggested that Argentina could become a full democratic polity only if all citizens could participate in market relations and their elected representatives could govern them. The boycott further implied that the market was not the adversary of state and society, something to be ruled from the outside by democratic institutions, or even embedded within them, but an integral part of democracy itself.

Critics of the Shell and Exxon boycott, it should be noted, also employed a contrast between democracy and dictatorship to denounce it. In an unexpected articulation of usually conflicting political interests, gas station owners and workers joined Shell executives and Kirchner's rivals in condemning the boycott as undemocratic. They did so for two reasons. The first was best expressed by the president of the Asociación de Estaciones de Servicio Independientes (Association of Independent Service Stations) when he stated, "The government should have applied the law and harshly punished the companies for forming part of an oligarchy, rather than going around insulting these [companies] who could care less, and leave us as the only ones harmed." Another small business leader stated, "In this fight between the government and Shell, the only ones who are losing are the station owners and workers, who are losing the tips that make up an important addition to their salaries." He continued, "This is not a problem for Shell, because they export what they don't sell in the internal market. The problem is for the station owner, who has a signed contract with the oil company and is obligated to fulfill it." These statements did not dispute the contention that oil companies illegitimately governed the market, but asserted that they should be dealt with solely through juridical means. These critics called the boycott undemocratic because it punished hardworking citizens who upheld their contractual obligations but did not penalize the criminal party, which could make more money selling its fuel in foreign markets than in Argentina. Service station owners and workers based their objections on a formal definition of democracy as "the rule of law" and also argued that the boycott was unjustly excluding them from the political community of the nation.[19]

Shell and Exxon representatives cited the above objections but also declared that Kirchner, not the oil companies, acted dictatorially by telling citizens what to do and thereby impeded the proper functioning of the free exchange of both ideas and petroleum in the marketplace. They did not, however, point to a problem with the boycott mentioned by the gas station owners and workers: that these transnational corporations financially benefited from the month-long boycott. Argentine law required them to satisfy the domestic market before they exported fuel, but if consumption of their products in Argentina decreased, then they could export more fuel and sell it at a greater profit than they could within Argentina (see the introduction). As Sawyer (2001) has shown in another context, oil companies are exquisitely intricate assemblages that reposition their parts to meet, and frequently benefit from, unexpected events like this boycott.

In contrast to the business leaders who drew on the neoliberal discourse about the free market and its unrestricted flows, state and NGO representatives portrayed the gasoline market as a site for political participation that needed to be made free through greater democratic government, not through further restrictions on state regulation. After the privatization of the national oil industry had replaced state regulators with corporate ones, the boycott leaders called for reregulation by citizen consumers and their democratic representatives. The boycott supporters who carried the day in mid-2005 portrayed Shell's actions not only as the stubborn trace of a discredited way of conducting business, but also as blocking the replacement of government through dictatorship with government through participatory democracy.

Defending the Right to Consume

The boycott interpolated Argentines as consumer citizens responsible for democratizing the fuel market, but it did so through differently classed techniques. Consumer advocacy organizations facilitated and represented middle-class participation in the boycott as an act of educated democratic choice akin to voting. In the eyes of these car-owning Argentines, the boycott not only helped them save some money, but also fought against the residues of neoliberalismo that continued to threaten their nation. They purchased commodities in a manner that reflected their sentiments of national belonging and concern for the common good, as well as their common economic interests. Yet few of them attended the march and rally described in the introduction. Poorer Argentines, who were accustomed to using buses, trains, bicycles, horse-drawn carts, and their feet for transportation, turned out for the march and rally in large numbers. Most of the Argentines who participated in the boycott through street protest were members of piquetero movements, and they explained their participation in demonstrations, rallies, and gas station blockades in terms of the defense of their economic rights. Several of the piquetero leaders pushed further than their compatriots in consumer advocacy organizations to suggest that if the petroleum market was to become a democratic forum in which all citizens participated, then petroleum consumption had to be extended to those who could not afford to own or operate petroleum-powered vehicles. This difference in their justification for the boycott suggests that the tensions between the liberal and the Peronist moral economy mapped onto a class divide.

While consumer advocates taught middle-class citizens to use their gasoline purchases as votes, piquetero leaders enlisted the poorest segments of the population in the gas station occupations and rallies in front of Shell headquarters by portraying these protests as direct actions to combat a threat to democracy. Luis D'Elía, the colorful leader of the movement called the Federación de Tierra y Vivienda (Housing and Land Federation, hereafter FTV), was possibly the most outspoken piquetero supporter of the boycott.[20] He argued that the foreign oil companies represented the newest threat of authoritarianism in Argentina by repeatedly describing Shell and Exxon's price increase as a *golpe del mercado* (literally "market strike"), echoing the term *golpe del estado* (coup d'état). He reinforced the comparison between oil companies and illegitimate military organizations by stating that "in this country, the petroleum companies have made coups, have put in place dictators, have created hyperinflations," thus equating the overthrow of President Yrigoyen in 1930, the hyperinflation of the early 1990s, and the price hikes in 2005.[21] He described the march and rally in downtown Buenos Aires as a "battle against the privatized companies and their dictatorship of the market." Later, he went further and asserted that the threat of a coup had already been realized and transnational corporations had taken over the country's oil market. On behalf of the FTV movement, he declared, "We are going to mobilize against the privatized companies that represent the dictatorship of the market." Expanding Kirchner's more subtle military metaphors, D'Elía implied that while the national military shattered Argentine democracy during the twentieth century, foreign companies destroyed democracy at the turn of the twenty-first. The middle-class voted with their pocketbooks, while the piqueteros were the heroic foot soldiers of democracy.

FUNDA, the piquetero movement to which the Sunshine Community Center belonged, was among several that supported the boycott by occupying Shell gas stations and joining marches and rallies. Javier Ruiz-Soto, the FUNDA regional coordinator, told me that the movement's leadership immediately decided that they would "do a demonstration [*medida de fuerza*] in support of the government and in repudiation of Shell's actions" in which "each [municipal] district took over its service station." Antonio López, another FUNDA leader in the municipality of Avellaneda, recounted that at these station occupations "we did not let a single car enter for more or less one hour." A few weeks later, FUNDA members of all ages were picked up by the rickety old buses the movement had hired to take them from the poor neighborhoods and shanty settlements of metropolitan Buenos Aires to join the march and rally for "energetic sovereignty and against the increase in prices" in Buenos Aires's symbolic center.[22] After marching through downtown to the Congressional Palace, FUNDA members listened to speeches for an hour or more before heading back home to the poor neighborhoods and shanty settlements that ring the capital.

Unlike their wealthier compatriots who were encouraged to choose among differently branded commodities, the piqueteros were encouraged to participate in the boycott in order to defend their right to consume commodities at all. Though the vast majority of FUNDA members were not gasoline consumers, none was outside of petroleum's circuits. They relied on petroleum products of all kinds—from the propane canisters they used as cooking fuel in shanty homes and communal kitchens, to the diesel trucks that delivered groceries to community centers, to the plastics of their clothes and shoes, to the asphalt under their feet at the demonstration. While we waited for a truck of groceries to arrive at the "reclaimed" building that served as FUNDA's informal base in Avellaneda, Antonio explained why FUNDA participated in the boycott, using the example of the foodstuffs we would unload when the truck arrived:

> Imagine this: you collect a [state welfare] plan of 150 pesos [a month], which is not sufficient in the slightest. If oil increases, transportation goes up for you. And obviously, the price of rice, flour is going to rise. They are going to continue collecting 150, and nevertheless, all the basic products in the basket of minimal goods for a family [*canasta familiar*] are much more expensive . . . You know that if Shell raises its prices, everyone else automatically raises their prices, not in the people's favor . . . Well then, when the president said that one should not buy, we went as a social movement to defend the only thing that those who do not have anything have, because the companies don't care, historically they did not care, and I don't believe they will ever care.

Antonio portrayed the boycott as a collective self-defense move by impoverished people with limited possibilities for supporting their families in post-privatization Argentina. Furthermore, he described the boycott as a reaction to Shell's disregard for the consequences of its action to the Argentine people. The actors who participated in the boycott were once again portrayed as a collective subject bound, at least partially, by the nation-state. FUNDA leaders like Javier and Antonio were not advertising experts who guided impoverished Argentines in remaking their individuated "selves" through market choices, but people who organized their fellow citizens (and some resident aliens) to ensure that at least minimal petroleum consumption remained an entitlement of citizenship.

FUNDA called on its members to make the petroleum market democratic, and petroleum consumption inclusive of all Argentines, through speech acts that condemned the transnational corporations and supported the Kirchner administration. Although they understood the boycott as acting for, not acting through, commodity consumption, they deployed a discourse of democracy versus dictatorship similar to that of the Kirchner administration, consumer advocates, middle-class boycott participants, and other piqueteros. In line with D'Elía's portrait of a "market coup," FUNDA members called the protests outside Shell's headquarters *escratches*, the term coined to describe the popular trials held in the street to adjudicate and sentence participants in the military dictatorship who had been legally pardoned by the state. At the escratches against Shell, protesters chanted "Shell, garbage, you are the dictatorship!" (*Shell, basura, vos sos la dictadora!*) and wrote *golpistas* ("overthrowers" or "usurpers") on the front of the company's building. They further compared Shell to the quintessential illegitimate state and market actors when they scrawled "pirates" on the pavement of its service stations.[23] Like wealthier Argentines, the pique- teros suggested that giant transnational oil companies were not rightful market regulators; however, piqueteros did not imagine themselves taking on this role in the way that middle-class Argentines did.

I now shift attention back to FUNDA's Sunshine Community Center to more closely analyze the cultural meanings of petroleum consumption in Argentina and the ambiguous manner in which the national community of consumption was extended to poor Argentines in a way that increased their participation in inequitable global capitalist circuits that they could not con- trol. Chapter 4 describes the development of the Sunshine Center in the context of neoliberal structural adjustment. Here, I focus on the center's involvement with state welfare programs and the experience of one woman, Carmen Santos, who was trying to use such programs to incorporate herself, her family, and her neighbors into the middle class through petroleum consumption.

Fueling the Sunshine Communal Kitchen

The Sunshine Community Center was simultaneously a site where FUNDA members practiced communal self-provisioning and where they helped or- ganize a larger group of unemployed, underemployed, and other impover- ished people to claim rights from state and corporate entities. Though several FUNDA leaders had been members of the Peronist movement, they were criti- cal of the personalized network through which food, medicine, housewares, and odd jobs were exchanged for support for politicians whose policies and programs contributed to people's impoverishment. According to FUNDA's official history, the organization emerged as a national piquetero movement during the nationwide protests that erupted at the end of 2001 in response to years of the downward economic spiral caused by neoliberalismo. However, the movement's roots reach back to efforts during the Menem years to address the immediate needs of impoverished Argentines while simultaneously organizing them for political action and linking them to the unions that refused to cooper- ate with the Menem administration's privatizations and concomitant weaken- ing of labor laws.[24]

Following the uprising that toppled Menem's successor de la Rúa, the Peron- ist leader Eduardo Duhalde held the presidency for a year and a half before Kirchner took office. The Duhalde administration offered the piquetero movements a limited number of slots in welfare programs (*planes sociales*) to distribute to their members in exchange for an end to the organization of demonstrations by the movements. FUNDA was among those that accepted this deal, and it reduced its direct actions against state and provincial authorities. While FUNDA continued to demand that everyone was entitled to a minimum of support, the Sunshine Center became a site where about a dozen women, and a few men, lucky enough to win placements in the program exchanged "volunteer" labor for 150 pesos a month or bags of food.

After advocating voting with blank ballots in the initial presidential election in 2001, FUNDA joined several other piquetero movements and unions in backing Kirchner in the runoff election. The piquetero movements that did this became Kirchner administration allies, and their members became known as "soft" piqueteros who denounced violence and favored dialogue and incremental change. Some FUNDA members even repudiated the label *piquetero* for the more docile term *social movement* that Antonio López used in his explanation of FUNDA's participation in the boycott quoted above. Although both state representatives and FUNDA leaders carefully avoided practices that resembled the "patron-client" exchanges in which other Peronist politicians engaged, the continuation of state assistance was at least partially predicated on FUNDA's ongoing demonstration of support through participation in events like the boycott. The boycott, therefore, represented a reversal of FUNDA's earlier agreement with the state. Now the movement was encouraged to participate in demonstrations, rather than refrain from them, in order to continue to garner welfare plans for its members.

The Kirchner administration began rewarding FUNDA for its support with increased access to assistance programs long before it took part in the national boycott of Shell and Exxon. Nevertheless, through a circuitous turn of events around the time of the boycott, the national Ministry of Social Development offered FUNDA the chance to make the Sunshine Center's community kitchen a site for a food-support program called the Fondo Participativo de Inversión Social (Participatory Fund for Social Investment, hereafter FOPAR).[25] FOPAR usually supplied groceries, cooking implements, and other materials for "volunteers" to prepare hot meals at large and well-established soup kitchens for children (*comedores infantiles*), which Sunshine decidedly was not.

Though FOPAR would enable the Sunshine members to better serve children in desperate need of nutritious food, the participants in the communal kitchen did not view the program as an unambiguous good. One afternoon, conversation around the cooking fire turned into debate over whether Sunshine should accept the Ministry of Social Development's offer. As we took turns stirring the stew and drinking mate, the women discussed the advantages and disadvantages of FOPAR and how it would change their cooking routines. On the one hand, Carmen Santos argued that FOPAR provided significant quantities of provisions, such as beef for preparing *milanesas* (breaded beef cutlets), that would allow them to better address the rampant malnutrition in Goldendas. On the other hand, others stressed how difficult it would be to participate in the FOPAR program because the ministry had strict rules, required a great deal of volunteer labor, and encouraged state and community surveillance of the community center. To fulfill the "transparency" requirements, for instance, they would have to submit the name and identification numbers of each child who ate at the communal kitchen, keep track of how frequently they came, and document that no food was fed to anyone else. All meals would need to be eaten in the Sunshine Center shack, so they would have to end the common practice of taking a *tuper* (plastic container) to someone who was sick, stayed late at school, or felt embarrassed to eat at the communal kitchen.

Among the many considerations about FOPAR, the switch from cooking outdoors on a wood-burning fire to cooking indoors on a propane gas stove was a particular topic of debate. The group divided between women who disdained cooking on the wood fire and women who saw advantages to it. A relative newcomer to the communal kitchen, Adela Molinari, complained that the smoke from the scrap wood fires made her cough. The more experienced fire cooks told her that she would get used to the smoke and the cough would soon go away. Gas was dangerous and would have to be monitored carefully for leaks that could cause deadly fires, someone else added. However, using gas would allow them to cook indoors, thus enabling them to open the kitchen in bad weather. But, longtime Sunshine Center participant Ramona Costanera pointed out, it would take more time to boil water on the stove than on the hotter open fire. She argued that if they switched to cooking on the gas stove, they would have to start cooking earlier in the day, taking more time away from their household chores, childcare, and other work. Maybe it would be better to continue boiling water outside even when they had a gas stove, Ramona suggested as a compromise. Other women nodded their heads in agreement. Carmen, however, stepped in as a vocal supporter of gas cooking.

Carmen did not dispute the disadvantages of gas cooking but countered her friends' arguments on other grounds. She said that she was embarrassed to go places after cooking at the Sunshine Center's fire pit because the person sitting next to her on the bus knew what she had been doing. The smoke stays in your clothes and especially your hair, she said as she swung her long ponytail in front of her nose and sniffed disapprovingly. The smoke smell made it obvious that she came from a shanty neighborhood, marking her as poorer than her fellow passengers, not to mention members of the family for whom she worked as a part-time maid. While cooking over a wood fire was a sign of poverty, using a gas stove helped her pass as a middle-class woman, at least while outside Goldendas.

Whether influenced by this discussion or not, the Sunshine coordinators decided to accept the FOPAR program at the communal kitchen. A few weeks later, we began cooking dinner each day for at least one hundred neighborhood children on a propane-powered stove in the Sunshine Center (see Figure 8). While everyone seemed pleased by the change, their prior debate over the

Figure 8. Two women pause while frying *milanesas* (breaded beef cutlets) in the Sunshine Community Center after the center began receiving support from a government program that allowed them to cook indoors on a gas stove rather than outdoors over an open fire. The propane canister can be seen to the right side of the stove.

FOPAR program illustrates the constraining terms by which FUNDA members were included in consumer citizenship. Their ability to use hydrocarbon fuel in the Sunshine Center was closely tied to their involvement in national politics, especially their support for the Kirchner administration. Accepting FOPAR limited their political actions, yet it only marginally incorporated them into the petroleum-consuming polity. Cooking with gas at a community center did not make piqueteros into consumer citizens who could choose among branded fuels in order to assert a political position, as wealthier Argentines could. The tension between Goldend as residents' desire for consumer citizenship and the reality of class-based subjectification is even more evident in the Sunshine Center's bakery cooperative.

Cultivating Propane Citizenship

Among the women and men I knew in Goldendas, Carmen Santos had the greatest aspiration toward becoming a middle-class housewife. She was born into a family precariously positioned on the fringe of the lower middle class in the northern province of Salta, but she had fallen into poverty as a child when her mother left home. When I asked her why she had moved to Buenos Aires after she married and her first son was born, she explained: "My family does have good job opportunities and such, but many times one wants to better oneself, progress in one's own life by oneself. And in order to progress in life, I believe, one has to hit oneself harder so that one can learn more, right? And so I decided to come here to move forward, move forward by myself and for myself." She expressed a belief common among migrants who have pursued upward mobility by moving to urban centers: personal initiative, dedication, and labor lead to individual progress. This belief was encouraged by the neoliberal discourse about self-responsibility and entrepreneurship that was explicitly used in relation to the emprendimiento owners discussed in Part I and more subtly communicated to other Argentines. Her emphasis on herself as an individual contrasted with the communal language that Sara Santos and other FUNDA leaders used to discuss "moving forward" as a nation.

Carmen did not intend to live in a shanty neighborhood when she and her husband, Dom, arrived in Buenos Aires in 1992. Dom had trained as a nurse in Salta, but after spending a week unsuccessfully seeking employment in the city, they moved to Goldendas where his great aunt, Luz Elena, was already living. Dom's brother Teo and his wife Sara later joined them, and both women were key figures in founding the Sunshine Community Center (see Chapter 4). Unlike many who moved to the shanty neighborhoods in and around Buenos

Aires, Carmen did not abandon her hope of regaining a place in the community of consumer citizens. She was the only one I knew there who dreamed of buying a house with land title in the Buenos Aires region rather than of returning to the rural province where she grew up.

When I met Carmen and Dom in 2005, their household stood out as one of the best-off in Goldendas. They lived with their sixteen-year-old son, twelve-year-old daughter, and two well-groomed dogs of recognizable breed, unlike the rest of the shanty mutts. Dom's eleven years of steady and legal work in a local factory had facilitated greater comforts than most Goldendas residents could afford, but not a home on the legal side of Dock Sud. Like its neighbors, their house was constructed out of a patchwork of scrap wood, cinder blocks, and metal sheeting and connected to the main alley through a chicken wire gate and narrow dirt footpath. Yet the house had a concrete floor, a refrigerator, a gas stove and oven, and a telephone. The outhouse they shared with Dom's aunt Luz Elena was covered in white tiles and had a sink and shower with running water. Although the house was in a shanty settlement, it contained some of the trappings of middle-class domesticity, which enabled Carmen to emulate the ideal of the middle-class housewife she so desired to be.

Carmen was an outgoing woman with seemingly boundless energy who balanced a part-time job as a maid in the capital, her work caring for her own children and house, and her responsibilities as the coordinator of the bakery cooperative that was housed at the Sunshine Center as part of another Ministry of Social Development program. Unlike Sara, Carmen preferred laboring in the center to attending FUNDA's political meetings, although she participated in piquetero demonstrations when called on to do so. On most days, she began making dough at Sunshine at four or five in the morning, and when I arrived an hour or two later, her hair bun was coming undone and her clothes were lightly dusted in flour, as she led the other bakers in rolling, cutting, shaping, and baking rolls. She simultaneously oversaw the baking, sold bread to Goldendas residents, and weighed and guarded the loaves for FUNDA's communal kitchens in the area. She also kept records of these transactions, including providing bread on credit to be repaid with the buyer's next state assistance payment. When she took a break from this work, Carmen often gave advice to whoever was at Sunshine about how best to use gas, like her trick of baking bread at home in a double pot on the stove with a preheated lid and some water at the bottom to keep it from burning, rather than using a gas-hungry oven.

Carmen deployed the skills she had learned using a propane canister to cook at home to keep the bakery cooperative fueled with the government's insufficient funding of the program. First, she closely monitored the flow of gas, keeping the temperature as low as baking would allow and turning the oven off while the last batch of rolls was still inside. Second, she routinely checked for gas leaks in the jerry-rigged series of black rubber hoses, thin metal pipes, and rusty valves that stretched across the back wall of the shack. Leaks were quite common, and the problem was exacerbated by Carmen's strategy of gently rocking the canisters back and forth to get out the last bit of gas. Third, she consulted with Pato and a few other men about when and how to replace these hoses and pipes—at Sunshine, baking was women's work, but center maintenance was a male activity. It often took several days for them to decide what repair was needed, gather the money for a new part, find the least expensive place to buy it, borrow the necessary tools, and make the repair. Despite these dedicated efforts, the propane was extremely difficult to control because one could not tell what was inside each inscrutable metal canister or when the invisible gas was seeping out.

Carmen usually bought propane from one of the local stores that offered black market canisters for somewhat less than what the Shell, YPF-Repsol, and other brand names sold for in legally recognized stores. But, she complained, these canisters were half full of water and therefore did not last as long as the brand name ones. The least expensive source for quality canisters was the big supermarket chains, but they charged too much for delivery, if they would agree to send their truck to the edge of the shanty settlement at all. The best way for the bakery cooperative to buy propane canisters was by using some of the propane FOPAR intended for cooking at the Sunshine Center's soup kitchen. With this strategy, it did not matter how much the canister cost as long as it came with an official receipt with a tax identification number printed at the top. However, the Sunshine Center could submit only two receipts for canisters a month, and the money from the ministry had to be used first to fuel the stove where they prepared the children's food. By cooking meals that demanded less gas, such as fried foods instead of baked ones, the Sunshine leaders could stretch the gas and submit a receipt for the bakery every once in a while. This strategy required sophisticated calculations, both to make sure the stove would not run out of gas at the expense of the bread oven and to know in advance to buy a canister from a store that gave official receipts rather than from the cheaper black market dealers. Needless to say, this did not always work out as projected despite Carmen and Sara's careful efforts.

Adela Molinari, one of the bakery's regular participants, impressed upon me Carmen's crucial role in managing the bakery. When Carmen went to visit her family in Salta for Christmas, Adela said with a self-effacing laugh, the bakery stayed open for only a day or two. The other women readily admitted that they did not have her combination of culinary expertise, financial accounting skills, and team management capability. Carmen clarified why the bakery shut down without her in somewhat different terms:

> It didn't work because nothing lasts when we don't have income in this bakery. We make money to buy [supplies], but sometimes I have to buy more flour, shortening, yeast, and gas. Therefore, I turn over the work I have outside of this; I invest it here. Let's say we lack 100 pesos for gas, I put in 30, 40, or 50 pesos. But this is my own money; it's not my husband's or anything. I used to have problems with my husband because I took from his money. However, having my own work is how I am saving a little extra money of my own, which it doesn't matter if I win or lose because it's mine. I put it here, and well, this is how [the bakery] works.

Running the bakery not only required Carmen's varied set of skills, but also a constant input of short-lived supplies, especially the expensive propane canisters. Her statement, "I turn over the work I have," with the omission of words such as "my earnings from," indicates how she saw her paid domestic labor as a maid in someone else's house as directly enabling her leadership of the bakery. Rather than being a step toward affording a legal residence and becoming a middle-class housewife who labors in her own home, the bakery drained away the money Carmen earned as a replacement housewife in a wealthier woman's home. While she understood her contribution as an "investment," that is, current capital that would reap future returns, I observed Carmen pour more and more of her earnings into merely keeping the bakery from closing. She had the skills and dedication to make herself into a consumer citizen, yet they were not sufficient to enable her to join the middle class because her self-improvement plan also depended on the hydrocarbon fuel market. Her continual use of her personal money to purchase gasoline canisters and other supplies for the communal bakery kept her entrenched in the shanty settlement, thus leaving her dream of reentering the middle class unfulfilled.

Carmen's purchasing practices more closely resembled the kind of frugal, calculating, and assertive consumer citizenship that Perón advocated for housewives during the economic downturn of the early 1950s than the commodity choice that the consumer advocacy organizations of the 2000s suggested to middle-class car owners. For instance, contemplating a choice between YPF-Repsol's white canisters and Shell's yellow ones was usually beyond Carmen's means. Instead, her citizen responsibility took the form of a labor discipline in which she rose extremely early in the morning to follow a self-imposed schedule of unpaid work in the cooperative bakery, followed by housework in her own home, interrupted to pursue similar labors in the capital several afternoons a week. Yet Carmen was a consumer citizen in the sense that she pursued her goals of financial self-sufficiency and legal homeownership by promoting and practicing petroleum consumption. Her reasons for advocating Sunshine's acceptance of FOPAR, her techniques for maximizing the available propane, and her dedication to buying hydrocarbon fuel despite exceedingly limited funds illustrate how important petroleum consumption was to her self-improvement project and her sense of self. These acts also reveal how consumer citizenship is both gendered and classed. Despite the significant changes between the Peronist administrations of the 1950s and the 2000s, both their representatives have hailed petroleum consumption as a symbol of the ideal female middle-class citizenship.

Carmen interwove entrepreneurial feats and ideas of individual responsibility with collective action and ideas of communal progress. Though she used the pronoun "I" more than other FUNDA leaders, who preferred "we," she did not operate a bakery with a wood oven in front of her house, like some shanty residents did. She managed a cooperative that was part of a social movement that explicitly engaged national and municipal politics. She combined her bakery labors with participation in other FUNDA projects and thus demanded her *and* her neighbors' inclusion in the national polity and right to consume petroleum. Yet her market-based techniques failed to achieve the consumer citizenship she sought and instead contributed to her class-based subjectification.

Conclusion

Studies of neoliberalism have insightfully analyzed the unstated ideas that organize and govern market interactions, yet they have tended not to consider their quotidian effects. Examining together the boycott of Shell and Exxon gas stations and the production of food at the Sunshine Community Center enables me to connect the discursive and labor practices of neoliberalismo on the ground in metropolitan Buenos Aires. Their connection reveals how fuels produced by private companies working through globalized processes were deployed to regenerate a national polity, to define legitimate market regulators, and to enhance social inclusion in postprivatization Argentina. The participants in the boycott and in the community center differently articulated Peronist and liberal moral economies in attempts to transform the consumption of petroleum into a democratic action. Representatives of consumer advocacy organizations equated purchasing gasoline with voting, while leaders of piquetero movements argued that more direct action was needed to save Argentina from the oil companies' threat of an economic coup d'état. For middle-class Argentines, participating in the construction of a democratic polity meant choosing among oil companies that had been invested with vastly different significances but that made materially indistinguishable products through a concentrated, cooperative, and privatized global industry. For poor Argentines, contributing to building a democratic polity meant supporting the Kirchner administration and gaining access to hydrocarbon fuels and other supplies through government programs that allowed their children to eat a daily hot meal. Contrary to what the scholarship on consumer citizenship would suggest, Carmen Santos and her fellow Goldendas residents demanded entitlement to petroleum consumption not as autonomous individuals, but as classed subjects of the nation-state.

Argentines' assertion of entitlement to petroleum consumption in national terms indicates that contests among moral economies are closely linked to struggles over citizenship and the state as much as they are tied to shifts in the dominant economic regime. This framing blurs the conceptual divide between citizenship as based on law and nationalism as based on emotion. It instead encourages investigation of how state recognition, national belonging, and consumer citizenship are constructed together through cultural processes of exclusion and inclusion. On the one hand, the community center and the boycott underscore the decisive role of state agents in shaping the goals, economic activities, and ideals of a range of citizens. On the other hand, the Kirchner administration's successes and failures can be attributed to its use of governing techniques that worked on and through transnational oil companies and national social movements. Though FUNDA members described their involvement in the consumer boycott and welfare programs in terms of defending their inclusion in the national community of consumers against those who threatened to push them farther outside of the commodity-nation, these political projects subtly adopted a neoliberal stance toward citizenship and consumption. The boycott, in particular, narrowly defined "democratic participation" as the ability to purchase equivalent fuels produced by a handful of privately owned giant transnational companies. Chapter 4 continues this discussion by placing the Sunshine Community Center within the context of the transformation of the oil industry and examines the kind of citizenship that Shell attempted to inculcate in Dock Sud.

4 Creating Bonds

A LETTER FROM SHELL ARRIVED, quite unexpectedly, at the Sunshine Community Center in Goldendas in March 2005. I had started volunteering there shortly after the beginning of the national boycott of Shell and Exxon stations and helped each day to prepare a hot meal for the one hundred or so children who ate at the center (see Figure 9). It was a chilly morning and the wind from the Río de la Plata blew through the cracks in the center walls and hurt my fingers, already sore from my unskilled efforts at peeling carrots with a bent table knife. That morning as we were cutting vegetables, one of the longtime members casually mentioned that Sara Santos, the center's head coordinator introduced in Chapter 3, had received this strange letter from Shell. I put down my knife, got out my notebook, and asked for more details. I soon learned that someone at Shell had invited the Sunshine Center to submit a proposal for the company's new community development program. This program aimed to establish "corporate-community partnerships" between the oil company and organizations working to improve life in the region adjacent to the Polo Petroquímico Dock Sud, which housed Shell's only South American refineries. The women told me that they were thinking of asking for funding for a nutrition program for the Sunshine Center. That sounded quite appropriate to me, given my experience in the neighborhood thus far.

At the beginning of my fieldwork in Goldendas, I was uncomfortably aware that I towered over women and men there even though I am not tall by North American standards. Malnutrition was responsible for their stature. Ironically, many Goldendas residents told me that they had come to Dock Sud to create a better future for their children than the life of poverty and ill health they knew

Figure 9. Goldendas children with cups of warm milk and pieces of bread from the communal kitchen at the Sunshine Community Center.

in the north of Argentina. Yet these children were suffering many of the same problems in the capital as their parents had experienced growing up in rural areas, including insufficient nourishment to grow to full stature. Children ate at the Sunshine Center because there was not enough food at home, and what food the family had was given first to the breadwinners in the household. The communal kitchen leaders hoped that Shell could help them better access government programs for undernourished children and thus improve the health of the area's many young residents.

We went back to cutting vegetables and chatting about other matters, but I knew that I would closely follow the trail of this letter. It could reveal a great deal about the relationship between oil companies and their neighbors that was developing in the privatized industry. How did Shell envision its relationship to Argentina? And how did Argentines relate to Shell now that the company was no longer a supplier for YPF Estatal but a major player in a globalized yet also increasingly concentrated oil industry? Shell was not the only company producing hydrocarbon fuels or petrochemicals in Dock Sud, but it was the largest and best-known entity and took a leading role in most complex-wide, and many nationwide and industry-wide, initiatives. Shell's actions thus set a precedent for other companies in the oil sector and beyond. The Shell and Exxon boycott had demonstrated the contested place of foreign oil companies in contemporary Argentina but also had reinforced the idea that Shell was more than just a corporation operating in the country. It stood for the global industry, the private market, the oil giants. A boycott was an infrequent event, while the relationship between the petrochemical complex and the Dock Sud neighborhood was ongoing. Shell's community relations effort in Dock Sud thus offered an avenue for exploring how private oil companies were forging a place for themselves in Argentina, particularly defining their rights and responsibilities in relation to their neighbors, through sometimes friendly and sometimes violent interactions with them.

Shell's new community relations program in Argentina, called Creating Bonds, was framed in terms of "corporate-community partnerships" that were supposed to be based on equality and friendship between the partners. But what did these partnerships really look like on the ground? What kind of relationship between the oil company and the Dock Sud neighborhood did the new program create? What does it reveal about the meanings of "the corporation" and "the community"? In addition, what can Creating Bonds demonstrate about transnational oil companies' strategies for managing people, health care, and the production of both energy and toxins? In order to answer these questions, I examine the changes in Shell's public relations endeavors in Argentina within the context of the history of Dock Sud and the transnational business movement known as corporate social responsibility (CSR). I argue, in short, that the shift to CSR, and the associated development of the Creating Bonds program in Dock Sud, was effective in creating a new position for Shell in Argentina because it remade the company's public face into a feminine one.

The Critical Study of Corporate Action

CSR is a movement that developed within the business world to turn corporations into "good citizens" and their profit-seeking activities into "compassionate capitalism." Scholars have rightly critiqued CSR for being ineffective in making substantial changes in the business practices of the companies that endorse it. Michael Watts (2005) has pushed further to argue that CSR has provided the mechanisms for corporations, and oil companies in particular, to claim social permission to continue to work in a socially exploitative and environmentally destructive fashion. In addition, the CSR movement's approach of voluntary codes, self-monitoring, and self-reporting—without outside verification or enforcement—has hindered efforts to regulate corporate practice through state or international law. Watts's study of Shell's actions in Nigeria shows that "global companies conduct business in conjunction with failed states, creating conditions in which egregious human rights violations can occur and have occurred" (401; see also Zalik 2004b). I concur that Shell's CSR program has helped create a "license to operate" in Argentina as elsewhere. Yet, in evaluating CSR programs, scholars have focused on the programs' failures to achieve what they promised and have given insufficient attention to the very real effects that particular corporate vocabulary and images *do* have. I highlight in this chapter how gender is a crucial but unrecognized aspect of CSR discourse and practice that plays a pivotal role in shaping Shell's influence in Dock Sud.

Whereas critical studies of CSR expose how corporations avoid legal regulation, anthropological analyses of the law illustrate how corporations' legal standing in the Global North has been used to construct and maintain unequal power relations around the world. Rosemary Coombe (1998) has described how intellectual property law enables corporations to circumscribe processes of cultural representation and subject formation through their ownership of commodity signs. For instance, corporate lawyers have effectively claimed that because a trademark indexes "the aura of the corporate persona," only its authorized representatives can deploy it (61). While intellectual property authorizes corporate ownership of meaning that corporate actors did not solely generate, limited liability releases them from responsibility for their actions by constructing corporations as agents distinct from the people who own and manage them. Suzana Sawyer (2006) has shown how this enabled Chevron-Texaco to deny responsibility for environmental and health damages from its subsidiaries' operations in Ecuador. Yet she also highlighted how the plaintiffs' descriptions of the company as a person rendered technical arguments comprehensible in a way that helped them hold Chevron-Texaco responsible for their ill health. I join Sawyer in emphasizing that legal discourse works in multiple ways that are unanticipated from the text of the law, yet I shift focus away from formal juridical sites toward overlooked sites, such as shanty settlements, where corporate power is also constructed, deployed, and transformed through the everyday practices of framing liability, shifting responsibility, and "empowering" community leaders.

A robust understanding of corporate power requires careful attention to corporate uses of affect in conjunction with the law. I build on recent anthropological work on advertising that illustrates how corporations generate profits through the production of affective images, discourses, and qualities for commodities. For instance, William Mazzarella (2003) has shown how advertising firms transform the legal concept of a trademark into the more valuable notion of a brand, and Robert J. Foster (2008) illustrated how the success of the Coca-Cola Company owes more to the company's management of an affectively charged brand than to its production of caffeine-charged sweetened water. He showed how both the creative labors of Coke drinkers and the company's "corporate citizenship" projects contribute to good feelings about Coke products, and thus translate into corporate profits. I advance the work of showing how corporations generate profits through the production of affect by highlighting the gender dynamics of this process.[1]

In order to analyze the very real effects of Shell's CSR program in Argentina, I extend the concept of *faciality* (Benson 2008a) because it can highlight how altering the public portrayal of a company can expand its political and economic power.[2] I use "facialize" to refer to the production of faces as reified sites of social difference and grounds for making ethical judgments on the basis of this difference. Faciality explains how the perception of particular human faces can reinforce the inequities of large-scale power dynamics, but I study this process from the opposite angle than Peter Benson did. Whereas he showed how the perception of farmworkers' faces legitimizes their subordination, I examine how the perception of corporate representatives' faces buttresses their and their company's dominion. I also emphasize how the process of facializing is deeply imbued with gender.

Shell's CSR Program

The transnational Royal Dutch Shell Group reconfigured its philanthropic work into a CSR program as part of its effort to repair its public image after the disastrous Brent Spar and Ogoniland incidents in 1995 (Watts 2005).[3] This project was introduced in Argentina only after the political-economic collapse of 2001, which, as Chapter 3 recounts, left many Argentines suspicious of foreign companies. Shell's CSR "makeover" was formulated distinctly for two different audiences: middle-class consumers, investors, and employees in Argentina, Europe, and North America; and Dock Sud residents. Its aims and effects, likewise, were distinct for these two audiences.

For the first audience, publications such as the landmark CSR report "Profits and Principles—Does There Have to Be a Choice?" represented Shell as caring about human welfare and the natural environment without disclosing quantitative information about its social spending or environmental contamination record (Livesey and Kearins 2002: 236). Its scrapbook design with handwriting-esque fonts, rough-edged textboxes, and colorful snapshots represented the company as "striving to live up to our responsibilities" following criticism that it had failed "to defend human rights, to protect the environment, to be good corporate citizens"(Knight 1998). The smiling faces of the recipients of Shell funding in the Creating Bonds year-end reports similarly portray the goodwill of the company for investors, consumers, and employees situated far from its Dock Sud refineries. The sympathetic images of dark-skinned women and children in CSR reports supplement the stiff portraits of mostly white male executives and action shots of workers found in the company's financial reports. CSR thus facialized Shell in a new way by deploying particular human visages with socially coded features to portray the company as an upstanding citizen and caring neighbor, thereby enabling it to continue to do what many of its investors, consumers, and employees would probably regard as unethical (if not also illegal) business practices if they visited places like the Niger Delta or Dock Sud.

The rest of this chapter explores how individual employees facialized Shell for the second audience, composed of the impoverished people who live alongside the petrochemical complex in Dock Sud. A Shell executive in Argentina told me: "We do not do exploration, production, or research [in South America]; instead, our largest business is refining. Because of this, we call the refinery in Dock Sud the heart of our business." Many people in Dock Sud complained that this "heart" was hardened to area residents, and the Shell-Exxon boycott revealed widespread discontent with the company. The growing disparities between the profitable oil enclave, on the one hand, and the settlements housing unemployed and marginally employed people, on the other hand, were closely tied to Argentina's experiments with neoliberal state and economic restructuring described in the previous chapters (see also Svampa 2005; Auyero and Swistun 2009). Shell dealt with this situation by establishing "partnerships" with community groups in Dock Sud. But who were Shell's partners? Before examining the process of creating collaborations between an oil company and its neighbors, I chart the construction of the Goldendas settlement and the Sunshine Center, crucial foci in "the community" with which Shell aimed to establish its partnerships. Their history shows another side of neoliberalism that complements the one seen from the Patagonian oil towns.

Living like a Turtle

Dock Sud long had been an industrial zone, transportation hub, and vibrant residential neighborhood when it was transformed by neoliberalismo. The shanty settlement of Goldendas, where the Sunshine Center sits, was created during the early years of Menem's rule. At that time, industrial and agricultural production in the provinces was declining and state welfare supports were being eliminated, but the situation in the Buenos Aires region still looked promising to many. Poor people from across Argentina and neighboring countries who were seeking a place to live near the national capital transformed a swamp with disputed ownership into a housing block.

Luz Elena Santos, a longtime Goldendas resident, told me that when she moved to this part of Dock Sud in 1993, people were not living in what today is a neighborhood of more than one hundred homes. "Here has been filled in . . . all of this is landfill," she said, slowly sweeping her arthritic hand in a small circle to indicate the area surrounding her house. Because no one in Goldendas owns title to the land, she told me with a chuckle, "the land is not mine; nothing is mine except for the house." She concluded that she lived "like a turtle." She watched Goldendas rapidly fill with precarious houses as employment opportunities evaporated and consumer prices skyrocketed. The newcomers from the north of Argentina included her nephew Teo Santos and his wife Sara, who later became the coordinator of the Sunshine Community Center.

The people who established shanty homesteads in the area around the Dock Sud Petrochemical Complex in the 1990s were not the first illegal occupants there. Shell, in fact, took over a piece of land on the eastern side of the Dock Sud Canal in 1913 without state approval (Pikulski, Orquiguil, and Larrain 1991: 24–25) and has operated in that location with varying degrees of noncompliance with the law ever since. The company began its Argentine business by importing fuels from Mexico, unloading them at the Dock Sud port, and selling them to the meatpacking plants in Dock Sud; it then added domestic and industrial clients in the provinces (Solberg 1979: 6–7). This business grew significantly after World War I disrupted ship traffic across the Atlantic. With the founding of YPF in 1922 and the subsequent movement toward state control of the oil industry, Shell continued its refining and retail sales business through contracts with the state-owned company. It built a refinery on the neck of land between the Dock Sud Canal and the Río de la Plata, began producing fuels there in 1931, and expanded its capacity several times since then (see Map, Inset A). While industrial production declined nationally during the

1980s and 1990s, the petrochemical industry grew. In this period, a small number of large Argentine and transnational producers replaced the state-owned enterprise and its numerous small contractors (López 1994). By 2005, Shell was the largest occupant of the petrochemical complex and an important funder of NGOs and public institutions in the Avellaneda municipality. However, the company, which had once supplied jobs for many area residents, no longer was a major employer. Just as YPF SA and then YPF-Repsol had replaced workers with computer-driven machinery in Northwest Patagonia, Shell had mechanized its operations in Dock Sud.

Despite the few available jobs in the petrochemical complex, numerous Dock Sud residents waited outside the gates each morning to see whether any of the local temporary labor agencies that Shell subcontracted were hiring that day. Consistent work was rare, but every few months Shell or one of the other companies in the petrochemical complex would shut down a section of the plant and hire large numbers of temporary workers to conduct a thorough scrubbing of the installation. Juana Rossi, a woman in her forties who had lived her whole life in Dock Sud, recounted how at these times, "they hire laborers to work nonstop—mornings, afternoons, and all night. You can earn in a few days what you normally earn in a month." Bleary eyed and covered in thick black soot, her husband once brought home food and other "gifts" from Shell in addition to his pay, but in recent years he was given only cash. Shell's investments in Argentina had not translated into significant employment, but company coffers benefited from Argentina's high unemployment rate and the state's weakening of labor laws and feeble regulatory enforcement.

At the same time that the Menem administration enacted neoliberal structural adjustments, it dismantled many of the achievements of Argentina's large labor movement, despite the Peronist Party's history as the champion of industrial workers (see Chapter 3). In the place of the labor unions, the Peronist Party established neighborhood centers to mediate between leaders and their popular base. These centers were run by *punteros*, informal agents of the Peronist Party, and *manzaneras*, neighborhood block captains who worked for the punteros. As state services passed from labor right to personalized assistance (Auyero 2000), punteros and manzaneras provided food, medical care, construction materials, and other items in exchange for the party loyalty of Argentines in places like Goldendas.[4] However, this personalized welfare system could not deal with the massive rise in unemployment, skyrocketing consumer prices, and rapid economic decline that followed the privatization of state enterprises and the other neoliberal "reforms." As we have seen, this situation gave rise to the piqueteros, participants in national social movements composed of neighborhood-based groups of impoverished people, frequently led by wealthier and more educated allies, who used street protest to demand citizens' economic and political rights, particularly their entitlement to dignified employment. The piqueteros trace their emergence back to La Pueblada (see Chapter 2), even though there were other important precursors (Svampa and Pereyra 2003). Their political tactics—blockades of roads and bridges, occupations of government buildings, supermarket raids, mass political meetings (*asambleas populares*), tent camps, and communal soup kitchens (*comedores comunitarios* or *comedores populares*)—were subsequently deployed across the country as the political-economic collapse accelerated and half the national population fell below the official poverty line.

During this tumultuous period, Sara Santos, Luz Elena's niece by marriage, joined a group of Dock Sud residents and university student allies who established a communal soup kitchen in a Dock Sud plaza and then began serving cups of warm milk on the Santos's patio in Goldendas as well. Although their appeals for material support from municipal authorities and the Peronist Party were rebuffed, they received donations from local businesses, which supplemented the food they and their university allies contributed. As Mercedes Medina, an early participant in the communal kitchen, recounted, "One place gave us meat; from another came vegetables; after that we [women] made things to sell and bought pasta, or whatever, so we could feed a hundred children." While these many women and a few men attempted to collectively meet their families' most urgent needs, they joined the thousands of piqueteros in protesting the lack of jobs and inequitable distribution of resources in the country. Sara told me that "from the beginning we knew that we were supporting a national political project; we were not just thinking about doing soup kitchens." She helped organize thousands of Dock Sud residents to take over municipal buildings and block the bridge that connects Dock Sud to the city of Buenos Aires in order to "demand [*reclamar*] what is ours" from both state and corporate entities. Their discourse of self-help sometimes conflicted with their demand that the state take responsibility for their welfare.

Brewing Stews of Contention

The piqueteros identified the Dock Sud Petrochemical Complex as making extraordinary profits from the privatization of the national oil industry but failing to "respond to their low-income neighbors," as one man put it. They first organized blockades of the complex through a longtime Dock Sud institution, the Demarchi Neighborhood Promotion Society (*sociedad de fomento*). They blocked the access road to the refineries until a Shell representative gave the leaders a small amount of cash and then repeated the action a few months later. As Nancy Pontegras, a subsequent president of the Demarchi Society, described the situation, they negotiated with Shell "to loosen the noose" around the necks of the people precariously hanging onto life in the shadows of the profitable oil enclave. Although Sara Santos explained these actions in terms of class conflict, she concurred: "It always ended up that Shell arranged with a couple of institutions from Dock Sud on our behalf, so that we would shut up and [go] each to his house." She further explained that Shell's "custom" was to offer local organizations money in the name of "paternal sponsorship" (*padrinazgo*). In this way, Shell "begins to absorb them, and . . . the institutions become managed by Shell." This fatherly practice of providing for basic needs with a heavy hand was a hallmark of the paternalist company (see Chapter 1). It soon would be replaced by a feminized notion of care organized around a contradictory mix of friendship, "empowerment," and discipline.

As Sara helped organize her neighbors to "demand what is ours" from both state and corporate entities, she joined the national piquetero movement FUNDA, and the communal kitchen that began in her patio became its Goldendas affiliate. FUNDA began gaining prominence in Dock Sud, and as it did, its leaders attempted to transform the exchange of money for docility into a social and environmental justice campaign that emphasized the differential effects of the greater integration of the Argentine oil industry into global circuits. Most residents of the Dock Sud shanty settlements lived with a "toxic uncertainty" produced by corporate actors with state complicity that paralyzed them from taking individual or collective action (Auyero and Swistun 2009). Yet not all were so paralyzed. Sara saw her political actions against Shell as a reaction to the toxic rivers of Goldendas.

She told me about her experience with Shell as she simultaneously supervised her three children, cleaned her house, and prepared our lunch. Cooking oil was popping in the frying pan as she described the beginning of her interactions with Shell officials as motivated by filial sentiments: "In the beginning, we started with the matter of the pollution here in the Dock. By then we had many cases of kids who were born already having respiratory problems here in the neighborhood. And all the more [reason to start with this issue] when it touches you closely. It touched me very closely since one of my girls is asthmatic because of all this pollution—her, Anabela. . . ." Sara did not finish this statement but instead bent her head toward her youngest daughter who was playing on the floor. She did not mention Anabela's more serious lead poisoning because she did not want to remind her daughter about this problem for which she had been promised, but never received, treatment.[5] Continuing her story, Sara explained how she helped unite her neighbors who faced similar situations: "We started with this issue by joining together all the neighbors who had exactly the same problems; the children had the same problems, and also the older folk. Well, from there we started to connect with other organizations that also were involved in the pollution issue . . . like Nancy from the Demarchi Society. That way we began to walk across many doorsteps, and everyone asked us how much [money] we wanted for shutting up." In refusing to take money from Shell, FUNDA leaders insisted that the oil company had an obligation to make a long-term commitment to their welfare.

When I spoke to the FUNDA coordinator for the municipality, Javier Ruiz-Soto, one night after a regional strategy meeting, he similarly argued that cash was insufficient: "We first took on the problem with Shell as a matter of medical assistance . . . and we also asked for the inclusion of our members in jobs." Unlike the environmentalists who advocated closure of the petrochemical complex, FUNDA leaders argued that Dock Sud residents deserved a portion of its profits as compensation for the negative health effects of corporate practices such as venting toxic gases into the night air. However, this argument was secondary to their contention that their right to jobs be fulfilled by whichever entities—state or corporate—had the means to do so. FUNDA thus positioned its members as citizens in relation to the oil company in a manner that suggested a form of relationality distinct from both the juridical one that environmentalists promoted and the affective one that we will see Shell fostered through Creating Bonds.

Paula Dominguez, a longtime Sunshine Center participant, described an action that exemplified FUNDA's strategy regarding the oil companies. The participants in sixteen communal kitchens blocked the road across the Dock Sud Canal until a Shell manager arrived at the scene and invited the protest leaders to his office. Paula recounted how she and hundreds of others were sitting in the street drinking mate when their representatives emerged from the petrochemical complex with a note signed by the corporate executives. The protesters had demanded that the companies stop polluting the air and water, but they did not "listen to us because they are mega-companies [*firmas pesadas*]." She noted that it was less expensive for them to donate food and medicine to the communal soup kitchens and to promise to "pay more attention to us" than to switch to more environmentally sound technologies. Although the pledged provisions never were delivered, the event made apparent that Shell representatives had modified their strategy from offering FUNDA the cash payments they gave other piquetero groups to promising material goods like those they gave social service organizations—and like those the Peronist punteros and manzaneras distributed on behalf of the state. This marked the beginning of a change in Shell's strategy for governing Dock Sud's disruptive residents from one primarily based on bribery to one that emphasized establishing personal relationships.

The "Visible Face" of Shell

The Shell representative who met with the FUNDA leaders was the plant's security manager, a retired coast guard officer named Bruno Camacho. His responsibilities not only included supervising the maintenance of the refinery facilities, but also maintaining the company's relationship with the people living on the other side of the barbed wire fence. Although residents identified several different shanty settlements in Dock Sud, Shell's community relations officers perceived a single shantytown and understood it as both a space of insecurity to monitor and a space of community to be assisted. During an interview in his office behind the refinery's heavily guarded gate, Bruno proudly reported that he delivered (used) computers to the municipal hospital, fire extinguishers to local schools, and propane canisters to soup kitchens. With the emergence of the piqueteros, Bruno's role expanded to include meeting with the representatives of the road blockades. The cash handouts and material donations he distributed were part of the company's effort to make sure that the petrochemical complex was safe from Dock Sud. As in Nigeria (Zalik 2004a; Watts 2005) and Indonesia (Welker 2009), donations and social programs were important security measures.

It soon became clear that Shell's "gifts" were unable to halt the demands that erupted during the political-economic collapse of 2001 and threatened the profitable oil enclave. In this moment of turmoil, Bruno explained, "the company had a need to communicate to the community" because "it had had some problems, some complaints, or some social actions, that is, some demands from the neighbors." To this end, he began offering tours of the refinery complex for local schools and other groups, giving neighbors a carefully orchestrated view of the complex. Each week or so, schoolchildren were driven through part of the refinery in a school bus, with Bruno standing behind the driver holding a microphone.

I joined a group from a Dock Sud elementary school on one of Bruno's tours of the refinery one beautiful spring day. He lauded how after a devastating fire in the Dock Sud Canal in 1984, Shell put in place "the highest security technology."[6] As the bus passed between storage tanks and near the docks, he pointed out the fire and environmental response systems, explaining how the equipment for cleaning up spills in the river worked like a vacuum cleaner, something none of these children had at home. When we passed malodorous blacks clouds billowing from one of the refinery smokestacks, a student asked whether it was toxic. "No, no," Bruno quickly replied. "It would be dangerous not to burn off the gas." Turning to the two teachers sitting in the front row, he commented that the "more serious danger" was children playing in the streets around the complex and getting in the way of the trucks. We were outside of the petrochemical complex walls at that time, and just as he said this, two boys holding rags approached a truck driver to see whether he would pay them a few cents to clean the truck. "See," Bruno said, pointing them out.

After touring the control room full of computers, we were shepherded into a lunchroom where we were served snacks. The children were given booklets about Shell full of colorful pictures and games before they left. In the process of communicating messages about Shell's policies and activities, this seasoned military man became "the visible face" (*la cara visible*) of Shell in Dock Sud, as one colleague put it.

The tours of the refinery illustrate that Shell's new strategy for interacting with Dock Sud residents represented the company in a more personal way than did its signature yellow-and-red scalloped shell on the T-shirts he gave local sports teams, the logo on the side of propane canisters, the trucks barreling down the streets, or even the cash payments and donations Bruno handed out. Greater communication was a first step in the company's move toward establishing intimate, affective, and feminized relations with Dock Sud residents. Acts like giving tours of the refinery not only presented "information," but also gave the abstract idea of a foreign oil company a human face. What is more, these actions gave the corporation's legal arguments about its blamelessness for poverty and illness in Dock Sud a corporeal and personal manifestation in a place far from the sites where its glossy brochures usually circulate.

The change in community relations strategy accelerated in 2002 when the executive board of Shell's South American division established a new Department of Community and NGO Relations to take over some of Bruno's community relations responsibilities. The new department was charged with bringing Shell's South American operations into alignment with the company's global effort to brand itself as a leader in CSR. The person they hired to direct it, Yasmín Nobleau, was as youthful and smooth as Bruno was mature and gruff.

She was an impeccably groomed woman in her mid-thirties with previous experience in social work, a master's degree in nonprofit administration, and the presentation style of a marketing executive. She beautifully represented the re-formed caring self that Shell was working hard to create across the world (Livesey and Kearins 2002). The hiring of Yasmín signaled a break from remnants of the company paternalism that once had characterized the relationship between oil companies and area residents.

Creating New Bonds

The staff of the new Department of Community and NGO Relations reconfigured Shell's philanthropy programs in Dock Sud as part of the company's effort to address the problems with the public perception of Shell that were evident from the road blockades of the petrochemical complex and then were dramatically displayed once again during the boycott in 2005. Yasmín first sought to learn more about the Dock Sud area, which she, like most of her social class, saw only from the highway as she drove from the city to the beach. Her initial research confirmed that Dock Sud was a place where, as she told me, "the population presents a high rate of unsatisfied basic needs," yet she did not see the petitions that the piqueteros handed to Bruno during protests or the requests that community organizations submitted at other times as adequate evidence of what the community needed from the company. Instead, Shell hired a sociologist named Filipe Aguilar as a project consultant to assist the community relations staff in administering what Yasmín called a "diagnosis of the area." "To us, it seemed super smart that it would be the community that tells us what are its necessities," she explained, but "they understood that we are not going to be able to contribute to everything."

Yasmín reported that the company's research showed that employment, health, pollution, security, and education were the most pressing concerns of Dock Sud residents. Next, she and her staff reworked these research results to reflect the values expressed in Shell's CSR statements, including "protection and care of the environment," "employment and income generation," and "improving the health of the population" (Shell Argentina 2006). How they did so was quite revealing. For instance, the piqueteros' demand that Shell offer employment at the refineries to more area residents was translated into a pledge to encourage entrepreneurial income-generating opportunities in "the local community" and thus outside of the petrochemical complex. Whereas Shell previously had built a neighborhood health clinic, it now awarded grants to NGOs to provide health education. Therefore, in the same moment that the Shell staff began inviting residents into the petrochemical complex for tours, the Creating Bonds program redefined "community needs" in ways that placed their solutions outside of the refinery walls.

Despite this distancing work, Yasmín portrayed Creating Bonds as deepening the personal relationship between the oil company and what she called "the community." Speaking for the company she had only recently joined, she declared that for Shell's seventy-five years in Argentina "we have always had a development that is very, very close to the community."[7] However, she qualified, "before it was more philanthropic, working more immediately on the most basic needs." Her example of the company's former approach was the donation of paint to a community center whose building was falling down. In contrast to "a very immediate action" like this, Yasmín explained Shell's new attitude: "We are not only financiers. It is not like we give them a check and they do their project, but instead we try to become their partners in the elaboration of the project, and in the development of the project." She added that her staff not only visited Shell's grantees more frequently, but also monitored and evaluated their projects "jointly with them." When I asked her to further explain the difference between a philanthropic donation and a CSR project, she told me: "A donation [is] I write you a check . . . It is only money, and the link is finished. That is to say, I know that I know you [sé que te conozco], but the truth is that I never visited you, nor know well what you do. I supported you in an immediate matter and that's it. In contrast, a project implies, first of all, from the design until the conclusion, a knowledge of you [un conocerte]." Yasmín thus described CSR as implying an intimate relationship between the giver and the receiver. Her comments illustrate how, as she sought to reshape Dock Sud residents into company partners, she also was working to reshape the company's public persona into a compassionate neighbor. With Creating Bonds, she told me, "Shell is not a brand; it's a face, a person" (Shell no es una marca; es una cara, una persona).

Gender was a crucial element in this effort to make Shell into a citizen and a friend. As Yasmín partially replaced Bruno, the company took on a more normatively female role in Dock Sud. Whereas he had provided things, she nurtured relationships. For example, Yasmín involved herself in the minutiae of how Creating Bonds projects were executed. She consulted with organization leaders about details such as what materials they should buy and where they should buy them. She reported that project coordinators called her cell phone on weekends as an example of how their interactions extended beyond the spatial and temporal boundaries of usual business relationships.[8] More like a Peronist manzanera than a company official or union boss, she tasted the meals served at soup kitchens, telling me, "If I don't like the food, the kids might not either." In addition, twenty other Shell executives became advisors for each of the Creating Bonds projects. Because a chemical engineer could not offer advice on teaching autistic children, for instance, this "advising" was really about establishing ongoing personal communication between the company and the community. While the discourse of partnership that the Shell staff used implied relationships of equality, it was clear to all involved that the impoverished people living in Dock Sud were not the equals of the company or its representatives by any measure. Instead, the Shell professionals tried to show that the company possessed feelings like compassion and to demonstrate that it had affective attachments to "the Dock Sud community," rather than paternal responsibility for it.

An important way that Creating Bonds nurtured a new relationship with Shell's community partners was by training them to meet their own needs by using a discourse and techniques of "empowerment." The concept of empowerment, Aradhana Sharma (2006) has noted in another context, signals the diffusion of governance from historical centers of power, such as welfare states, onto individuals and community groups.[9] In Argentina, empowerment shifted everyday governance away from paternalist companies as well as state institutions. The Creating Bonds program was designed, in Yasmín's words, to empower Dock Sud residents so that "they would not only be asking for things, but also offering what they know how to do and the resources that they might have." Company officials taught that Shell was a friendly and caring neighbor who was concerned about its neighbors' well-being yet wanted to foster their independence. As a group of grantees and I learned during a training session, empowerment meant providing many hours of unpaid "volunteer" labor. Shell only provided funds for purchasing material supplies, like the paint that Bruno had formerly given out directly, and for compensating outside experts, not for paying local residents who did the organizations' daily work or who provided occasional labor. Shell's empowerment training meshed well with the discourse of neoliberalismo that advocated purging the population of asistencialismo, a term used to intimate the passivity of people who expect that materials and services will be given to them, whether the assistance being offered is material goods, education, or medical services.

Creating Bonds mostly funded health and environmental education activities that taught that people were responsible for the health of their own bodies and those of their children. One program instructed young mothers in the shanty settlements to avoid pollution by drinking bottled water and by keeping their children from playing on the ground. Like Foster (1996) showed of Shell's advertisements in Papua New Guinea, the company's CSR programs in Argentina implied that people were autonomous individuals who could control what entered their bodies and the environment around them. Corporate support of health education thus shifted the burden of illness from the industries that produce toxins onto those who ostensibly elect to place themselves and their families in a contaminated environment. This actively trained Dock Sud residents to rethink their expectations of the company, in other words, to strive to make themselves into self-sufficient people, autonomous from the company. This way of thinking denied their lived reality, in which pollution from the refineries gradually damaged their health and the development of their children, and on occasion, company trucks hit their neighbors.

The Shell staff dovetailed its lesson in individual responsibility with one in communal self-sufficiency by encouraging its grantees to create an independent community. Though local leaders identified their organizations' greatest need as funds, the pamphlet explaining Creating Bonds guidelines instructed potential project leaders that they "need[ed] to cooperate" with organizations, state entities, and corporate entities other than Shell. Projects selected for Creating Bonds support had to demonstrate that they would cover half of their costs by soliciting funding from other sources and by matching Shell's gift with volunteer labor and loaned infrastructure. The Shell staff further encouraged this kind of collaboration by offering twice the money to projects that linked several entities as opposed to projects that involved only one organization. These measures provided, according to Yasmín, "an exit strategy that assures that you [Shell] are not always supporting the same ones, but instead that you are in some manner teaching them that later they can go it alone." As I have previously shown, neoliberal economic projects do not replace dependence with autonomous individualism but instead encourage novel forms of filial and communal relationality. In this case, Creating Bonds' lessons in individual responsibility and community self-sufficiency worked together to generate new forms of community in Dock Sud. At the same time, the program replaced the image of the "market dictator" with a sympathetic face.

The re-facialization of the company illustrates the shift away from a normative fatherly role of provider and disciplinarian toward a feminized one. Yet the new feminized face of Shell is a woman in high heels and designer suits who hardly fits the image of maternalism. Yasmín is an unsettled amalgamation of the businesswoman and the caring friend. She and her staff supervised and audited community projects like a corporate manager would do to business projects.

They replaced verbal requests with written documents and cash payments with bank disbursements. They introduced businesslike meetings, training sessions, budgets, timelines, and deadlines. The corporate representatives also attempted to teach the project leaders how to measure their work, calculating the number of people served and otherwise gauging their effects using quantitative assessment techniques. Through the introduction of these professional methods, the Shell community relations staff distanced themselves from the projects they funded by making it clear that they expected the project leaders to identify and figure out solutions to their own problems. Yasmín reiterated that the Shell staff would suggest potential solutions to their community partners but would not solve problems for them. This woman who represented corporate success was attempting to convince the impoverished residents of Dock Sud that they too could become successful, even professional, people, if they would just take responsibility for their own lives.

Yet the Shell representatives also sought to establish personal relationships with community members that resembled normative female friendships based on emotional support and trust. Yasmín and her assistants wanted the Dock Sud residents to share stories of their personal struggles with them and offered them sympathy and encouragement in return. This strange kind of intimacy certainly was not based on balanced reciprocity. In several respects it was the mirror image of the relationship that Donna Goldstein (2003) has described in Brazil, but which occurs throughout the Americas, in which professional women pour out their troubles to their maids but know little of the maids' life struggles.

Creating Bonds had the double mission of remaking Shell into a good corporate citizen and caring neighbor who improved the lives of its fellow Argentines and of remaking its "partners" into NGOs with whom the corporation could cooperate but for whom it was not responsible. As Nancy Pontegras from the Demarchi Society put it, Yasmín's role was "to work with the community to iron out the wrinkles." The metaphor of ironing points to the way in which Creating Bonds enabled the exploitative and polluting activities of the oil industry by domesticating the company in the neighborhood. Nancy wryly suggested that the company converted iron, like oil, from a hazardous industrial material into a mundane domestic tool that makes things nicer, but only superficially. The development of the Creating Bonds program paralleled the shift in Peronism from state- and union-based welfare to personalized welfare networks and privatized health care. Yet the work of the new Department of Community and NGO Relations also fit with the increasing professionalization of philanthropy in Argentina and the neoliberal notion of self-responsibility.[10]

At the same time that Creating Bonds mirrored changes occurring in Argentina, it also involved discursive modifications to make the program align with transnational notions of CSR and corporate citizenship that would speak to customers, investors, and critics beyond the country's borders. The Creating Bonds framework closely resembled the "community development program" that Shell staff designed in Nigeria, particularly in its emphasis on "partnerships" with NGOs and the change from "giving things" to supervising the work carried out by subcontractors and volunteers (see LaPin 2000). Thus, Shell in effect outsourced development in Argentina and around the world, decreasing its costs and undermining claims for compensation from the company (for Nigeria, see Zalik 2004a). The Creating Bonds staff also employed affective techniques to establish friendly relations between the company and neighborhood residents and thereby undercut opposition to its operations. This shift from a male to a female face did more than hide the company's profit-seeking beneath a veneer of sympathy; it weaned Dock Sud residents of their expectations of assistance from the oil company.

The Sunshine Health Room

Shell's partnership with FUNDA to build a health room at the Sunshine Community Center epitomized the company's new strategy for governing Dock Sud by fostering an incongruous amalgamation of individual responsibility, communal autonomy, and sympathetic friendship with Shell. When Yasmín invited the Sunshine Center to present a proposal to Creating Bonds in its third funding cycle, it marked the first year that a piquetero movement was included in the program. Until that point, Creating Bonds exclusively funded NGOs, schools, and other well-established charitable organizations; FUNDA clearly did not fit into these categories. One FUNDA leader speculated that Shell was experimenting by "giving a project to a social movement that is prominent in the area to see if taking this approach would restrain the conflict they were having." FUNDA had reduced its activism during Kirchner's presidency, but its members still participated in protests that the president supported, including the national boycott of Shell and Exxon. Yasmín frankly asserted that Shell wanted to support the "softer" tendencies within FUNDA and to undermine the "more intransigent line" that helped organize the boycott. In other words, Creating Bonds would, she hoped, transform FUNDA from a politically engaged piquetero movement into an "anti-politics machine" (Ferguson 1994) that would provide social services to Dock Sud residents without engaging them in activism.

Although Shell's invitation was extended only to the Sunshine Center, the FUNDA regional coordinator gathered members of several community centers and a few professional allies, including a doctor, to design their proposal. The group that met in the center that day saw Creating Bonds as a tool to help them move away from simply serving cups of warm milk or stew and toward more profoundly addressing the causes of malnutrition in the area. Moreover, it could help them gain greater access to state assistance programs, especially food rations for malnourished children.[11] They outlined a proposal to use Shell funding, in combination with money from the Ministry of Social Development, to rebuild the Sunshine Center out of sturdier materials and to add and equip a health room at the front. The Sunshine Center's Proposal stated:

Health Clinic for Prevention and Promotion of Health
The principle objective is to create in the neighborhood a space for Health Promotion and Prevention, for the fulfillment of talks, workshops and spreading information about many health concerns. This is aimed at boys and girls and young mothers. Also, first aid services will be offered in this "Health Room" under the supervision of doctors and nurses who already collaborate in solidarity with our institution through trainings and [medical] attention to the neighbors. The equipment we request will be designated for those activities aimed at consolidating the work that we have long carried out in the neighborhood through the training of health promoters. They are just our own neighbors who have trained to carry out health promotion and prevention duties by giving talks and workshops about, for example, addictions, HIV, infant sicknesses, respiratory illnesses, etc. Also, the health promoters carry out nutritional checks on a monthly basis, which assist the food unit provided by the national Ministry of Human Development, for 40 boys and girls who live in the neighborhood and have been found to be malnourished or underweight. All this work that has been carried out through the community center's health section will be seen to be reinforced and supported by this project once we are enabled to build [*montar*], in a more formal and less rudimentary form, our objective of HEALTH PROMOTION AND PREVENTION in the neighborhood. The activities that we will carry out will mainly be first aid services, large-scale neighborhood diffusion activities for the prevention of the most common illnesses (respiratory, nutritional, etc.), training in raising the consciousness of families about their right to access the health system, which encourages neighbors to carry out periodic checks in the area hospitals, and question-

naires to determine the main necessities in the neighborhood and the design of collective proposals to solve these problems.

FUNDA's application to Creating Bonds reshaped the piqueteros' demands that Shell clean up its operations and provide local employment into a constrained NGO-esque request for money to purchase building materials and medical equipment so they could provide nutrition education and services to themselves, by themselves. Furthermore, the collaboration between several communal kitchens that had emerged through street protests was replaced by a collaboration that included a single communal kitchen–turned–community center, volunteer medical professionals, and state medical agents. The organizers did this in order to qualify for the approximately $3,400 available for "network" projects, rather than the $1,700 that "individual" projects received. In describing their proposed health room, the FUNDA leaders maintained a delicate balance between excluding statements that Shell representatives would find unacceptable, such as identifying the petrochemical complex as the source of the widespread respiratory illnesses, and including FUNDA principles, such as collectively designing programs to address the causes of the health problems in the area. Yet the Sunshine leaders envisioned nutrition workshops at the center that would resemble the ones FUNDA conducted in other neighborhoods, in which women trained as "health promoters" not only instructed their neighbors in how to stretch their meager resources to feed their families, but also taught them that dignified employment and a clean environment were citizenship rights.

These leaders thus saw the health education workshops as extending, not counteracting, the demands they made at road blockades, at a time when this more disruptive technique was becoming less effective. The FUNDA leader Javier Ruiz-Soto articulated their intention to use Shell funding to pursue their citizenship rights when he stated: "We don't see this as them giving anything to us; we see [the money] as a small part of what is rightfully ours. . . . They are giving us a small part of what they owe Dock Sud for what they cause. Ten thousand pesos do not cover the death of even one kid." Sara Santos further explained that they envisioned Creating Bonds as an opportunity to "empower what we had long been doing." By emphasizing FUNDA's history of activism, Javier and Sara gave citizenship and empowerment decidedly different meanings than did Yasmín. However, when the Creating Bonds grantees were announced at a press conference, a Shell official handed a representative from each organization a gigantic symbolic check amid the flash of cameras, and they appeared as grateful recipients of Shell's outsized generosity. This image was reproduced in the publicity sent to people who were removed from the political grounds in Dock Sud and helped facialize the company in benevolent terms to people far away from Argentina, which, in turn, enabled the continuation of harmful practices there.

Breaking Ground

The health room groundbreaking ceremony expressed a message of communal partnership that disregarded, if not opposed, amicable partnership with the oil corporation that partially funded it. FUNDA leaders presented the health room to the residents of Goldendas in terms that would have made Shell executives fume, if they had known. The flyer that Sunshine participants circulated among their neighbors inviting them to celebrate the initiation of construction declared that "this project has been presented by our movement, before the Shell company, to protest [*reclamar*] the unsanitary conditions that our neighborhood suffers, in part induced by the activities that this company develops in the area."

As I walked up the main alley of Goldendas on that crisp Saturday afternoon in June 2005, Shell employees were nowhere to be seen, but a group of children who regularly ate at the Sunshine soup kitchen came running to usher me into the community center. I immediately saw that it had been thoroughly cleaned and rearranged for the presentation of the health room project. The table that usually sat in the center of Sunshine's main room had been moved outside to make room for the guests. Someone had swept into a pile the broken pieces of brick, cement, and cinder blocks that were in front of the building and had gotten rid of the scraps of paper, toys, plastic, and other debris that kids and dogs tracked in. Stacks of brand new red cinder blocks, bought to begin the construction, surrounded the fire pit where meals were still being cooked at the time. The walls inside the community center were hung with the illustrations that health promoters had made for their health education workshops with markers and magazine cutouts on the back of outdated FUNDA posters. One portrayed a food pyramid and another included an acrostic about the elements of good nutrition that was used to help members evaluate the food assistance they received from state agencies and other donors. A physician named Dr. Martín, who had collaborated in designing the Creating Bonds proposal, arrived with large sheets of butcher paper showing the results of the FUNDA national health survey. He hung them from the ceiling beam that divided the area in the back of the building, also newly filled with bricks, from the front space where a small crowd was gathering between the chairs and benches.

The ceremony began when Sara Santos called the group to attention and briefly recounted the history of Sunshine, emphasizing the Goldendas residents' collaborative role in developing the FUNDA movement in Dock Sud, from handing out cups of warm milk on her patio to finishing paying for the shack in which we were sitting. She stated that "our aim, our dream" was to rebuild the Sunshine Center's structure out of cinder blocks, to expand the space for activities, and to make the community center less precariously situated in the physical and political landscape of Dock Sud. Her speech crescendoed to a close by declaring that they were now reaching these goals, which represented not only an achievement for Goldendas, but also a step toward "a different Argentina." Her words echoed a slogan frequently used by Kirchner supporters, yet it also illustrated that the piqueteros did not represent a shift from a politics of redistribution to one of recognition, but instead these two were intimately linked.

Echoing Sara's definition of their needs, goals, and accomplishments, Dr. Martín presented the results of FUNDA's national health survey and discussed the movement's struggle to make health care accessible to everyone, not just those "with money in their pockets." Jenni Herrera Salazar, one of the university students who had been involved with the communal soup kitchens in Goldendas since before they had become part of FUNDA, spoke last. She talked about the movement's effort to replace corrupt politicians who, among other faults, overlooked Shell's violations of environmental laws. In their speeches about community improvement through cooperative effort, no one mentioned Shell.

When the speakers finished, several women proudly carried around trays of luxurious snacks rarely consumed in Goldendas—triangular ham and cheese sandwiches, empanadas, and mini pizzas—which they had made for the event. We then toasted the initiation of construction of the health room with cups of soda and enthusiastic cheers. After the crowd thinned, Dr. Martín showed Sara and a few other women the contents of a cardboard box: a modest assortment of first-aid supplies that he had brought as a contribution to building the Sunshine health room. Finally, the dozen or so of us who still remained carried the bricks that were stacked around the fire pit into the back of the community center before departing. In sum, through the making of posters and giving of speeches, the preparing of food and carrying of bricks, the health room groundbreaking ceremony embodied collaboration among neighbors that did not depend on, and even excluded, Shell. However, dismissing Shell was far more difficult once the project was under way and construction at the Sunshine Center began (see Figure 10).

Figure 10. Construction of the health room begins in front of the Sunshine Community Center. The men are building a frame for the walls, which will abut the neighboring house to the left. A roof support stands in the foreground on the right. The roof of the center is so low that someone has used it to store a wicker basket.

"You Always Have Weeds"

The Shell public relations staff's effort to transform its relationship with Dock Sud residents through partnerships with community organizations did not proceed in the manner that company executives had hoped. Conflicts over the terms of Shell and FUNDA's joint project emerged even before construction at the Sunshine Center began. Their representatives argued over how the money would be dispensed and what it could be used for, not to mention each other's ongoing involvement in national politics. Despite Yasmín's talk about getting to know Dock Sud residents personally, she and her colleagues rarely entered the shanty settlements. Shell employees mostly spoke to their community partners from the safe distance of their offices in downtown Buenos Aires, behind the guarded walls of the petrochemical complex, or via cell phone. After Yasmín came to inspect the center, the women at Sunshine snickered for weeks about how she picked her way up the alley path in spiky high heels and a designer suit. Yasmín, for her part, spoke of them as though they were children, calling Sara, for instance, by the diminutive "Sarita." The FUNDA coordinators skipped Creating Bonds training sessions, and Shell refused to dispense the promised funds. Construction fell far behind Creating Bonds' strict schedule of project deadlines. A year and a half after the groundbreaking ceremony, the reconstruction of the Sunshine Center was still not complete. Though the area in front of the community center had been enclosed in cinder-block walls, the new room had neither a floor nor a roof and thus was not being used for health or any other activities. It was clear that neither Shell's nor FUNDA's vision for the health room would reach fruition.

Yasmín vehemently declared the Sunshine health room the biggest disaster of the twenty projects that Creating Bonds funded that year. The glossy year-end report Yasmín handed me in her office squarely placed responsibility for any failures in the projects on the community organizations. Though the report listed the obstacles facing the Sunshine health room as including an unsuitable location, a lack of planning, and insufficient volunteers to carry out the construction, Yasmín told me that the greatest problem was something else: "FUNDA is a political movement—with different branches—that has a lot of social activity within it, but social activity clearly linked to political interests, so it was very hard for us to be able to work with them . . . I believe the biggest obstacle over there was that their true interest and motor is not a social motor . . . it is really more political, and for power, for power." When I pushed her to explain what she meant by "power," she replied: "There are many political activists [*militantes*] involved. And for a long time now they have been working for the government, bringing people to different demonstrations. These people's interest is to position themselves politically, to earn a state salary at the charge of 'I'll bring people for you.'" She summed up her experience with FUNDA with a nature metaphor: "When you are working very closely with the community, you always have weeds that go cropping up." By using gardening to represent politics, Yasmín suggested that FUNDA's actions were out of place in a social landscape in which Shell cultivated local organizations to grow in an apolitical direction and away from Shell.

Yasmín framed the problem in terms of FUNDA's failure to develop the right interests, yet FUNDA leaders framed it in terms of the unjust distribution of resources and hazards. Sara and Javier asserted that some of what Yasmín had written in her report was true, for instance, that the community center was situated on a swampy piece of land. But Goldendas' sodden landscape could be addressed by pouring a higher concrete floor if only the money from Shell had not run out before they finished purchasing all the construction materials, not to mention the medical equipment and supplies they needed. Sara added that the greatest obstacle facing the completion of the health room was the improving economic situation in Argentina in 2005. Paying construction workers was not among the acceptable uses of Creating Bonds funds because, as mentioned previously, the organizations were supposed to have a cadre of volunteers to provide labor as part of the organizations' contribution to their partnership with Shell. At the time that FUNDA submitted its proposal, most of the neighborhood construction workers were unemployed or underemployed, and several were willing to exchange labor for a hot meal at the center. However, as these men found more opportunities for paid employment, they no longer volunteered to build the health room. In other words, it was not their lack of skills or their political interests, but Shell's insufficient and tightly controlled funding that caused the halt in construction at the Sunshine Center. The fiscal rules of the Creating Bonds program seemed to compromise Shell's stated goal of improving health in the neighborhood and its unstated goal of improving public opinion of the company. Yet even in failed projects like this one, Creating Bonds still subtly supported Shell's message of communal self-sufficiency and corporate nonresponsibility and discouraged political alliances that could challenge the company.

The Shell staff not only placed blame for the failure of Creating Bonds projects on its "community partners," but subtly used the notion of partnership to hold those partners responsible for the unchecked illness and poverty in Dock Sud. Yasmín confided that her biggest problem was "generating a link of trust, and that's besides the fact that they see [me] as a capitalist who is going to put up the Shell letters on their door." She explained that in 2005 they had "advanced a little" so that Dock Sud leaders "now know [me] as a spokesman." However, she aimed for a more intimate relationship in which they would view her as "someone who they can talk to like an equal." She wanted them "to really see that you understand what they are talking about, and that you speak the same language that they do, and have their friendship." Yet, at the same time that Yasmín and her colleagues tried to become the peers of the community leaders, they policed a wide gulf between the company and the community. To quote Yasmín once more:

> You have to stay very connected with the people, and with the project in question, but also not lose focus of the legal aspect that this is a business. And [keep in focus] that a business is not an NGO, it's a business. And so you have to always be managing and taking care that the organization's purpose is the common good, and its work is about the community, and the business's purpose is to make a profit. Because, if not, the director sitting in London is going to say to us "it's all very pretty, but this girl spends money that we do not have." That is the reality that has to be generated within a business.

Yasmín thus asserted that interactions between the partners had to be personal but not so close that the boundary between "the people" and "the business" became blurred. Each of the partners had a different role. By legal mandate, she pointed out, Shell had to create financial profits for its shareholders, and NGOs had to serve a community that did not include Shell. It followed that these organizations, and not the oil company, were accountable for improving the environmental and economic situations in Dock Sud. It is also significant that Yasmín contrasted the company with an NGO and not a state agency, for comparing it with the state would have evoked the paternalist conception of obligation that she was working hard to eliminate. Her comments implied that the Sunshine Center, and by extension FUNDA, had failed to fulfill its legal mandate, while Shell had more than executed its own. Moreover, her comment illustrates how affective attachments are carefully circumscribed by a profit motive that seeks to reduce the company's financial costs at almost any social cost. The regendering of Shell's face meant that the company was *less* responsible for the people living near its installations.

The Monster's Hand

Despite the prevailing characterization of the health room project as a failure, Sunshine Center leaders saw how it succeeded in governing Dock Sud residents in subtle ways. Several pointed out that Creating Bonds reinforced Sunshine's ostensibly apolitical activities and divided it from other FUNDA centers. They commented to me that Shell gave FUNDA money to build a health room not only in the hope that they would "shut up," but also so that they would "fight amongst themselves." The program's divisiveness was evident, for instance, when a delegation from another FUNDA center came to the Sunshine Center to complain that it was "getting all the attention" and resources and asked that the Sunshine coordinators hand some cooking supplies over to them. Shell used Creating Bonds to splinter the piqueteros so they could no longer gather large numbers of people for protests. In Sara's words, the company "throws us a piece of meat" and "like a pack of hungry dogs we wrestle over it." Creating Bonds' funding thus supported Shell's message of communal self-responsibility while discouraging political alliances.

Paula Dominguez offered an even bleaker assessment when she angrily declared: "Now we are not blockading, we are not doing protests, we are not doing anything. We are asking for what is our right. So why do we also have to contribute? Why do we have to put up the room so that they come and see that the room is up, so that they can send all the materials that they promised that they would send? Don't you see?" She summed up her estimation of Creating Bonds thus:

> We have been fighting for three years over the Shell affair. But we are—how can I explain it to you? We are a paper cut. In comparison with the whole body, we are a paper cut. So, [Shell says] we are going to treat this little hurt on the finger because it is going to take hold of the whole hand, take hold of the entire body. Well then, how do we treat this? With medicines, with donations, with blah, blah, blah.

Paula pointed out that many words had been exchanged between FUNDA and Shell representatives ("blah, blah, blah"), but the promised medicine was still undelivered and the health room unfinished. While corporate representatives like Yasmín used the image of "a face" to portray Shell as caring about its less fortunate neighbors, company critics like Paula used the metaphor of the paper cut to suggest that Shell was a hard-hearted giant that experienced the anger and suffering of the impoverished shanty settlement dwellers as a trivial pain. Paula also pointed out how responsibility for addressing the pollution from the petrochemical complex had shifted away from the company (not to mention the state) to FUNDA and the Goldendas residents. Yet her comment also indicates that even Shell critics envisioned the oil company in personlike ways. Shell might not have had a sympathetic face in her estimation, but it still had a body that could be hurt. The women and men affiliated with the Sunshine Center never accepted the Shell staff's portrayal of the company as a caring friend and good neighbor but instead saw in Shell's actions a devious and calculating adversary who successfully diffused political activism. Nonetheless, the Creating Bonds program was effective in undoing the expectation of company paternalism, in stemming protests against the company, and in "empowering" poor people to view systemic environmental, health, and welfare problems as their own.

Conclusion

An enormous amount of labor is needed to create an attractive public persona for a company such as Shell. While glossy CSR reports represent the oil company to middle-class consumers, investors, and employees in Argentina, Europe, and North America, individual employees work hard to facialize Shell for the impoverished people who live alongside the Polo Petroquímico Dock Sud. In Shell's presentations to these two audiences, the image of the company was similarly feminized. In 2002, a suave young woman partially replaced a gruff older man as Shell's community representative in Dock Sud. Yasmín took Bruno's attempts at "communicating to the community" through refinery tours and moved them beyond the walls of the petrochemical complex. While Bruno chastised the children who tried to earn a little money cleaning the oil trucks in the parking lot of Polo Petroquímico Dock Sud, Yasmín set up workshops to teach their parents that they should not let their children spend time in such areas in the first place. In doing so, she attempted to represent the sympathetic and concerned face of the company for those who experienced the environmental contamination, perilous traffic, and other hazards produced by the refineries. The gendered quality of this staffing change might have been coincidental, but it reinforced a broader regendering of company discourse, image, and practice. Both in person and in publications, female faces supplemented the male ones that were widely seen as callously pursing profits with indifference to others, in Argentina as in many other places.

The regendering of Shell's face reinforced the larger shift away from company paternalism, the kin-based metaphor for capitalist organization based on the normative father-son relationship. Not only did the oil company increasingly use female faces to represent itself, but its agents also took on some normatively female roles in relation to the company's "community partners," while disavowing others. Shell moved away from the fatherly role of direct financial supporter to a feminized role of educator and concerned friend. Whereas Shell officials once mainly handed out paychecks to laborers and material goods to schools and soup kitchens, now they principally handed out advice, worksheets, and limited expense reimbursements to the leaders of NGOs. Instead of lauding how the company supported the people living in the regions in which it operated, company officials now talked about how they empowered them to improve their own lives. Moreover, the Creating Bonds program neutralized opposition less by giving or withholding cash and other resources, as Shell staff had in the past, and more by training, encouraging, and counseling Dock Sud residents in how to obtain these things for themselves. Shell's CSR program thereby reworked the familiar role of *patrón* (boss)—the stern, distant, and financially necessary father figure that many large companies in Latin America had taken on since the colonial period.

As Creating Bonds remade Shell's public persona in Argentina, it reimagined the recipients of its philanthropy as the company's partners—that is, local people who worked with corporate employees in the joint project of improving both the neighborhood and the company's image. The discursive and labor practices of corporate-community partnership implied a symmetric relationship in which both parties were distinct actors with corresponding, if different, roles and obligations to a common project. In Dock Sud, the oil company took on the task of guiding, advising, and partially funding community development projects, while delegating the actual work of education and service provision. The example of the Sunshine Center health room illustrates that CSR not only outsourced labor to unpaid "volunteers," but also replaced corporate liability with personal and communal responsibility. The public relations staff worked hard to show that Shell was concerned about the well-being of Dock Sud residents and the quality of their environment but insisted that it was not their responsibility to fix "local" problems. Instead, they claimed to empower their neighbors to address the poverty and illness in Dock Sud themselves. In doing so, the Creating Bonds program drew on the transnational "ecoliberal" discourse about cooperation in the face of environmental problems that whitewashes different actors' positions in creating and experiencing the hazards of industrial capitalism (Di Chiro 2003). As an example of this, Shell supported education campaigns that taught Argentines about nutrition and the dangers of ingesting lead, while deflecting responsibility for the rampant malnutrition and lead poisoning in the residential area near its plant. The Creating Bonds program thus papered over the vast disparities between a corporation that reported profits of more than $26 billion in 2005 and its "community partners," many of whom were supporting large families on less than $1,000 per year.[12]

In Part I of this book, I showed how enduring the kin-based relationships have been in the Neuquén oilfields. Here, in Dock Sud, it is clear that they were not as deeply entrenched. The Creating Bonds program more easily remade the relationship between the company and its neighbors from paternalism and patronage to corporate-community partnership. While the former positioned the company's workers and neighbors as dependent children, the latter suggested their independence. In addition, while paternalism implied long-term commitment, partnerships entailed short-term contractual relationships. This did not necessarily mean a deterioration in relations, for kinship bonds can be as exploitative as any other relationship. But it did indicate a shift in its temporal frame from a relationship that cannot be simply ended to one that is more easily created and more easily terminated. In the place of paternalism and patronage, Creating Bonds introduced an incongruous combination of individual responsibility, community autonomy, and intimacy with Shell. The move away from a normatively masculine form of power reduced costs, limited protests, and transferred liability away from the company.

The design of Creating Bonds involved discursive, financial, and administrative modifications in Shell's approach to community relations in Dock Sud to make this program line up with the transnational notions of CSR and corporate citizenship that would speak to customers, investors, and critics beyond Argentina. Since the CSR movement emerged in the 1980s—with its declarations of moral principles, voluntary codes of conduct, and self-reporting mechanisms—it has served as a "counterweight" to international policies and national laws, such as the U.S. Alien Tort Claims Act, which are more threatening to companies like Shell (Watts 2005: 395). CSR thus shifted the terrain of struggle away from the formal juridical domain, where challenges to oil companies have met some limited successes (Sawyer 2006; *New York Times*, May, 22, 2009), and toward the more pliable field of public opinion. Here, debate centers around questions of goodwill, intent, and moral character, rather than rights and responsibilities. Shell officials used CSR programs in places like Dock Sud to rebrand the company as a concerned citizen with good intentions and a friendly disposition. They drew on gender in particular to re-present Shell, in Argentina and abroad, as a morally upstanding person and benevolent neighbor, thus investing the company with social legitimacy. This approach is not entirely novel; it continues, but reconfigures, a long history of "creating the corporate soul" through imagery (Marchand 1998). The recent trend in CSR extends this process to impoverished populations largely ignored by marketing campaigns aimed at middle-class consumers.

Shell's public relations work in Argentina demonstrates how corporate actors molded representations of the company for different audiences, but it equally shows that the outcomes of these efforts are far from certain. While the new vision of Shell as a good citizen might be credible enough for the majority of its employees, consumers, and investors to continue to do business with the company, it was not persuasive for many people in Dock Sud. The Shell community relations staff was unable to make many Dock Sud residents perceive the oil company as an upstanding citizen and friendly neighbor. Yet this did not mean that the Creating Bonds program failed. In fact, it effectively stemmed demands on the company and protests against it and, more generally, diffused corporate liability for the health and welfare of the population living close to its installations. When Goldendas residents are told they should drink bottled water they cannot afford, they are taught that their health problems are caused by their poverty, not by the petrochemical complex's pollution. Shell agents also accomplished this reeducation by replacing a philanthropy program that was rooted in patronage and paternalism with a CSR program that used sympathy, education, and empowerment techniques to manage disruptive neighbors.

The FUNDA leaders asserted that Creating Bonds' funding of the Sunshine Center health room constituted only partial compensation for the harm that Shell caused Goldendas residents. They argued that the transnational corporation, like the Argentine state, had an obligation to guarantee citizens' rights to health care and dignified employment. By engaging in a partnership with Shell, however, FUNDA inadvertently endorsed Shell executives' claim that the company was more like an ordinary citizen than like the state and therefore had only limited obligations to others.[13] Moreover, the participation of organizations like FUNDA in the personification of oil companies like Shell subtly reinforces corporate power by singling out a particular company as an immoral individual. The suggestion that each company has a distinct persona and that Shell's nefarious actions are caused by its depraved character individualizes a systemic problem. The labeling of individual companies as "bad citizens" implies that other companies are as their CSR reports present them: good corporate citizens. The facialization of transnational corporations by company officials and their critics alike makes more difficult the larger project of remaking global capitalism, the oil industry's place in it, and the grossly unequal distribution of benefits and hazards across the social landscape.

Conclusion

The Neoliberal Family and the Corporate Effect

A MOTHER DESPERATELY TRYING to provide hot meals for her children. A workman struggling to remake himself into a small-business entrepreneur. A president attempting to combat inflation. All these people found themselves entangled in the global circuits of oil, and each labored to mold them to different ends. *Resources for Reform* has explored how the lives of Argentines of different backgrounds and experiences have intersected with the increasingly globalized and concentrated oil industry. Argentina's dramatic experiment with privatizing its venerable national oil company in the name of neoliberal reform offered an avenue through which to examine the multiple interconnections among the transformations in the global oil industry, Argentine society, and people's everyday lives, intimate relationships, and sense of self. The twists and turns in the story of oil and neoliberalismo told in this book confound any simple or linear explanation of these transformations. The book highlights both the unexpected lines of continuity between the neoliberal and preceding regimes of rule, and the surprising shifts in subjectivities and relationships.

Since I concluded the research for this book, some things have changed, but many more have remained the same. Néstor Kirchner was succeeded in the presidency by Cristina Fernández de Kirchner, his wife, amid speculation that they would pass the presidency between them for many years into the future. However, he died suddenly of a heart attack in October 2010. Meanwhile, President Fernández de Kirchner has continued to govern through techniques that might be characterized as "anti-neoliberal neoliberalismo." She, like Menem, has issued decrees of "urgency and necessity" in her attempt to influence the private oil market and manage fuel prices without engaging in the legislative process. She, like Néstor Kirchner, has railed against privatization as destroying democracy.[1]

The difficult relationship among the state, the private oil companies, and the Argentine people has continued as well. Despite government sanctions and fines, Shell has persisted in raising its fuel rates, by February 2011 reaching 127 percent of its price during the boycott six years before (*La Nación*, February 8, 2011). While fuel shortages have become common in Argentina, Shell's transnational parent company, Royal Dutch Shell, continues to report staggering profits for most quarters. The transnational corporation Repsol, which in late 2011 owned a little more than half of YPF, reported that its profits had more than tripled between 2009 and 2010.[2] In Argentina, YPF announced in May 2011 that it had discovered 150 million barrels of shale oil in the Neuquén oilfield. Once again, the residents of the region have high hopes that this find will return Northwest Patagonia to its former prominence and relative wealth. They, however, remain disappointed by the actions of private companies and government agencies. The emprendimientos that have survived still struggle to make a place for themselves in the globalized oil industry, and the YPFianos continue to worry about whether the legacies of YPF that they dedicated their lives to building will be passed on to future generations.

Around the country, the piqueteros continue both their street protests and their communal provisioning. In July 2011, residents of Dock Sud imposed a thirty-six-hour blockade of the road to the Polo Petroquímico Dock Sud, halting truck traffic to and from the refineries in order to demand that state agencies install basic infrastructure, such as sewage pipes, in the crowded shanty settlements bordering the refineries. Once more, the piqueteros challenged the complicity of state officials in favoring the projects of prosperous corporate citizens over the daily struggles of poor human citizens. The struggles that grew out of the reconfiguration of the Argentine state, economy, and society in the name of neoliberalismo are far from over.

Neoliberal Redux

Recent anthropological work has shed a bright light on the contingency and dynamism of neoliberalism and has illustrated how it has been assimilated into new situations. This scholarship has highlighted the calculative mechanisms, quantitative evaluations, and commodification that are important techniques that state and nonstate actors use to govern themselves and other people under neoliberal regimes. Still, scholars continue to glide over the distinctions among neoliberalisms and, in the process, to suggest that both a calculative market-based regime of rule and, similarly, a calculative entrepreneurial subjectivity are global norms. My examination of the lives of YPFianos in Neuquén Province and the piqueteros in the Buenos Aires metropolitan area demonstrates that the neoliberal processes carried out in the Argentine oil industry did not generate the ascendancy of either quantitative economic rationality or autonomous individuals. Neoliberalismo did not turn Argentines into "active individuals seeking to 'enterprise themselves,' . . . according their life a meaning and value to the extent that it can be rationalized as the outcome of choices made" (Rose 1996: 57). Instead, processes of state and economic restructuring presented dilemmas that people addressed by merging calculative *and* caring practices, detached *and* loving affect, and nurturing *and* dispassionate governing techniques. In doing so, these processes generated thoroughly relational and affective subjects who, in turn, embodied novel formulations of agency and sociality. *Resources for Reform* thus contributes to our understanding of neoliberalism by analyzing the affective dimension that, with few exceptions, other scholars have largely neglected. It not only illustrates how the neoliberal project of privatizing the Argentine oil industry reinforced affective governing techniques, but also indicates how this project dissolved distinctions between affective and calculative governing methods.

The anthropological literature on affect tends to obscure the production of inequality, while this book links affect to political economy, examining how sentiments work in combination with other productive forces to shape capitalism. I argue that affect is not a force of reproduction limited to the domestic domain, but a force of production that shapes the state and corporate domains as much as the domestic one. This attention to affect further reveals lines of continuity between neoliberal and previous methods of government that are not evident from studying the introduction of new technical mechanisms alone. Part I illustrated that, although the privatization of YPF dismantled familial privileges in the oil industry and encouraged dispassionate calculations about equipment, employment, and benefits, it did not replace affective attachments with an imported model of disinterested rationality. Instead, state oil workers continued to call themselves YPFianos after the state-owned oil company for which they once had labored. Additionally, and perhaps more importantly, they reconfigured their affective ties to YPF and to each other to fit the restructured oil industry as they formed emprendimientos. At the same time, the corporate managers from the oil companies that contracted their services placed themselves in paternal or avuncular positions in relation to the new business owners. As one emprendimiento director described it, the YPF SA representatives taught the emprendimiento partners to run their businesses in ways that bound them as "dependents" of the transnational company, much as YPF Estatal had positioned workers as "children" of the paternalist state company. This illustrates how a private oil company used affective techniques to sustain exploitative business activities. Yet, the YPFianos who were able to sustain emprendimientos through the privatization process did so by developing business practices that were at the same time generous caring acts and prudent financial computations.

Part II similarly demonstrated that neoliberalismo worked through techniques with affective and calculative dimensions. When Shell reformulated its public relations strategy in response to the piqueteros, its staff implemented "corporate-community partnerships" that sought to do more than squelch protest. Its new Creating Bonds program aimed to portray Shell as a caring neighbor and a good citizen, both to the impoverished people living near its refineries and to consumers, investors, and employees living far from them. Individual company employees attempted to form intimate relationships with the leaders of its partner organizations, using affective, educational, and fiscal techniques both to "empower" and to discipline the residents of Dock Sud. The feminization of Shell's public persona worked to soften the company's image as it simultaneously shifted responsibility for ill health and poverty from the oil company onto shanty settlement residents. Throughout this book, I have recounted other instances of the blurred boundaries between affective and calculative techniques in the neoliberal governing of people and natural resources in Argentina. Investigating only the juridical and administrative changes would have made the privatization seem merely a break with a preceding regime of rule, but attending to kinship and affect demonstrates how a neoliberal project worked to sustain previous governing relations as well.

The Argentines described in this book have made and remade neoliberalismo partially, collectively, and frequently unintentionally. They are not following a grand plan or acting out an ideology but are dealing with particular problems, large and small, as they arise. It is important to recognize that differently situated people have been able to shape the emergence and development of large-scale projects like the privatization of the Argentine oil industry in different ways and to different extents. Nonetheless, neither neoliberalismo nor the oil industry is an external structure that exists in a domain beyond everyday people's daily lives, affecting them from the outside. Both neoliberalismo and the oil industry are made and remade through the quotidian micropractices of laboring, learning, communicating, playing, caring, and a multitude of other activities. The fact that everyday people create neoliberalismo—not only react to it—does not mean that they can easily change or dismantle it, but it does mean that it is not a phenomenon in the world separate from them.

The reality that processes of political-economic and social transformation are shaped by the particular histories and contexts in which they are elaborated also means that each is distinct. These processes cannot be explained by a singular logic of capitalism or the interests of a set of powerful actors such as "the Oil Giants." Yet we are witnessing a convergence of events around the world that seems to suggest a singular cause. How can we explain, for instance, why countless state companies and services—in the former Soviet Union, Europe, Asia, Africa, and across the Americas—have been converted into privately owned corporations in the years since the end of the Cold War? Why has "privatization" become one of the hallmarks of neoliberalism around the world? What accounts for the reality that the emergence of global neoliberalism coincides with the increase in the size, wealth, and political might of transnational oil corporations, but not an increase in their number? Why is there today more collaboration among oil companies than competition between them? If these changes were not caused by an underlying logic or global agent, then what explains the remarkable coincidence of recent events? One of the central challenges faced by scholars who reject single causal definitions of neoliberalism is how to account for the similarity of phenomena at different sites.

Several anthropologists have turned to Gilles Deleuze and Félix Guattari's notion of "assemblage" to describe the simultaneous commonalities and inconsistencies among neoliberal projects the world over. While this analytic accounts for the ever-shifting connections among discourses and techniques, it is not well equipped to explain processes that, like the transformation of the oil industry, involve the nexus of numerous agencies and actions over the course of more than a decade. I look instead to Ludwig Wittgenstein's concept of "family resemblance" to offer an approach to understanding the relationship among neoliberalisms and to accounting for their staying power despite hostility to them on multiple fronts.

Neoliberalism constitutes a family resemblance in the sense that diffuse processes and specific projects carried out in different contexts have enduring features that mutually overlap with one another in numerous ways. These resemblances make neoliberalisms alike even though they do not all share a single origin, ideology, list of policies, or hidden code determining their development or final form. The neoliberal family is as differentiated and internally inconsistent as any other family; nonetheless, its members are well attached to each other for they have been associated for a significant period. To continue the kinship metaphor, the members of the neoliberal family speak the same language, and they financially support and symbolically sustain, but also clash, with each other. In its Argentine home, neoliberalismo has "married" novel concepts such as entrepreneurship and empowerment, with older ones such as patronage and paternalism. This marriage has endured for several decades now, although it is not always a happy one. Many neoliberal projects in Argentina and elsewhere share an inclination toward quantification, commoditization, and evaluation through market mechanisms, yet they also show a tendency to work through kinship sentiments and affective attachments to nations and communities. One strength of understanding the connections among neoliberalisms as family resemblance is that it acknowledges that some likenesses are noticeable in particular places and moments, while others rise to prominence in other contexts.

My analysis of neoliberalism in terms of family resemblance also explains the connections among my different concerns in this book. Neoliberalismo brings together the several shifts I documented: from state-led development to corporate-managed economic activities, from production as the principal basis of political organization to consumption as the grounds for citizens coming together as a nation, from labor relations characterized by long-term care and discipline to ones characterized by short-term and temporary contracts, from oil considered as a national treasure and strategic resource to its treatment as individual property and a form of money. My examination of the relationships among a sometimes unified, sometimes disarticulated group of people, institutions, events, discourses, ideas, and practices enables understanding of how neoliberalismo works as a generative phenomenon that has remade many different aspects of social life, and whose changes seem to be remarkably enduring. My attention to kinship and affect together with commodification and calculation demonstrates the inseparability of the semiotic *and* material forces that have worked together to create and re-create neoliberalismo. This analysis has important implications for how we understand the seemingly inexorable power of transnational corporations, for business entities too combine symbols and substances, discursive representations and physical entities.

Individuals and Corporations

Resources for Reform advances the longstanding anthropological tradition of scrutinizing the quotidian workings of corporate power beyond the "box" of office politics and business culture by focusing on people who are formally positioned outside of corporations as much as, if not more than, those who work within them.[3] Exploring the experiences and perspectives of oil town resi-

dents, refinery neighbors, oil company employees, subcontractors, and temporary workers revealed the wide web of power relationships in which business
firms are involved. I thereby illustrate that corporate power does not follow a
unidirectional path in which a foreign and invincible corporation impacts the
lives of regular people who have no real effect on the corporation itself. One
example of this is the inadvertent role the emprendimientos played in making
the privatized YPF into a profitable transnational corporation. Without these
subcontracting microenterprises doing the labor of producing oil, YPF SA
would have had to rely on transnational firms, namely, the oilfield service corporations made famous by the scandals involving Halliburton, to do this work
at much higher prices than the emprendimientos charged. Although YPFianos
did not always faithfully carry out the official privatization scheme, they still
helped to reduce wages and job security and to eliminate benefits and expectations of long-term care from oil companies. These changes attracted transnational firms to Argentine soil, and consequently the majority of the wealth that
the YPFianos helped generate went to professional employees and shareholders, not to Argentine workers. An ethnography focused on company executives,
government policymakers, IMF bankers, and the like would not have revealed
this crucial aspect of corporate power.

The reality that emprendimiento owner–workers, day laborers, and volunteer health promoters are all crucial to the financial success of oil companies
suggests that the boundaries of the corporation are not clear. What is a corporation? How does it make change in the world? Can a corporation act in the same
way that a person does? What kind of agency does it embody? I conclude this
book with some reflections on the meanings of two seemingly distinct forms of
personhood referenced but not fully examined in the preceding chapters—the
individual and the corporation—and explore how they have converged and di-
verged from each other in scholarly texts and in the oilfields and shanty settlements of Argentina. Are people and corporations comparable entities in any
sense? What does it mean for a person to be considered an individual? For a
corporation to be one as well? And how does the state fit into this picture?

We have inherited a European tradition that is strongly invested in an idealized conception of the person as an individual. The word *individual*, in both
English and Spanish, comes from the Latin *individuus*, meaning something
that cannot be divided into further parts. Like atoms are to the physical world,
this tradition implies, individual humans are the most basic building blocks
of the social world. This definition assumes that people exist prior to society
and are its creators, rather than are created by it. In addition, when people are

envisioned as individuals, they are regarded as unique and autonomous agents who each own their own bodies, thoughts, and actions. In this conception, a person's connections to other people and things are detachable additions to the essential core of who she or he is. Individuals are therefore distinct from the world around them. They move through the world and shape it, and are also influenced by it, but they are not part of it. This conception of the individual long has been criticized for ignoring the profound ways in which people are enmeshed in complex webs of interconnections that mold their very being. The idealized notion of the individual thus neglects the social forces that form people's ostensibly unique identities, their personal achievements, and even their ability to think and act. In short, critics argue that people are not self-sovereign agents but cultural creations. Peronism expressed some of these ideas in its critique of liberal citizenship and its arguments for a corporatist state (see Chapter 3) but still maintained a largely European understanding of personhood.

While historians have traced the emergence of the conception of the individual within European societies, anthropologists have mapped its rarity from a comparative perspective. Marcel Mauss (1985) famously charted a social history of personhood that pointed out the modernity and exceptionality of the understanding of a person as an independent, self-sovereign, and indivisible individual. He argued that a person is more often understood as an "organizational fact" than a "complete entity" (14). His examples, drawn from North America, Australia, India, and China, emphasized that people are more commonly regarded as made up of their connections to ancestors, spirits, objects, animals, and other humans. He distinguished this composite conception of personhood from the Greek, Roman, and Christian ones that evolved into the liberal notion of the individual. Anthropologists working in widely varied settings have continued to illustrate that people do not, and cannot, live up to the liberal ideal of the individual that so many around the world cherish and aim to embody.

While the understanding of people as made up of their connections is more common outside of European societies, the notion that personhood can be composite is not entirely absent from the liberal tradition. Composite personhood has been deployed in a startling context: to define a corporation as a person. Mauss (1985) pointed out that Roman law recognized an entity such as a university as a "collective person" (a person of persons) and that the Christian Bible suggests that people are "all one person, . . . in Christ Jesus" (19). Ernst Kantorowicz ([1957] 1997) extended this history and traced how the concept of corporate personhood traveled from Christian theology to the Tudor legal doctrine of the king's two bodies, to the English parliamentary state. In these instances, a corporation is a special kind of person composed of two inseparable bodies: the mortal body of the ruler who is replaced periodically and the eternal body politic of government that is constructed of a changing group of subjects. The former is material and temporary, the latter intangible and perpetual.[4] This amalgamation has been the legal grounds for some of the most powerful entities in history: the church, the kingdom, the state, the empire, and, I would argue, today's transnational business firms. In particular, both nation-states and business corporations have been theorized and legally treated as composite persons with a somatic yet perpetual existence. This conception has reached far beyond the northern societies that claim the liberal tradition as their own. Fernando Coronil (1997) has revealed how the notion of a composite yet indivisible body undergirded the emergence of the Venezuelan nation-state. The idea of composite personhood also has enabled colonial business ventures since the emergence of colonial corporations, such as the British East India Company, in the seventeenth century.

Recently, the conception of business corporations has shifted away from the tradition of conceiving them as composite persons and toward reimagining them as sovereign individuals. This move was first advanced in the second half of the nineteenth century by German legal scholars who, in grappling with the growth of the nation-state, envisioned corporations as possessing human capacities, qualities, and distinct identities (Lamoreaux 2004: 43–45; Gindis 2009). This legal tradition, known as "real" or "natural entity theory," grew in the United States throughout the twentieth century as the courts redefined corporations as "natural persons" who possess the constitutional rights and privileges of citizenship. Corporate lawyers have used the idea that corporations are individuals to strengthen the doctrine of "limited liability," which defines corporations as persons separate from those who own them and thus releases these owners from responsibility for the crimes and debts of the company whose profits they reap. In 2010, the U.S. Supreme Court ruled that corporations even have the same right to free speech as other citizens. As business corporations are being reenvisioned as individuals, they are being treated correspondingly as rights-bearing citizens equal to other citizens in ways that, in fact, increase their power *over* other citizens. Anthropological studies have emphasized how the legal "fiction" of corporate personhood has increased inequality but have not fully analyzed how the seemingly abstract concept of corporate personhood has been actualized on the ground far from the courtrooms where it is formally adjudicated.

Let us return to contemporary Argentina where events from the privatization of YPF to La Pueblada, to the boycott of Shell and Exxon, to the development of the Creating Bonds program demonstrate both the importance of oil companies as crucial actors in political contestation and social transformation and the widespread recognition of their importance by the majority of the Argentine population. It is now well established that corporations occupy a powerful position in daily life, economic and political relations, and the national imagination across the world. Events like the Argentine boycott show something that is less recognized: that oil companies are being portrayed, discussed, and I would argue at least partially conceived as individuals-writ-large. In the streets, gas stations, community centers, and homes in Argentina, corporations appear as powerful and autonomous individuals. For YPFianos, YPF-Repsol was an "assassin" and "giant" thief. From the perspective of boycott leaders and participants, foreign oil companies were undemocratic "market dictators" and "national traitors." In the words of company representatives, corporations were "good citizens" and "caring neighbors." Suzana Sawyer (2006) similarly documented how oil company officials, news reporters, peasants, and *indígenas* from the Ecuadorian Oriente region all referred to Chevron-Texaco as an individual person. Therefore, across geopolitical and ideological lines, oil companies have been described in terms that reflect the liberal conception of a person as an individual; that is, they are portrayed as independent and indivisible historical agents that act upon the world and are not made up of or by it.

At the same time that the Shell and Exxon boycott in Argentina reinforced the idea that a corporation is an individual, the event also provided ethnographic evidence that oil companies act more like composite entities than singular individuals. The boycott's detrimental effects on gas station franchisees, who were contractually obligated to purchase fixed quantities of fuel and sell them at set prices, is one illustration that oil companies are composed of differently positioned pieces, not of autonomous or organic wholes that (who?) act as one. The amalgamated, and thus easily disassembled, constitution of corporations was also evident when Chevron-Texaco executives disowned responsibility for the environmental and health effects of the company's Ecuadorian subsidiary (Sawyer 2001) and when Coca-Cola directors first created a system of semi-independent local franchises around the world, later replaced them with a consolidated and standardized system, and then switched back to using franchises again (Foster 2008). Despite the great amount of labor that is invested in trying to actualize individual personhood for corporations, these efforts continually fail to create the autonomy and integrity that the ideal of the individual suggests. Moreover, the figures of the subcontractor, the consultant, and the temporary worker point to the emergence of a global economic network in which the "bodies" of individual companies are unstable. Ethnographic evidence thus reveals the multiple respects in which business corporations do not embody the ideal of the individual any more than humans do. If corporations are not individuals-writ-large, how are we to understand people's experience of them as powerful agents? What explains the palpable agency of corporations in the world?

The Corporate Effect

The critical study of the state offers analytical tools for scrutinizing the workings of transnational corporations, especially the apparent contradiction between the portrayal of business corporations as individual agents and their organization as porous webs of mutable parts. Scholars already have noted that corporations often take on the roles and privileges of state institutions and agents in times and places where the latter are absent. Although companies do sometimes reoccupy spaces abandoned by the state and mimic their actions, the history of the Argentine oil industry illustrates a more complex and bidirectional resemblance between state and corporate practice. First, in the twentieth century, the paternal state and the paternal company mirrored each other in a way that makes it impossible to identify which one is the original and which the reflection. Both housed, educated, healed, and, in the process, disciplined citizens. In fact, parastatal companies such as YPF thus illustrate that it is not always possible to determine where the state ends and the business begins. Then, at the turn of the twenty-first century, both state and corporate social services were eliminated in the name of ending *asistencialismo*, and welfare support given through official institutions was replaced by assistance given through personal connections to state or corporate representatives. The behavior of Shell's representatives in Dock Sud had much in common with that of the Peronist punteros and manzaneras. This is because both the state and the oil companies were heavily invested in defining, promoting, and executing neoliberalismo. Yet despite these overlaps between state and corporate practice, there is a curious disconnect between the sophisticated theorization of the agency of states and the insufficient theorization of the agency of corporations.

Anthropologists and other scholars have shown the great amount of cultural, discursive, and bureaucratic labor needed to construct "the state" as a coherent and unitary entity that can act on its citizen-subjects. Just as people continually fail to live up to the ideal of the individual, this work demonstrates, so too the state fails to embody the sovereignty that liberal theory attributes to it. Scholars have documented how states are made up of numerous pieces that work together at some times and at cross purposes at others. Instead of the state being envisioned as a singular agent, it is better conceived as the result of practices of organization and representation that "create the effect of an enduring structure apparently external to those practices" but really generated by them (Mitchell 1999: 78; see also Adams 1988). Timothy Mitchell (1999) has retold the history of U.S. involvement in oil extraction in the Middle East in order to illustrate that the boundaries of the state are not as stable as they usually seem. Whereas he highlighted the legal, financial, and military activities used to generate and sustain the state, anthropologists point to the importance of affective (Stoler 2004) and biopolitical (Ferme 2004) processes at work. This scholarship shows from multiple angles that the state is not a bounded entity, fixed structure, or even a sphere of action, but a contingent *effect* of diverse governing activities—actions that all need to be constantly repeated in order for the "fiction" of the state to be maintained.

Mitchell's term the "state effect" (1999: 78) suggests the possibility of a parallel but imperfectly analogous phenomenon that I call the *corporate effect*. This conceptualization reveals that business corporations are composed of the individualized "faces" of corporate personhood and the disarticulated "bodies" of corporate organization, much like the modern nation-state is made up of a "state-idea" and a "state-system" (Adams 1988). I follow Mitchell in arguing that corporations—states and businesses—are constantly being remade as coherent entities, though I am also mindful of the lessons from the feminist scholarship I discuss in Chapter 2 that such effects are the result of contingent cultural processes, not manifestations of the needs of capitalism. The powerful coupling of the abstract notion of "the company" and the material manifestation of incorporated business firms is thus the effect of a contingent fusion of several different developments in the contemporary moment. These processes include the integration of oil production around the world into a concentrated network dominated by a very small number of giant corporations that manage numerous subcontractors combined with the globalization of national oil markets worldwide. The expansion of the legal fiction of corporate personhood, the granting of citizenship rights to these "persons," and the rise of corporate social responsibility movements are also crucial developments that helped create a corporate effect. These processes work together to enable oil companies to seem to be singular agents that can act on employees, consumers, neighbors, and others as they simultaneously allow these corporations to be organized as a fluctuating assemblage of expendable parts. Although these processes can seem inexorable, it is important to remember that the corporate effect that is being produced is not a stable structure but a fusion of facade and organization that is constantly being erected. In order to maintain the effect of oil companies' power, particular symbols, subjects, and substances are repeatedly generated and regenerated. The news is full of examples of oil companies' muscular exercise of control, yet corporate power can also be quite subtle, intimate, and vulnerable. This means that it is more open to modification than it seems, for it is constructed out of uncountable micropractices of numerous people—employees, subcontractors, day laborers, consumers, investors, and neighbors—unwittingly working together. While I do not want to suggest that the corporate edifice is easily toppled, I do suggest that it is unstable. *Resources for Reform* has illustrated that the seemingly invincible corporations that inhabit the contemporary world result from contingent historical processes. I have emphasized the contingency of this process because I want to affirm that it is open to future change. The historical path we have followed recently—one of increased consolidation of transnational oil companies and the growth of their political, economic, and social power—is not inevitable. It is constantly reimagined, recreated, and reinforced. The ongoing processes of remaking oil companies and securing their power offer avenues for imagining and forging a different future.

Notes

Introduction

Portions of the introduction and Chapters 1 and 2 previously appeared in Elana Shever (2008), "Neoliberal Associations: Property, Company, and Family in the Argentine Oil Fields," *American Ethnologist* 35(4): 701–16.

1. Naming this oil company is more than a bit confusing. Yacimientos Petrolíferos Fiscales translates as Oilfields for State Revenue. I use the anachronistic term YPF Estatal to refer to the national oil enterprise that existed from 1922 to 1992. YPF SA refers to the privatized oil corporation from 1992 to 1999. (SA stands for *sociedad anónima*, which is equivalent to "incorporated" in English.) YPF-Repsol refers to the company after Repsol, the former national oil company of Spain, purchased the controlling shares of YPF SA. This corporation is usually called Repsol-YPF or simply Repsol outside of Argentina, and sometimes within it. An overview of Repsol's formation can be found in Gavaldá 2003: 14–15.

2. For an important corrective to the assumption that money is a universal medium of exchange, see Senders and Truitt 2007, especially the chapter by Julie Chu.

3. I use the designation "Patagonia" to refer to the southern region of Argentina, despite the fact that Patagonia encompasses both Chile and Argentina, in order to avoid the awkward repetition of "Argentine Patagonia" throughout the book.

4. The only comparable state enterprise in the world at the time was in the Soviet Union (Solberg 1979), where industry was being privatized across the board.

5. Kirchner did not actually win the election over Menem. As the two candidates with the largest percentage of votes in a race in which no one held the majority, they were scheduled for a runoff election, but Menem withdrew amid predictions of a landslide defeat.

6. I draw on Anna Tsing's clarification of the term *project*. She writes that projects are "organized packages of ideas and practices that assume an at least tentative stability

through their social enactment, whether as custom, convention, trend, clubbish or professional training, institutional mandate, or government policy. A project is an institutionalized discourse with social and material effects" (2001: 4).

7. Some of the many critical studies that emphasize the failures of privatization projects around the world include Verdery 1996; Coronil 2000; Rofman, Baima de Borri and Cesilini 2000; Svampa 2005; and Ferguson 2006.

8. Examples of this kind of scholarship can be found in Gordon 1991; Barry, Osborn, and Rose 1996; and Miller and Rose 2000. Elizabeth Dunn (2004) draws from this tradition but employs ethnography to show that when a baby-food factory was privatized in postsocialist Poland, foreign norms of rationality and subjectivity were introduced but not faithfully replicated on the ground.

9. Some excellent examples of the ethnography examining governing by nonstate actors include Paley 2001; Roitman 2005; Sharma 2008; and Postero 2007.

10. Sawyer's study of oil extraction in the Ecuadorian Oriente (2004) is one of the few that examines corporate actors.

11. The Neuquén oilfield holds nearly half of Argentina's proven oil and gas reserves (Sturzenegger 2004: 50). The other two important oil regions are on the Bolivian border in the north and along the Patagonian coast in the south.

12. I have given this shanty settlement a pseudonym and not revealed its location on the map in order to protect its inhabitants from suffering any negative consequences of my description in this book.

Chapter 1

1. I have given this man and all my other informants pseudonyms, and in some cases changed personal details, in order to protect them from suffering any negative consequences of my description in this book. The names of their microenterprises are also pseudonyms. I do not give pseudonyms to public figures such as Carlos Menem or to transnational oil companies such as Repsol. However, the transnational business consultancy Morningside Advisors, discussed later in this chapter and the next, is a pseudonym.

2. *Emprendimiento* is coined from the verb *emprender*, to embark or launch.

3. See footnote 1 in the introduction for an explanation of the difference between YPF Estatal, YPF SA, and YPF-Repsol. Note that I employ the term *transnational* with reservations because it implies that nations are isomorphic with states and that the corporation transcends the boundaries of these entities. Yet the word is useful because it readily highlights one of the most salient changes brought by privatization, that is, the conversion of YPF from a company that extracts oil only from the Argentine subterritory to part of one that works in more than thirty countries.

4. This is an anachronistic statement since "the First World" is a Cold War concept, yet it is important to recognize that the reasons that Memen's statement resonated so strongly for Argentines is because making the country more like Europe or North America had long had been a promise that seemed just out of reach.

5. This assertion can be found in sources that cross theoretical divides. See, for instance, Bourdieu 1998 and Harvey 2005 cited in Freeman 2007. The growing anthropological scholarship on entrepreneurship emphasizes the value placed on "flexibility" and its gendered quality (Isik 2010).

6. This point draws from Susan McKinnon's critique of the assumption that kinship and economy have become separate spheres in modern societies (McKinnon and Cannell 2010).

7. While some scholars emphasize how contemporary kinship practices question the equation of father with genitor and encourage innovations in familial composition, others focus on how technologies can reinscribe normative notions of paternity, authority, and property. Sarah Franklin (2003), for one, argues that in vitro fertilization and cloning reconfigure biological reproduction into a novel resource for the production of capital accumulation and the constitution of "technoscientific fatherhood" (104). While Franklin focuses on questions of property, Lawrence Cohen (2001; 2005) highlights the crucial role of care in articulating kinship, law, and biomedical technologies through his analysis of organ transplant in India.

8. The Mapuche have struggled ever since for rights and recognition in a state and popular culture that ignores their very existence (Briones and Lanata 2002; Briones 2005).

9. For a summary of Alberdi's vision, see Chapter 16 of *Basesy Puntos de Partida para la Organización Politica de la República Argentina* [1852] 1979, reprinted in Nouzeilles and Montaldo 2002: 95–101.

10. See also Gadano 2007. Both Solberg and Gadano point out that Luis Huergo, the engineer who headed the Petroleum Bureau within the Ministry of Agriculture from 1910 to 1913, expressed some of these ideas sixteen years earlier.

11. For a discussion of kinship as the giving and receiving of care in another context, see Borneman 1997.

12. Ong (2006: 163–65) and Benson (2008b) emphasize the regulatory and disciplinary techniques of contract production, but not the affective ones. Ferguson (2006: 204–7) points out that contracting was a common colonial governing technique.

Chapter 2

1. *Público* can mean available to everyone; published or disclosed; an audience; or an individual spectator, reader, or client, in addition to state-owned.

2. Kregg Hetherington (2009) describes the distinctive meaning of "privatization" in rural Paraguay and the corresponding changes in laws, meaning, and land use. Despite the differences between the Argentine and Paraguayan cases, his article provides further evidence that legal "reforms" made in the name of increasing citizens' property ownership can result in cementing their exclusion from it.

3. The easy availability of foreign loans, in which funds from Middle Eastern oil profits were funneled through U.S. banks, also facilitated the enormous military expenditures that sustained the dictatorship's control. YPF's debt multiplied sixteenfold be-

tween 1976 and 1983, reaching $6 billion by the fall of the dictatorship (Gavaldá 2003: 28). The state's foreign debt rose another 106 percent between 1980 and 1989, to reach $16.4 billion by the end of the decade (Manzetti 1999: 82). For a general discussion of how petrodollars became invested in the Global South, see Harvey 2005: 27–31.

4. Menem issued 336 executive decrees, while only 35 had previously been issued since the signing of the 1853 constitution (Llanos 2002: 87). Yet Argentina has been characterized by strong presidential authority since the creation of that constitution, which granted the president the authority to initiate legislation and to make decrees without the consent of Congress. The dictatorship that punctured the democratic regimes of the twentieth century further strengthened the executive branch. This did not change following the return to constitutional democracy in 1983, and presidents have assumed roles that the constitution assigned to Congress, including creating new laws and modifying or repealing existing ones (Llanos 2002: 20).

5. The CGT splintered into three factions: the largest one supported Menem in exchange for political appointments and economic concessions, a smaller one remained oppositional, and a third one created an alternative federation (Murillo 1997: 82–88). After the majority of unions decided to negotiate with the Menem administration, a much weakened CGT reunited under the leadership of the first faction and joined the coalition of actors supporting neoliberal structural adjustment. The actions of the CGT were widely interpreted as an indication that Menem had effectively swayed the Peronist majority to support his reform program.

6. Problems with the state developmentalist approach became painfully clear during the 1980s debt crisis. In Argentina, state protection of domestic industries had created an elite class of national business owners with guaranteed contracts, high profits, and little motive to lower commodity prices or to provide quality services. This was particularly apparent in the oil sector where YPF paid some of its contractors more for refining gasoline than it charged its consumers at the pump. Neoliberal advocates effectively used this history to portray privatization as the only solution to state insolvency and economic decline, and thereby made it seem inevitable.

7. Cavallo was exemplary of this new class of economic experts. He received a second doctorate in economics from Harvard University in 1977 and then returned to his native Córdoba to collaborate with business leaders there and establish a think tank (Fundación Mediterránea) that produced policy papers calling for the privatization of state-owned companies. He was able to execute some of its ideas on the national stage when he briefly served as president of the Central Bank near the end of the military dictatorship, but more effectively under Menem (Teichman 1997: 35). Following two years as Menem's foreign minister, Cavallo reached the height of his influence when he took over the Ministry of the Economy in 1991. He brought with him a team of economic experts who had training and experience similar to his (Llanos 2002: 90–91).

8. See Acuña 1994; Gerchunoff and Cánovas 1996; Manzetti 1999; and Etchemendy 2001 for more detailed accounts of this process.

9. These numbers, which were often repeated to me by YPFianos and other Argentines, are also published in Manzetti 1999: 115.

10. When I arrived to do fieldwork in Plaza Huincul and Cutral Có a decade after La Pueblada, many residents were angered by the researchers who briefly came to the towns to investigate the protest and never returned. To differentiate myself from them, I discussed La Pueblada only when people raised it with me. Despite this restriction, the event came up frequently in my discussions with YPFianos and other town residents, who were both proud of its fame and frustrated by its failure to significantly change their situations. My quotations here draw not only from my own interviews, but also from the most ethnographically rich and analytically insightful of the studies of La Pueblada, Auyero's analysis of the event as a "search for recognition" (Auyero 2003: 9). I also consulted Sánchez 1997; Klachko 2002; García 2003; and the archives of several national and regional newspapers.

11. Like Morningside Advisors, the Cellis and Associates law firm and the Muller-Lange Group are pseudonyms.

12. YPF SA's revenue was estimated at $5.6 billion the previous year. The company controlled almost half of the retail market in Argentina and had three billion barrels of proven reserves. This put YPF-Repsol on the list of the top ten oil companies in terms of petroleum reserves and production capacity in the world.

13. Diana Kapiszewski, personal communication, 2005.

14. To legally qualify as a PyME, a company must have annual revenues less than 86.4 million pesos (approximately $25 million) a year. This gives them limited tax advantages.

Chapter 3

1. FUNDA stands for Families United for a New Democratic Argentina, a pseudonym I created for a prominent piquetero movement. The Sunshine Center is also a pseudonym.

2. For cultural citizenship, see Rosaldo 1994; Ginsburg 2005; and Rofel 2007. For flexible citizenship, see Ong 1999. For biological citizenship, see Petryna 2002. For indigenous citizenship in South America, see Gordillo 2006; and Postero 2007. For insurgent citizenship, see Holston 2008. For consumer and corporate citizenship, see Mazzarella 2003; Özyürek 2004; Jain 2006; Foster 2008; and García Canclini [1995] 2001.

3. The argument that citizenship is tightly bound to consumption as well as to nationalism is not entirely new. Anderson's *Imagined Communities* (1983) can be read as a treatise on the importance of discursive consumption in the construction of citizenship in Latin America. Whereas newspapers were decisive in the construction of Argentine-ness among the urban elite in the eighteenth and nineteenth centuries, an oral tradition of stories, songs, games, and jokes was crucial for rural people (de la Fuentes 2000). Radio and film significantly contributed to the formation of national belonging among a much wider audience in the twentieth century (García Canclini [1995] 2001:

89–90, 109–12). García Canclini ([1995] 2001) points out that "the exercise of citizenship has always been associated with the capacity to appropriate commodities and with ways of using them" (15). He suggests that scholars reconceive Anderson's "imagined political community" as "an interpretative community of consumers" in which citizens differently interact with the discourses and objects that circulate through transnational circuits.

4. These competing conceptions of personhood are further discussed in the conclusion. For insightful discussion of possessive individualism, see MacPherson 1962 and subsequent interpretations by Strathern 1999 and Rofel 2007. For Melanesian understandings of personhood, see Strathern 1988.

5. Inspired by the writings of Michel Foucault, I join those scholars who theorize liberalism as a modern form of political intervention, yet I understand it as a "family" of interventions that resemble each other in important ways while also reflecting the particularities of their specific historical trajectories and geographic settings. In Argentina, too many studies reduce the history of the twentieth century to a battle between the opposing ideologies of Peronism and liberalism, while ignoring the ways in which their ideas and practices overlapped. Out of the vast literature on Argentine liberalism, the works that have most influenced my understanding are Halperín Donghi 1980; Halperín Donghi 1988; Adelman 1999; and Sábato [1998] 2001.

6. Esteban Echeverría, one of the leading figures in the Generation of 1837, proposed a form of graduated citizenship that differentiated between *el pueblo*, constituted by all inhabitants of the geographical region, and *los ciudanos* (the citizens), those among the inhabitants who proved themselves capable of exercising government. As the historian Jeremy Adelman (1999) eloquently asserts, "Echeverría's 'democratic' clarion call is consistent with a broader political trend to wind down the effects of revolution, [to] scupper any transition from political to social claims-making, and to rebuild polities that endorse the rights of property and not of broad social membership" (178).

7. For instance, suffrage was extended to adult males in the wake of independence, then further restricted in the 1820s and 1830s (Sábato [1998] 2001: 4).

8. See Sábato [1998] 2001 for a description of how organizations such as mutual aid societies, social clubs, immigrant associations, trade guilds, and philanthropic committees mobilized sizeable numbers of people for political demonstrations, celebrations, and commemorations.

9. The enormous literature on Peronism swings from condemnations of it as fascist to celebrations of it as socialist revolutionary to careful historical studies that bring out its ambiguities. The works that most influenced my interpretation of Peronist citizenship include James 1988; Plotkin 2003; Milanesio 2006; and Elena 2007.

10. The institutions already expressing criticism of the liberal regime included civic organizations that had grown into trade unions and forcefully demanded a greater share of the wealth they produced. In addition, a small group of successful immigrant merchants challenged the established elites' privileged position in state and society. The lib-

eral statesmen saw a crisis looming, and in response, some advocated the deepening of democratic institutions while others questioned the validity of liberal principles. The former successfully advanced a law in 1912 that established secret ballots and mandatory voting for adult males. Four years later, the candidate from the Radical Party won the presidency for the first time. However, the latter grew into a powerful Catholic nationalist block that displaced the Radicals and ruled Argentina during the 1930s.

11. Mariano Plotkin (2003) demonstrates that the Eva Perón Foundation did not merely incorporate sectors of the population that the state otherwise could not; it also served as a counterbalance to the increasingly powerful unions.

12. The Spanish term *ama de casa* (literally "house lover") does not carry the same connotations that the English "housewife" does today.

13. Plotkin documents how businesses and unions gave "donations" to the Eva Perón Foundation in exchange for preferential treatment by the state (2003: 150–51).

14. For a discussion of the transnational routes through which tango came to stand for Argentina, see Savigliano 1995.

15. Petrobras was once Brazil's state company and is now a public/private transnational corporation.

16. The price of Shell regular gasoline went up by 2.9 percent on March 9 and lowered 3.4 percent on April 6. Although Exxon also lowered the price of its diesel fuel in early April, Shell did not modify its diesel fuel prices.

17. To investigate the enactment of the boycott in the media, I tracked a variety of news sources, including the conservative newspaper *La Nación*, the left-leaning paper *Página/12* (both published in Buenos Aires), *Río Negro* (published in Patagonia), and several national television and radio programs. Most of the statements by public figures I quote in the pages that follow can be found in multiple sources, so I provide references only to those that are unique.

18. This is not to say that state entities under the Kirchner administration did not use law to regulate economic relations as well.

19. Holston and Caldeira (1998) provide a useful critique of this limited definition of democracy.

20. For extensive discussion of D'Elía and the FTV, see Svampa and Pereyra 2003.

21. For a critical discussion of the role of foreign oil companies in the 1930 coup, see Solberg 1979: 153–55.

22. The march and rally were formally organized by the Argentine chapter of the Primer Foro Latinoamericano y Caribeño de las Trabajadoras y los Trabajadores Energéticos (First Latin American and Caribbean Forum of Energy Workers), which would be held in Caracas later that year.

23. Coronil (1997) analyzes the character of the pirate in Venezuelan popular imaginaries of oil industry actors as simultaneously "the adventurer in search of plunder and the impostor whose false appearances fails to conceal his or her ineptitude" (319). As in Venezuela, in Argentina pirates refer to unapologetic usurpers of both national mate-

rial resources and legitimate state authority. Also note the role of pirates in Shell's imaginary (Royal Dutch Shell 2005).

24. This history is deliberately vague so as to preserve the anonymity of the movement and its participants.

25. The Ministry of Social Development was headed, not coincidentally, by Néstor Kirchner's sister, Alicia Kirchner.

Chapter 4

Portions of this chapter and the conclusion appeared in Elana Shever (2010), "Engendering the Company: Corporate Personhood and the 'Face' of an Oil Company in Metropolitan Buenos Aires," *Political and Legal Anthropology Review* 33(1): 26–46.

1. My examination of Shell's effort to transform its community relations program and regender its public face draws insight from the scholarship on the gendering of the state. In particular, the situation in Argentina shares similarities with the one in India that Aradhana Sharma has explored (2006; 2008). I document a similar shift toward socially feminine forms of power by a corporation rather than a state agency.

2. Benson (2008a) links Emmanuel Levinas's discussion of the face as a site of ethics with Deleuze and Guattari's discussion of faciality as a representation of social power in order to argue that "faces are actively coded as allegorical signs and invested with cultural meanings in practices of everyday life" (596). Moreover, "generic facial representations are detachable images that can circulate as symbols of place, icons of a group of people, and tools of power and resistance" (597).

3. In 1995, it came to light that Shell was planning to sink an old oil storage and tanker loading buoy, called the Brent Spar, in the North Sea when it was no longer serviceable. The company changed its plans after public outcry over environmental risks. At the same time, Shell was supporting the authoritarian regime in Nigeria that was committing human rights violations, including violently repressing criticism of both the government and the oil company by the Ogoni people of the oil-rich Niger Delta. Ken Saro-Wiwa led a social movement called the Movement for the Survival of the Ogoni Peoples (MOSOP) that criticized the collusion between Shell and the Nigerian state. He and eight other MOSOP activists were executed after a sham trial. In 2009, Royal Dutch Shell settled the lawsuit alleging the company committed crimes against humanity for its involvement in the men's death by agreeing to pay $15.5 million to the victims' families and the Ogoni.

4. This governing technique was pioneered by Hilda "Chiche" González de Duhalde, who headed both the women's branch of the Peronist Party and Buenos Aires's Consejo Provincial de la Familia y Desarrollo Humano (Provincial Council for the Family and Human Development) during Menem's second term as president (Auyero 2000: 104).

5. A study funded by a Japanese NGO found that children living in Villa Inflamable, the shantytown closest to the Polo Petroquímico Dock Sud, were exposed to dangerous levels of lead, benzene, and toluene. Auyero and Swistun's ethnography of Villa Inflam-

able (2009) analyzes how different actors understood this study and the issue of pollution. Children in Goldendas were tested for lead poisoning through an accord between the mayor and Shell, but they were never treated because a new mayor refused to recognize his predecessor's agreement.

6. The incident that Bruno referred to was when an YPF oil tanker called the *Perito Moreno* exploded while sitting full of oil in the Dock Sud Canal in June 1984. The initial explosion killed the crew and the Dock Sud residents who had gathered by the docks to receive leftovers from the crew's party. The tanker continued to burn for two weeks, obliterating two quays of the Dock Sud Canal and everything around them, blowing out windows as much as a kilometer away from the canal, and spewing toxic debris into the air that blanketed Dock Sud in a layer of black soot. One longtime resident of the settlement closest to the petrochemical complex, then called La Costa ("the coast"), recalled that when she ran out of her parents' house, it felt "as if the flames burnt you up." She and her neighbors could not immediately flee the neighborhood because the only road leading out became impassible. While the dispute over environmental damages from the explosion dragged along legal avenues for years, the burned and rusting hulk of the tanker remained in the destroyed quay until 1996, when it was moved to the swampy end of the uncompleted canal; it finally was broken up and removed in 2005. In the meantime, the neighborhood was renamed Villa Inflamable ("flammable shantytown") to mark the event that most significantly shaped its history.

7. Her reckoning of seventy-five years began with the refinery's first production in 1931, not Shell's first illegal construction in Dock Sud in 1913.

8. Compare this to the golf games that are common extensions of business beyond the office.

9. Other scholars have argued that a Janis-faced form of empowerment, in which "NGOs may disempower those they seek to aid," is characteristic of neoliberal governance (Gledhill 2004: 335).

10. A similar process occurred in other Latin American countries where NGOs shifted from direct political action to cooperation with state institutions and foreign funders (Postero 2007). Existing studies tend to emphasize the importance of transnational donors but overlook the crucial role of corporations in this shift.

11. The FUNDA leaders knew that many families in Goldendas were eligible for state assistance but were not enrolled in the food rations program because their children had not been properly certified as underweight. Beatriz Rocio, the FUNDA health promoter in Goldendas, used a measuring stick constructed from pieces of fruit crates and an inaccurate bathroom scale to make initial measurements of the children. She then sent the parents of many of them to wait in long lines at the state clinic to obtain an appointment for an official measurement and return with their children at the designated time. The people gathered in the Sunshine Center that day saw Creating Bonds as a way to eliminate these visits to the state clinic, which presented an obstacle to their access to state services.

12. See the Shell global homepage at http://www.shell.com for official financial disclosures.

13. Activists' practice of holding corporations personally responsible for the environmental conditions, health, and welfare of people around the world not only recognizes the role of corporations in causing the problems but also responds to a moment in which nonstate entities have assumed, but not fulfilled, tasks that were previously the (also unfulfilled) responsibility of the state (Foster 2008: 163–65).

Conclusion

1. See, for example, her comments on the privatization of television stations (http://www.presidencia.gov.ar/discursos).

2. See http://www.repsol.com for financial disclosure information.

3. Nash's *We Eat the Mines and the Mines Eat Us* (1979) is a landmark for this tradition because of the way it integrates the critical examination of global capitalism with the study of established anthropological themes such as ritual and kinship.

4. One of the clearest elaborations of this idea is found in a sixteenth-century legal text:

> For the King has in him two Bodies, *viz.* a Body natural, and a Body politic. His Body natural (if it be considered in itself) is a Body mortal, subject to all Infirmities that come by Nature or Accident, to the Imbecility of Infancy or old Age, and to the like Defects that happen to the natural Bodies of other People. But his Body politic is a Body that cannot be seen or handled, consisting of Policy and Government, and constituted for the Direction of the People, and the Management of the public weal, and this Body is utterly void of Infancy, and old Age, and other natural Defects and Imbecilities, which the Body natural is subject to, and for this Cause, what the King does in his Body politic, cannot be invalidated or frustrated by any Disability of his natural Body. (Kantorowicz [1957] 1997: 7).

References

Acuña, Carlos. 1994. "Politics and Economics in the Argentina of the Nineties (or Why the Future No Longer Is What It Used to Be)." In *Democracy, Markets, and Structural Reform in Latin America: Argentina, Bolivia, Brazil, Chile, and Mexico.* W. C. Smith, C. H. Acuña, and E. A. Gamarra, eds. Pp. 30–73. New Brunswick, NJ: Transaction.

Adams, Philip. 1988. "Notes on the Difficulty of Studying the State." *Journal of Historical Sociology* 1(1): 58–89.

Adelman, Jeremy. 1999. *Republic of Capital: Buenos Aires and the Legal Transformation of the Atlantic World.* Stanford, CA: Stanford University Press.

Alberdi, Juan Bautista. [1852] 1979. *Bases y Puntos de Partida para la Organización Política de la República Argentina.* Buenos Aires: Centro Editor de América Latina.

Alexander, Myrna, Carlos Corti, and World Bank. 1993. *Argentina's Privatization Program: Experience, Issues, and Lessons.* Washington, DC: World Bank.

Anderson, Benedict. [1983] 1991. *Imagined Communities: Reflections on the Origin and Spread of Nationalism.* New York: Verso.

Auyero, Javier. 2000. *Poor People's Politics: Peronist Survival Networks and the Legacy of Evita.* Durham, NC: Duke University Press.

———. 2003. *Contentious Lives: Two Argentine Women, Two Protests, and the Quest for Recognition.* Durham, NC: Duke University Press.

———. 2005. "Protest and Politics in Contemporary Argentina." In *Argentine Democracy: The Politics of Institutional Weakness.* S. Levitsky and M. V. Murillo, eds. Pp. 250–68. University Park, PA: Penn State University Press.

Auyero, Javier, and Debora Swistun. 2009. *Flammable: Environmental Suffering in an Argentine Shantytown.* New York: Oxford University Press.

Babb, Sarah. 2004. *Managing Mexico: Economists from Nationalism to Neoliberalism.* Princeton, NJ: Princeton University Press.

Bakan, Joel. 2005. *The Corporation: The Pathological Pursuit of Profit and Power*. New York: Free Press.

Bandieri, Susana. 2005. "Asuntos de Familia—Construcción del Poder en la Patagonia: El caso de Neuquén." *Boletín del Instituto de Historia Argentina y Americana "Dr. Emilio Ravignani."* 28(2): 65–94.

Barry, Andrew, Thomas Osborn, and Nikolas Rose, eds. 1996. *Foucault and Political Reason: Liberalism, Neo-liberalism and Rationalities of Government*. Chicago: University of Chicago Press.

Bauman, Zygmunt. 1998. *Globalization: The Human Consequences*. New York: Columbia University Press.

Belini, Claudio. 2006. "El Grupo Bunge y la Política Económica del Primer Peronismo." *Latin American Research Review* 41(1): 27–50.

Benson, Peter. 2008a. "El Campo: Faciality and Structural Violence in Farm Labor Camps." *Cultural Anthropology* 23(4): 589–629.

———. 2008b. "Good Clean Tobacco: Philip Morris, Biocapitalism, and the Social Course of Stigma in North Carolina." *American Ethnologist* 35(3): 357–79.

Berle, Adolph, and Gardiner Means. 1932. *The Modern Corporation and Private Property*. New York: Macmillan.

Borneman, John. 1997. "Caring and Being Cared For: Displacing Marriage, Kinship, Gender and Sexuality. *International Social Science Journal* 49: 573–84.

Borneman, John, ed. 2004. *Death of the Father: An Anthropology of the End in Political Authority*. New York: Berghahn.

Bouquet, Mary. 1985. *Family, Servants and Visitors: The Farm Household in Nineteenth and Twentieth Century Devon*. Norwich, UK: Geo Books.

———. 2001. "Making Kinship, with an Old Reproductive Technology." In *Relative Values: Reconfiguring Kinship Studies*. S. Franklin and S. McKinnon, eds. Pp. 85–115. Durham, NC: Duke University Press.

Bourdieu, Pierre. 1998. "The Essence of Neoliberalism." In *Le Monde Diplomatique*. http://mondediplo.com/1998/12/08bourdieu.

Brenner, Neil, Jamie Peck, and Nik Theodore. 2010a. "After Neoliberalization?" *Globalizations* 7(3): 327–345.

———. 2010b. "Variegated Neoliberalization: Geographies, Modalities, Pathways." *Global Networks* 10(2): 182–222.

Brenner, Neil, and Nik Theodore. 2002. Preface: "From the 'New Localism' to the Spaces of Neoliberalism. *Antipode* 34(3): 341–47.

Briones, Claudia. 2005. "Formaciones de Alteridad: Contextos Globales, Procesos Nacionales y Provinciales." In *Cartografías Argentinas: Políticas Indigenistas y Formaciones Provinciales de Alteridad*. C. Briones, ed. Pp. 11–43. Buenos Aires: Antropofagia.

Briones, Claudia, and José Luis Lanata. 2002. "Living on the Edge (Still)." In *Contemporary Perspectives on the Native Peoples of Pampa, Patagonia, and Tierra del Fuego*. C. Briones and J. L. Lanata, eds. Pp. 1–31. Westport, CT: Bergin and Garvey.

Canitrot, Adolfo. 1994. "Crisis and Transformation of the Argentine State (1978–1992)." In *Democracy, Markets, and Structural Reform in Latin America: Argentina, Bolivia, Brazil, Chile, and Mexico*. W. C. Smith, C. H. Acuña, and E. A. Gamarra, eds. Pp. 75–102. New Brunswick, NJ: Transaction.

Carsten, Janet. 1997. *The Heat of the Hearth: The Process of Kinship in a Malay Fishing Community*. Oxford: Clarendon.

Cohen, Lawrence. 2001. "The Other Kidney: Biopolitics beyond Recognition." *Body and Society* 7(2–3): 9–29.

———. 2005. "Operability, Bioavailability, and Exception." In *Global Assemblages: Technology, Politics, and Ethics as Anthropological Problems*. A. Ong and S. Collier, eds. Pp. 79–90. Malden, MA: Blackwell.

Comaroff, Jean, and John Comaroff. 2000. "Millennial Capitalism: First Thoughts on a Second Coming. *Public Culture* 12(2): 291–343.

Contreras, Carlos Alberto. n.d. "Cutralco: Historia de su Origen Relato del Doctor Víctor Ezio Zani a Carlos Alberto Contreras." Unpublished manuscript.

Coombe, Rosemary. 1998. *The Cultural Life of Intellectual Properties: Authorship, Appropriation and the Law*. Durham, NC: Duke University Press.

Coronil, Fernando. 1997. *The Magical State: Nature, Money, and Modernity in Venezuela*. Chicago: University of Chicago Press.

———. 2000. "Towards a Critique of Globalcentrism: Speculations on Capitalism's Nature." *Public Culture* 12(2): 351–74.

Costallat, Karina. 1997. "Efectos de las Privatizaciones y la Relación Estado-Sociedad en la Instancia Provincial y Local: El Caso Cutral Có-Plaza Huincul." *Cuaderno Cepas* 7: 1–33.

De la Fuente, Ariel. 2000. *Children of Facundo: Caudillo and Gaucho Insurgency during the Argentine State-Formation Process (La Rioja, 1853–1870)*. Durham, NC: Duke University Press.

Di Chiro, Giovanna. 2003. "Beyond Ecoliberal 'Common Futures': Environmental Justice, Toxic Touring, and a Transcommunal Politics of Place." In *Race, Nature, and the Politics of Difference*. D. S. Moore, J. Kosek, and A. Pandian, eds. Pp. 204–32. Durham, NC: Duke University Press.

Dunn, Elizabeth. 2004. *Privatizing Poland: Baby Food, Big Business, and the Remaking of Labor*. Ithaca, NY: Cornell University Press.

Elena, Eduardo. 2007. "Peronist Consumer Politics and the Problem of Domesticating Markets in Argentina, 1943–1955." *Hispanic American Historical Review* 87(1): 111–50.

ENARSA. 2004. *Ley ENARSA*. Buenos Aires: Energía Argentina Sociedad Anónima. http://www.enarsa.com.ar.

Etchemendy, Sebastián. 2001. "Constructing Reform Coalitions: The Politics of Compensation in Argentina's Economic Liberalization." *Latin American Politics and Society* 43(3): 1–36.

———. 2005. "Old Actors in New Markets: Transforming the Populist/Industrial Coalition in Argentina, 1989–2000." In *Argentine Democracy: The Politics of Institutional Weakness*. Pp. 62–87. University Park, PA: Penn State University Press.

Favaro, Orietta, and Mario Arias Bucciarelli. 1999. "La Conformación de una Provincia Exportadora de Energía: Neuquén, 1950–1980." In *Neuquén: La Construcción de un Orden Estatal*. O. Favaro, ed. Pp. 225–51. Neuquén: Centro de Estudios Históricos de Estado, Política y Cultura, Universidad Nacional del Comahue.

Favaro, Orietta, and Graciela Iuorno. 1999. "Entre Territorio y Provincia: Libaneses y Sirios: Comercio y Política en el Neuquén." In *Neuquén: La Construcción de un Orden Estatal*. O. Favaro, ed. Pp. 57–80. Neuquén: Centro de Estudios Históricos de Estado, Política y Cultura, Universidad Nacional del Comahue.

Ferguson, James. 1994. *The Anti-Politics Machine: "Development," Depoliticization, and Bureaucratic Power in Lesotho*. Minneapolis: University of Minnesota Press.

———. 2005. "Seeing Like an Oil Company: Spaces, Security, and Global Capitalism in Neoliberal Africa." *American Anthropologist* 107(3): 377–82.

———. 2006. *Global Shadows: Essays on Africa in the Neoliberal World Order*. Durham, NC: Duke University Press.

Ferme, Mariane. 2004. "Deterritorialized Citizenship and the Resonances of the Sierra Leonean State." In *Anthropology in the Margins of the State*. V. Das and D. Poole, eds. Pp. 81–115. Santa Fe, NM: School of American Research Press.

Foster, Robert J. 1996. "Commercial Mass Media in Papua New Guinea: Notes on Agency, Bodies, and Commodity Consumption." *Visual Anthropology Review* 12(2): 1–17.

———. 2002. *Materializing the Nation: Commodities, Consumption, and Media in Papua New Guinea*. Bloomington: Indiana University Press.

———. 2008. *Coca-globalization: Following Soft Drinks from New York to New Guinea*. New York: Palgrave.

Foster, Robert J., ed. 1995. *Nation Making: Emergent Identities in Postcolonial Melanesia*. Ann Arbor: University of Michigan Press.

Franklin, Sarah. 2003. "Kinship, Genes, and Cloning: Life after Dolly." In *Genetic Nature/ Culture: Anthropology and Science beyond the Two-Culture Divide*. A. Goodman, D. Heath, and M. S. Lindee, eds. Pp. 95–110. Berkeley: University of California Press.

Freeman, Carla. 2007. "The 'Reputation' of Neoliberalism." *American Ethnologist* 34(2): 252–67.

Gadano, Nicolás. 2007. "Urgency and Betrayal: Three Attempts to Foster Private Investment in Argentina's Oil Industry." In *Populism and Natural Resources*. W. Hogan, ed. Cambridge, MA: Harvard University John F. Kennedy School of Government.

García, Analía. 2003. "Consecuencias de la Privatización de YPF en un Enclave Petrolero: Cutral Có y Plaza Huincul en el Marco de una Redefinición Institucional." Tesis de Licenciatura Buenos Aires: Universidad de Buenos Aires.

García Canclini, Néstor. [1995] 2001. *Consumers and Citizens: Multicultural Conflicts in the Process of Globalization*. G. Yúdice, trans. Minneapolis: University of Minnesota Press.

Garth, Bryant, and Yves Dezalay. 2002. *The Internationalization of Palace Wars: Lawyers, Economists, and the Contest to Transform Latin American States*. Chicago: Chicago University Press.

Gavaldá, Marc. 2003. *La Recolonización: Repsol en América Latina: Inversión y Resistencias*. Barcelona: Icaria Editorial.

Gerchunoff, Pablo, and Guillermo Cánovas. 1996. "Privatization: The Argentine Experience." In *Bigger Economies, Smaller Governments: Privatization in Latin America*. W. Glade and R. Corona, eds. Pp. 191–218. Boulder, CO: Westview.

Gibb, George Sweet, and Evelyn Knowlton. 1956. *The Resurgent Years, 1911–1927*. New York: Harper.

Gindis, David. 2009. "From Fictions and Aggregates to Real Entities in the Theory of the Firm." *Journal of Institutional Economics* 5(1): 25–46.

Ginsburg, Faye. 2005. "Blak Screens and Cultural Citizenship." *Visual Anthropology Review* 21(1–2): 80–97.

Gledhill, John. 2004. "Neoliberalism." In *A Companion to the Anthropology of Politics*. D. Nugent and J. Vincent, eds. Pp. 332–48. Malden, MA: Blackwell.

Goldstein, Donna. 2003. *Laughter Out of Place: Race, Class, Violence, and Sexuality in a Rio Shantytown*. Berkeley: University of California Press.

Gordillo, Gastón. 2006. "The Crucible of Citizenship: ID-paper Fetishism in the Argentinean Chaco." *American Ethnologist* 33(2): 162–76.

Gordon, Colin. 1991. "Governmental Rationality: An Introduction." In *The Foucault Effect: Studies in Governmentality, with Two Lectures by and an Interview with Michel Foucault*. G. Burchell, C. Gordon, and P. Miller, eds. Pp. 1–51. Chicago: University of Chicago Press.

Gorelik, Adrián. 1987. "La Arquitectura de YPF: 1934–1943, Notas para una Interpretación de las Relaciones entre Estado, Modernidad e Identidad en la Arquitectura Argentina de los Años 30." *Anales del Instituto de Arte Americano* 24: 97–107.

Guano, Emanuela. 2002. "Spectacles of Modernity: Transnational Imagination and Local Hegemonies in Neoliberal Buenos Aires." *Cultural Anthropology* 17(2): 181–209.

Halperín Donghi, Tulio. 1988. "Argentina: Liberalism in a Country Born Liberal." In *Guiding the Invisible Hand: Economic Liberalism and the State in Latin American History*. J. L. Love and N. Jacobsen, eds. Pp. 99–116. New York: Praeger.

Halperín Donghi, Tulio, ed. 1980. *Proyecto y Construcción de una Nación: Argentina 1846–1880*. Caracas: Biblioteca Ayacucho.

Harvey, David. 2005. *A Brief History of Neoliberalism*. New York: Oxford University Press.

Hayden, Cori. 2003. *When Nature Goes Public: The Making and Unmaking of Bioprospecting in Mexico*. Princeton, NJ: Princeton University Press.

Hetherington, Kregg. 2009. "Privatizing the Private in Rural Paraguay: Precarious Lots and the Materiality of Rights." *American Ethnologist* 36(2): 224–41.

Ho, Karen. 2009. *Liquidated: An Ethnography of Wall Street*. Durham, NC: Duke University Press.

Holston, James. 2008. *Insurgent Citizenship: Disjunctions of Democracy and Modernity in Brazil.* Princeton, NJ: Princeton University Press.

Holston, James, and Arjun Appadurai. 1996. "Cities and Citizenship." *Public Culture* 8(2): 187–204.

Holston, James, and Teresa Caldeira. 1998. "Democracy, Law, and Violence: Disjunctions of Brazilian Citizenship." In *Fault Lines of Democracy in Post-Transition Latin America.* F. Agüero and J. Stark, eds. Miami: North-South Center Press.

IMF. 1998. *Argentina: Recent Economic Developments.* Washington, DC: International Monetary Fund.

INDEC. 2001. "Censo Nacional de Población, Hogares y Viviendas 2001," Vol. 2006. Buenos Aires: Instituto Nacional de Estadística y Censos.

Isik, Damla. 2010. "Personal and Global Economies: Male Carpet Manufacturers as Entrepreneurs in the Weaving Neighborhoods of Konya, Turkey." *American Ethnologist* 37(1): 53–68.

Jain, Sarah Lochlann. 2006. *Injury: The Politics of Product Design and Safety Law in the United States.* Princeton, NJ: Princeton University Press.

James, Daniel. 1988. *Resistance and Integration: Peronism and the Argentine Working Class, 1946–1976.* New York: Cambridge University Press.

Kantorowicz, Ernst. [1957] 1997. *The King's Two Bodies: A Study in Mediaeval Political Theology.* Princeton, NJ: Princeton University Press.

Kirchner, Néstor. 2005. Discursos Presidenciales. Archivo de Documentos Gubernamentales de América Latina. Austin: University of Texas at Austin Latin American Web Archiving Project. http://lanic.utexas.edu/project/archives/lagda/indexesp.html

Klachko, Paula. 2002. "La Conflictividad Social en la Argentina de los '90: El Caso de las Localidades Petroleras de Cutral Có y Plaza Huincul (1996–1997)." In *Crisis y Conflicto en el Capitalismo Latinoamericano.* B. Levy and F. Lorenc Valcarce, eds. Pp. 169–221. Buenos Aires: Consejo Latinoamericano de Ciencias Sociales.

Knight, Peter. 1998. *Profits and Principles—Does There Have to Be a Choice? The Shell Report, 1998.* London: Shell International.

Kozulj, Roberto, Victor Bravo, and Nicolas di Sbroiavacca. 1993. *La Politica de Desregulación Petrolera Argentina: Antecedentes e Impactos.* Buenos Aires: Centro Editor de América Latina.

Laclau, Ernesto. 1979. *Politics and Ideology in Marxist Theory: Capitalism, Fascism, Populism.* London: Verso.

Lamoreaux, Naomi. 2004. "Partnerships, Corporations, and the Limits on Contractual Freedom in U.S. History: An Essay in Economics, Law, and Culture." In *Constructing Corporate America: History, Politics, Culture.* K. Lipartito and D. B. Sicilia, eds. Pp. 29–65. New York: Oxford University Press.

LaPin, Deirdre. 2000. "The Leveraged Buy-In: Creating an Enabling Environment for Business through Strategic Social Investments." Paper presented at the Society for Petroleum Engineers International Conference on Health, Safety, and the Environment in Oil and Gas Exploration and Production, Stavenger, Norway, 2000. Society for Petroleum Engineers.

Livesey, Sharon, and Kate Kearins. 2002. "Transparent and Caring Corporations? A Study of Sustainability Reports by The Body Shop and Royal Dutch/Shell." *Organization and Environment* 15(3): 233–58.

Llanos, Mariana. 2001. "Understanding Presidential Power in Argentina: A Study of the Policy of Privatisation in the 1990s." *Journal of Latin American Studies* 33(1): 67–99.

———. 2002. *Privatization and Democracy in Argentina: An Analysis of President-Congress Relations.* Oxford: Palgrave.

López, Andrés. 1994. "Ajuste Estructural y Estrategias Empresarias en la Industria Petroquímica Argentina." *Desarrollo Económico* 33(132): 515–40.

MacPherson, C. B. 1962. *The Political Theory of Possessive Individualism: Hobbes to Locke.* New York: Oxford University Press.

Manzetti, Luigi. 1999. *Privatization South American Style.* New York: Oxford University Press.

Marchand, Roland. 1998. *Creating the Corporate Soul: The Rise of Public Relations and Corporate Imagery in American Big Business.* Berkeley: University of California Press.

Marcus, George. 1998. *Ethnography through Thick and Thin.* Princeton, NJ: Princeton University Press.

Mauss, Marcel. 1985. "A Category of the Human Mind: The Notion of Person; the Notion of Self." In *The Category of the Person: Anthropology, Philosophy, History.* M. Carrithers, S. Collins, and S. Lukes, eds. Pp. 1–25. New York: Cambridge University Press.

Mazzarella, William. 2003. *Shoveling Smoke: Advertising and Globalization in Contemporary India.* Durham, NC: Duke University Press.

McKinnon, Susan, and Fenella Cannell, eds. 2010. "Vital Relations: Kinship as a Critique of Modernity." Unpublished manuscript. Santa Fe, NM: School of Advanced Research Advanced Seminar.

Megginson, William, and Jeffry Netter. 2001. "From State to Market: A Survey of Empirical Studies of Privatization." *Journal of Economic Literature* 39(June): 321–89.

Milanesio, Natalia. 2006. "'The Guardians Angels of the Domestic Economy': Housewives' Responsible Consumption in Peronist Argentina." *Journal of Women's History* 18(3): 91–117.

Miller, Peter, and Nikolas Rose. 2000. "Governing Economic Life." *Economy and Society* 19(1): 1–31.

Mitchell, Timothy. 1999. "Society, Economy and the State Effect." In *State/Culture: State Formation after the Cultural Turn.* G. Steinmetz, ed. Pp. 76–97. Ithaca, NY: Cornell University Press.

Mombello, Laura. 2005. "La 'Mística Neuquina': Marcas y Disputas de Provincianía y Alteridad en una Provincia Joven." In *Cartografías Argentinas: Políticas Indigenistas y Formaciones Provinciales de Alteridad.* C. Briones, ed. Pp. 151–78. Buenos Aires: Antropofagia.

Moore, Donald S. 2005. *Suffering for Territory: Race, Place, and Power in Zimbabwe.* Durham, NC: Duke University Press.

Moore, Sally Falk. [1978] 2000. *Law as Process: An Anthropological Approach.* Hamburg: Lit Verlag.

Mosconi, Enrique. 1984. *Obras del General Enrique Mosconi.* Buenos Aires: Yacimientos Petrolíferos Fiscales.

Murillo, María Victoria. 1997. "Union Politics, Market-Oriented Reforms and the Reshaping of Argentine Corporatism." In *The New Politics of Inequality in Latin America: Rethinking Participation and Representation.* D. Chalmers, C. M. Vilas, K. Hite, S. B. Martin, K. Piester, and M. Segarra, eds. Pp. 72–95. New York: Oxford University Press.

———. 2001. *Labor Unions, Partisan Coalitions, and Market Reforms in Latin America.* New York: Cambridge University Press.

Nash, June. [1979] 1993. *We Eat the Mines and the Mines Eat Us: Dependency and Exploitation in Bolivian Tin Mines.* New York: Columbia University Press.

Nicoletti, María Andrea, and Pedro Floria Navarro. 2002. "Building an Image of the Indian People from Patagonia during the Eighteenth and Nineteenth Centuries: Science and Christening." In *Archaeological and Anthropological Perspectives on the Native Peoples of Pampa, Patagonia and Tierra Del Fuego to the Nineteenth Century.* C. Briones and J. L. Lanata, eds. Pp. 133–43. Westport, CT: Bergin and Garvey.

———. 2000. *Confluencias: Una breve historia del Neuquén.* Buenos Aires: Editorial Dunken.

Nouzeilles, Gabriela, and Graciela Montaldo, eds. 2002. *The Argentina Reader.* Durham, NC: Duke University Press.

Ong, Aihwa. 1999. *Flexible Citizenship: The Cultural Logics of Transnationality.* Durham, NC: Duke University Press.

———. 2006. *Neoliberalism as Exception.* Durham, NC: Duke University Press.

Ong, Aihwa, and Stephen J. Collier, eds. 2005. *Global Assemblages: Technology, Politics, and Ethics as Anthropological Problems.* Malden, MA: Blackwell.

Özkan, Derya, and Robert J. Foster. 2005. "Consumer Citizenship, Nationalism, and Neoliberal Globalization in Turkey: The Advertising Launch of Cola Turka." *Advertising and Society Review* 6(1): n.p.

Özyürek, Esra. 2004. "Miniaturizing Atatürk: Privatization of State Imagery and Ideology in Turkey." *American Ethnologist* 31(3): 374–91.

Palacios, María Susana, and Norma Paris. 1993. "Municipio y Sectores Dirigentes: El Caso de Cutral Có (1933–1955)." In *Historia de Neuquén.* S. Bandieri, O. Favaro, and M. Morinelli, eds. Pp. 320–31. Buenos Aires: PLUS ULTRA.

Paley, Julia. 2001. *Marketing Democracy: Power and Social Movements in Post-Dictatorship Chile.* Berkeley: University of California Press.

Petryna, Adriana. 2002. *Life Exposed: Biological Citizens after Chernobyl.* Princeton, NJ: Princeton University Press.

Pien, Sandra. 1999. *Un Argentino Llamada Mosconi: Un Siglo del Petróleo en la Argentina y la Historia del Hombre que lo Convirtió en un Instrumento para el Desarrollo de la Nación.* Buenos Aires: Editorial Ghirlanda.

Pikulski, Maria Teresa, Oscar Félix Orquiguil, and Federico Fernández Larrain. 1991. *Dock Sud: Un Sentimiento.* Avellaneda: Editora Comisión Homenaje Centenario de Dock Sud.

Plotkin, Mariano. 2003. *Mañana es San Perón: A Cultural History of Peron's Argentina.* K. Zahniser, trans. Wilmington, NC: Scholarly Resources.

Porter, Michael. 1998. "Clusters and the New Economics of Competition." *Harvard Business Review* (November/December): 77–90.

Postero, Nancy. 2007. *Now We Are Citizens: Indigenous Politics in Postmulticultural Bolivia.* Stanford, CA: Stanford University Press.

Retort. 2005. *Afflicted Powers: Capital and Spectacle in a New Age of War.* New York: Verso.

Rock, David. 2002. "Racking Argentina." *New Left Review* (September/October): 55–86.

Rofel, Lisa. 2007. *Desiring China: Experiments in Neoliberalism, Sexuality, and Public Culture.* Durham, NC: Duke University Press.

Rofman, Alejandro B. 1999. *Las Economías Regionales a Fines del Siglo XX: Los Circuitos del Petróleo, el Carbón, y el Azúcar.* Buenos Aires: Planeta/Ariel.

Rofman, Alejandro, Marta Baima de Borri, and Sandra Cesilini, eds. 2000. *Privatizaciones e Impacto en los Sectores Populares.* Buenos Aires: Editorial de Belgrano.

Roitman, Janet. 2005. *Fiscal Disobedience: An Anthropology of Economic Regulation in Central Africa.* Princeton, NJ: Princeton University Press.

Rosaldo, Renato. 1994. "Cultural Citizenship and Educational Democracy." *Cultural Anthropology* 9(3): 402–11.

Rose, Nikolas. 1996. *Inventing Ourselves: Psychology, Power, and Personhood.* Cambridge: Cambridge University Press.

Rose, Nikolas, and Peter Miller. 1992. "Political Power beyond the State: Problematics of Government. *British Journal of Sociology* 43(2): 172–205.

Royal Dutch Shell. 2005. *The Shell Global Scenarios to 2025: The Future Business Environment: Trends, Trade-Offs and Choices.* London: Shell International.

Sábato, Hilda. [1998] 2001. *The Many and the Few: Political Participation in Republican Buenos Aires.* Stanford, CA: Stanford University Press.

Sánchez, Pilar. 1997. *El Cutralcazo: La Pueblada de Cutral Có y Plaza Huincul.* Buenos Aires: Editorial Agora.

Savigliano, Marta. 1995. *Tango and the Political Economy of Passion.* Boulder, CO: Westview.

Sawyer, Suzana. 2001. "Fictions of Sovereignty: Of Prosthetic Petro-Capitalism, Neoliberal States, and Phantom-like Citizens in Ecuador." *Journal of Latin American Anthropology* 6(1): 156–97.

———. 2004. *Crude Chronicles: Indigenous Politics, Multinational Oil, and Neoliberalism in Ecuador.* Durham, NC: Duke University Press.

————. 2006. "Disabling Corporate Sovereignty in a Transnational Lawsuit." *PoLAR: Political and Legal Anthropology Review* 29(1): 23–43.

Schwegler, Tara. 2008. "Take It from the Top (Down)? Rethinking Neoliberalism and Political Hierarchy in Mexico." *American Ethnologist* 35(4): 682–700.

Senders, Stefan, and Allison Truitt, eds. 2007. *Money: Ethnographic Encounters.* Oxford: Berg.

Sharma, Aradhana. 2006. "Crossbreeding Institutions, Breeding Struggle: Women's Empowerment, Neoliberal Governmentality, and State (Re)Formation in India." *Cultural Anthropology* 21(1): 60–95.

————. 2008. *Logics of Empowerment: Development, Gender, and Governance in Neoliberal India.* Minneapolis: University of Minnesota Press.

Shell Argentina. 2006. Programa Creando Vínculos: Lecciones Aprendidas, 2005. Buenos Aires: Shell Compañía Argentina de Petróleo Sociedad Anónima.

Shever, Elana. 2008. "Neoliberal Associations: Property, Company, and Family in the Argentine Oil Fields." *American Ethnologist* 35(4): 701–16.

————. 2010. "Engendering the Company: Corporate Personhood and the 'Face' of an Oil Company in Metropolitan Buenos Aires." *Political and Legal Anthropology Review* 33(1): 26–46.

Solberg, Carl. 1979. *Oil and Nationalism in Argentina: A History.* Stanford, CA: Stanford University Press.

————. 1982. "Entrepreneurship in Public Enterprise: General Enrique Mosconi and the Argentine Petroleum Industry." *Business History Review* 56(3): 380–99.

Somers, Margaret. 1993. "Citizenship and the Place of the Public Sphere: Law, Community, and Political Culture in the Transition to Democracy." *American Sociological Review* 58(5): 587–620.

————. 1994. "Rights, Relationality, and Membership: Rethinking the Making and Meaning of Citizenship." *Law and Social Inquiry* 19(1): 63–112.

Sommer, Doris. 1990. "Irresistible Romance: The Foundational Fictions of Latin America." In *Nation and Narration.* H. Bhabha, ed. Pp. 71–98. New York: Routledge.

————. 1991. *Foundational Fictions: The National Romances of Latin America.* Berkeley: University of California Press.

Stoler, Ann. 2004. "Affective States." In *A Companion to the Anthropology of Politics.* D. Nugent and J. Vincent, eds. Pp. 4–20. Malden, MA: Blackwell.

Strathern, Marilyn. 1988. *The Gender of the Gift.* Berkeley: University of California Press.

————. 1992. *After Nature: English Kinship in the Late Twentieth Century.* New York: Cambridge University Press.

————. 1999. *Property, Substance, and Effect: Anthropological Essays on Persons and Things.* London: Athlone.

Sturzenegger, Federico, ed. 2004. *Neuquén: Energía para el Desarrollo.* Buenos Aires: Planeta.

Svampa, Maristella. 2005. *La Sociedad Excluyente: La Argentina Bajo el Signo del Neo-liberalismo*. Buenos Aires: Taurus.

Svampa, Maristella, and Sebastián Pereyra. 2003. *Entre la Ruta y el Barrio: La Experiencia de las Organizaciones Piqueteras*. Buenos Aires: Editorial Biblos.

Teichman, Judith. 1997. "Mexico and Argentina: Economic Reform and Technocratic Decision Making." *Studies in Comparative International Development* 32(1): 31–55.

Thompson, E. P. [1971] 1991. "The Moral Economy of the English Crowd in the Eighteenth Century." In *Customs in Common*. Pp. 185–258. New York: New Press.

Treisman, Daniel. 2003. "Cardoso, Menem, and Machiavelli: Political Tactics and Privatization in Latin America." *Studies in Comparative International Development* 38(3): 93–109.

Tsing, Anna. 2001. "Nature in the Making." In *New Directions in Anthropology and Environment*. C. Crumley, ed. Pp. 3–23. Walnut Creek, CA : AltaMira.

Verdery, Katherine. 1996. *What Was Socialism, and What Comes Next?* Princeton, NJ: Princeton University Press.

Vitalis, Robert. 2007. *America's Kingdom: Mythmaking on the Saudi Oil Frontier*. Stanford, CA: Stanford University Press.

Watts, Michael. 2005. "Righteous Oil? Human Rights, the Oil Complex and Corporate Social Responsibility." *Annual Review of Environment and Resources* 30(9): 373–407.

Welker, Marina. 2009. "'Corporate Security Begins in the Community': Mining, the Corporate Social Responsibility Industry, and Environmental Advocacy in Indonesia." *Cultural Anthropology* 24(1): 142–79.

Westbrook, David. 2007. *Between Citizen and State: An Introduction to the Corporation*. Boulder, CO: Paradigm.

Wittgenstein, Ludwig. 1958. *Preliminary Studies for the "Philosophical Investigations."* Oxford: Basil Blackwell.

Yanagisako, Sylvia. 1979. "Family and Household: The Analysis of Domestic Groups." *Annual Review of Anthropology* 8: 161–205.

———. 2002. *Producing Culture and Capital: Family Firms in Italy*. Princeton, NJ: Princeton University Press.

Yanagisako, Sylvia, and Carol Delaney. 1995. "Naturalizing Power." In *Naturalizing Power: Essays in Feminist Cultural Analysis*. Pp. 1–22. New York: Routledge.

Zalik, Anna. 2004a. "The Niger Delta: 'Petro Violence' and 'Partnership Development.'" *Review of African Political Economy* 101: 401–24.

———. 2004b. "The Peace of the Graveyard: The Voluntary Principles on Security and Human Rights in the Niger Delta." In *Global Regulation: Managing Crises after the Imperial Turn*. London: Palgrave.

Index

Italic page numbers refer to illustrations.